Abortion, Politics, and the Courts

RECENT TITLES IN
CONTRIBUTIONS IN AMERICAN STUDIES
SERIES EDITOR: ROBERT H. WALKER

Abortion, Politics, and the Courts
Roe v. Wade and Its Aftermath

REVISED EDITION

Eva R. Rubin

Contributions in American Studies, Number 89

Greenwood Press
NEW YORK • WESTPORT, CONNECTICUT • LONDON

Library of Congress Cataloging-in-Publication Data

Rubin, Eva R.
    Abortion, politics, and the courts.

(Contributions in American studies, ISSN 0084-9227 ;
no. 89)
    Bibliography: p.
    Includes index.
    1. Abortion—Law and legislation—United States.
I. Title. II. Series.
KF3771.R8   1987   344.73′0419   86-22847
                        347.304419
ISBN 0-313-25614-4 (lib. bdg. : alk. paper)

Library of Congress Catalog Card Number: 86-22847
ISBN: 0-313-25614-4
ISSN: 0084-9227

First published in 1987

Greenwood Press, Inc.
88 Post Road West, Westport, Connecticut 06881

Printed in the United States of America

∞™

The paper used in this book complies with the
Permanent Paper Standard issued by the National
Information Standards Organization (Z39.48-1984).

10 9 8 7 6 5 4 3 2 1

Copyright Acknowledgments

    The author and publisher are grateful for permission to reprint a table from *Planned
Parenthood—World Population, Washington Memo*, June 18, 1976 (Washington,
D.C.: The Alan Guttmacher Institute). Reprinted by permission of The Alan Guttmacher Institute.
    Every reasonable effort has been made to trace the owners of copyright materials
in this book, but in some instances this has proven impossible. The publishers will
be glad to receive information leading to more complete acknowledgments in subsequent printings of the book, and in the meantime extend their apologies for any
omissions.

For Louis, Robert, and Raoul

Contents

Preface

The first edition of *Abortion, Politics and the Courts* was
completed in 1980 and published in 1982. I first became interested
in this intriguing subject in 1973, after reading the decision of the
Supreme Court in *Roe v. Wade*. I was, at the time, teaching a
seminar in constitutional law and wished to explore the constitutional doctrines used by the Court to support what was a surprising
decision. But I was also curious about the genesis of state abortion
legislation, as well as about the background of the new challenges
by women plaintiffs. I found myself belatedly reading feminist
literature. In 1973, the background material available on abortion
was scattered and fragmentary. I read what I could find, although I
was not satisfied that I really understood the dynamics of the
nineteenth-century campaign to criminalize abortion until much
later, when I read James Mohr's book, *Abortion in America*. I
presented my preliminary thoughts about the decision in a law
review article published in 1974 in the *North Carolina Central Law
Journal*.

As I continued to follow legal and political developments after
1974, I became more and more interested in the range of responses
to the decision, and I began to collect material with the idea of
doing some kind of impact study. The subject kept unfolding and
changing focus. A movement for legal reform dominated by

professionals became a feminist cause, then became an antiabortion crusade, and then helped generate an across-the-board reaction to government social policy by a new coalition of social conservatives. In recent years, the abortion issue has become part of a broader reexamination of family policy and the relationship of families to the state.

My professional interest in the subject is primarily with the political roles played by courts and the use of litigation to instigate changes in social policy. Although I have tried to give a reasonably objective account of this aspect of the abortion controversy, I do have some personal biases that probably should be made clear now. I believe that a right to limit reproduction is essential to the continuing improvement of the legal and social status of women, although, like most women, I accept abortion only as a necessary evil and hope that advances in contraceptive technology will eventually make such a drastic remedy unnecessary. I am also concerned about the world population explosion and think that fertility control is necessary to human survival on the planet.

In 1986 the country is in a holding pattern on the abortion issue. The courts have continued to respect the precedent established in 1973, opponents of abortion have been unsuccessful in their attempts to amend the Constitution, and public opinion has been consistent in supporting the need for abortion in some circumstances, while having reservations about its unrestricted use. This revised edition attempts to bring the account up to date and to use the subject matter to illuminate some of the ways in which disputes about divisive social and political issues seek resolution within the framework of the political system.

Abortion, Politics, and the Courts

Introduction

This study began as an account of a litigation campaign—the campaign by women's organizations to use the courts to overturn state criminal abortion laws—its historical antecedents and some of its political consequences. Thirteen years after *Roe v. Wade*, it seems important not only to describe the use of litigation as a method of changing public policy, but to make some attempt to assess the impact of *Roe* to see what we can learn about the consequences, intended and unintended, of a Supreme Court decision.

The use of litigation as one of the avenues for changing the direction of public policy is not new. Clement Vose's *Constitutional Change*, published in 1972, examined a number of organized attempts by interest groups to use the courts for such purposes during the nineteenth century. But it was really the decision in *Brown v. Board of Education* (1954), the result of an extended litigation campaign by the NAACP Legal Defense and Education Fund to overturn public school segregation, that suddenly revealed the possibilities of litigation as a political strategy.[1] The success of this effort encouraged other groups to consider using the courts as an alternate means of exerting leverage on the political system.

After *Brown*, it was initially suggested that litigation was a tactic particularly suited to instances in which politically disadvantaged groups with poor access to the legislative process could use court action to supplement other kinds of pressure for changes in social policy. But new studies of interest-group litigation, such as Lee Epstein's *Conservatives in Court,* have demonstrated that conservatives as well as liberals, groups with political clout as well as those with little influence, often take to the courts to advance their policy goals.[2]

Even though we have become accustomed to seeing interest groups employ the litigation tactic, there remain a number of questions about its use and its efficacy:

1. In what situations does litigation appeal to its sponsors as an appropriate strategy?

2. What kinds of political gains can an organization expect from a victory in court?

3. Are the kinds of changes that result from a winning lawsuit permanent?

4. Are there advantages or disadvantages that flow from policies promulgated by courts because of the special characteristics of court decisions and the nature of the litigation process?

5. Has any erosion of the adversary process, the structure of courts, or the nature of lawsuits resulted from the increased use of courts to solve policy conflicts?

Scholars who have examined social issue lawsuits find that there are significant differences between such proceedings and traditional lawsuits.[3] The traditional lawsuit was a contest between adversely situated parties with direct personal interest in its outcome. The newer public interest lawsuits are tailored to fit the format of an action at law but have different aims: to produce policy change rather than to vindicate the private rights of the parties. We are still trying to assess the impact of this kind of suit on the structure and function of the courts themselves.

Resort to the courts is rarely used to the exclusion of other strategies. Agitation for legislative action and programs to influence both public opinion and the electoral process may take place simultaneously with the legal manuevering. If litigation is selected, there are different ways that courts can be used. An extended effort over a period of time to bring a series of test cases is one possibility. This is the true *litigation campaign,* the classic model of which was provided by *Brown*. The death penalty cases also followed this model, though with a less satisfactory outcome.[4] *Bellotti v. Baird* is an example of the single test case approach, as it was filed to test the constitutionality of a Massachusetts law limiting the access of minors to abortion.[5] Since it costs less and requires fewer resources to join a case already in progress than to bear the entire financial burden of the litigation, an economy-minded strategy may suggest joining an ongoing lawsuit, either as an *amicus curiae* or an intervenor, rather than initiating litigation. This maneuver has been favored by antiabortion groups, who use *amicus curiae* briefs to add emphasis and direction to litigation, or intervene as additional parties, and rely on the government lawyers defending state abortion legislation to present the main case.[6]

There are risks and opportunities, advantages and disadvantages with any of these moves. If a series of cases is to be brought, control is essential so that weak cases can be avoided and strong cases promoted. There is a need for central organization with a definite strategy and the power to discourage bad cases.[7] Individual test cases are less expensive, but one case does not always bring the desired results, and an adverse ruling may create an insuperable obstacle to the achievement of the goals being sought.

Sizable resources are necessary to any type of legal strategy. Extended litigation campaigns require organization as well as social purpose. To control, organize, and manage a carefully selected sequence of cases, it is essential to have money, legal talent, and experience. Funding is especially important, for litigation is expensive. Anything more than the simplest lawsuit requires staff and equipment and money for filing fees, office supplies, salaries, duplicating machines, files, and telephones. Litigation extending over a series of years requires a permanent staff, office space, and an active network of lawyers, clients, and supporters throughout the country.

Because much of the chance for success in the case depends not only on the rightness of the cause, but on the presentation of important issues to the courts in a form they can accept, good lawyering is essential. Although broader issues and strategies must be kept in mind, a court will not make a favorable decision if it is not offered a clear and reasonable legal choice, firmly anchored in acceptable authority. Clement Vose described an early loss in the campaign to undermine the white primary that was due to an amateurishly prepared brief, one that did not give the Supreme Court a sound basis on which to rule—cases, statutory authority, and a precise request for an equitable remedy that the Court could grant.[8] Judges are likely to respond favorably to a good legal argument and approve a carefully crafted remedy.

Resources and legal skill alone are no guarantee of success. Timing and luck are also important. The Court must be receptive and open to the arguments being made. A mismatch between issues and the timing of their presentation may be fatal. Women's rights cases were invariably lost before 1971.

Although inspired in part by the successful civil rights campaigns of the 1950s and 1960s, the abortion rights campaign differed somewhat from earlier litigation efforts. It was very much an outgrowth of movement politics, the upsurge of feminist enthusiasm, ferment, and activity that began in the 1960s and matured in the 1970s.[9] It had little central organization and planning, relying on outside parties—physicians, women's groups, or state prosecutors—to generate cases. Organizational ties were loose and decentralized. It was not until after the Court's decision, when pro-Choice supporters began to respond to antiabortion activity with professional organizing attempts of their own, that national organization seemed essential. Before 1973, local and single-issue groups were the backbone of the movement. The backers of many of the cases in state and federal trial courts were loose coalitions of dozens of groups. Rather than a centrally located legal staff, lawyers skilled in abortion litigation travelled from one city to another to help with cases. However, the sheer volume of cases coming into the courts in the period from 1969 to 1973 turned out to be an important factor in getting a hearing in the Supreme Court.[10]

The Supreme Court's decision legalizing some abortions was a quick and stunning victory. As many women's rights advocates recognized later, it may have come too quickly and too easily, before proabortion forces had consolidated their gains and organized to repel counterattacks from their opponents. Karen Mulhauser, director of National Abortion Rights Action League (NARAL), expressed the opinion that "had we made more gains through the legislative and referendum processes, and taken a little longer at it, the public would have moved with us"; Roger M. Williams, writing for the *Saturday Review*, compared the campaign to "an armoured column that has raced deep into enemy territory, outstripping their lines of supply."[11] The Court's decision itself served as a rallying point for organizational growth on both sides of this volatile, emotional, and symbolic cause. Later, with the strengthening of the organization of women's rights groups, the nature of the struggle changed from that of movement politics— ruled by enthusiasm, esprit de corps, and vounteered services— to a defensive organizational battle designed to resist a rollback of the gains of the legalization campaign.[12]

Throughout the next decade, it was unclear what the ultimate impact of the Court's decision would be. Political pressure by Right-to-Life forces begat state legislation and further litigation. The issue became thoroughly politicized and spread from the states into the national electoral process, eventually serving as a symbolic issue and rallying point for social conservatives, Republicans, and religious fundamentalists—a coalition that helped put President Reagan in the White House.

From studying this sequence of events, what conclusions can we draw about the effects of a campaign to change public policy through litigation? In the context of the abortion cases, at least some tentative responses to the questions posed earlier are possible.

1. Why did women's rights activists choose this method of policy initiation? In the 1970s, the litigation effort here described seemed an appropriate strategy because legislative gains were unstable and were being subjected to increasing counterattacks and risks of reversal, even after initial successes in the state legislatures. Then, at a key moment, an important law review article written by Roy Lucas and published in the *North Carolina Law Review* supplied a blueprint for developing the legal and constitutional issues necessary for challenging abortion laws in court.[13]

2. As to the expectations of the sponsoring groups and what they hoped to obtain, the first objective seems to have been quick, tangible results. Success in court would invalidate all state abortion laws at one blow. Little thought seems to have been given to the need to plan beyond a favorable court decision. But it must be

remembered that the context was that of the women's movement and that the issue was women's rights—these women hoped for a moral victory backed by the authority of the courts—a vindication of women's reproductive rights as an essential element in the fight for equality. But the decision itself was challenged on moral authority and opened the whole subject up to moral debate and discourse.[14]

3. How permanent are results achieved in this fashion? *Roe v. Wade* was the result of a successful battle, but it did not win the war. If one looks at the political furor that ensued, one might conclude that the tactic was not successful. But the decision has not been reversed. And as Sylvia Law observed in her 1985 article, "Rethinking Sex and the Constitution," "Nothing the Supreme Court has ever done has been more concretely important to women."[15] The decision was not permanent because wins in the courts involve different actors and a different balance of political forces than victories in legislatures. Litigation amplifies the voices of some groups and mutes others. The dynamics of a legal battle are different from that of a legislative battle, and a victory in court is no guarantee of an end to political conflict.[16]

4. There are, however, some obvious advantages to achieving a victory through the judicial process. The decision of a court, especially of the Supreme Court, is enhanced by the prestige of the Court and the authority of the law and the Constitution. It announces constitutional and legal principles. It becomes precedent and is therefore viewed by other courts as having a presumptive right to be followed. If based on the Constitution, it cannot be reversed directly by legislation. On the other hand, judicial decisions are much narrower, and less detailed than legislative acts. More litigation is necessary to define their limits, and the application of one set of principles to other fact situations is often unclear. Judicial decisions on social issues are political decisions, much like those of other branches. Rather than resolve a controversy, a judicial decision is more likely to redefine its terms and then push the problem back into the political process in a modified form. But unlike the decisions coming from legislative bodies, a judicial ruling may run ahead of public consensus, and, if it does, it will meet opposition. A policy initiated under such conditions may

not have acquired the essential support of the public or of other branches of government.

5. There has been a great deal of speculation about the impact on the courts themselves of the flood of social policy cases. It has been claimed that the use of courts as a supplementary political branch is leading to politicization of the judiciary. As courts are involved in confrontational issues, perhaps they may suffer some loss in institutional authority.[17] Judicial policy making provokes political reprisals, and moves are initiated to control and restrict litigation, to raise its costs, to strip courts of jurisdiction, and to make increasingly political appointments to judgeships. A controversial decision often itself becomes the focus of political debate, and the judicial branch becomes the target of people displeased with its policies—not as a fortress that can be attacked directly, but one that can be sapped and undermined in subtle and ingenious ways.

Finally, *Roe v. Wade* provides us with raw material for examination of the fascinating subject of "impact." What types of impact did *this* decision have? What generalizations and perhaps hypotheses can be generated from close examination of the events that followed a controversial decision on an important issue of social policy? It is clear that impact cannot always be measured simply in terms of compliance, whether other courts have followed the decision, or whether political actors accept the Court's ruling. A decision like *Roe v. Wade* is a major political event, like an election. It is likely to have broad ramifications for many aspects of society—not only the political and governmental. The abortion decision wrought significant changes in the practice of medicine and medical research; affected religious organizations in important ways; touched many areas of family life; changed the context in which family policy was considered; initiated changes in the direction of legal development; created a semireligious, sometimes violent, protest group; and both helped and hindered the movement for gender equality. It provoked a realignment of political forces. Just as some crucial "realigning elections" symbolize and make visible shifts that have taken place in the political arena, so also some Supreme Court decisions both respond to and restructure social change. Perhaps decisions of this nature, and *Roe v. Wade* was certainly one, might be labelled "restructuring" decisions.

Chapters One and Two of this book discuss the background of abortion law reform and early litigation efforts. Chapter Three describes and discusses the Supreme Court's decision in *Roe v. Wade* and Chapter Four the political battles that immediately followed. Chapter Five describes the state legislative reaction to the decision through 1985 and the judicial response to some of the new state laws. Chapter Six examines political responses on the federal level and court cases generated by legislative action.

CONFLICT AND CONSTITUTIONAL DECISION

Reformers and Legislatures

1

The attempt to control abortions by law was a nineteenth-century development: laws making abortion a crime were passed by American state legislatures, beginning in 1821 and throughout the remainder of the century. These laws were an abrupt departure from earlier American practice. American courts had traditionally followed the old English common law, which did not condemn abortion before *quickening* (before the mother could feel the developing fetus move, at some time around sixteen to eighteen weeks). Although court decisions and writings explaining the common law's position on abortion are sparse and conflicting, most of the old cases deal with conduct causing miscarriage after the fetus has quickened.[1] For example, a treatise on criminal law written by William Hawkins, an English barrister, which was used extensively as a reference book by American lawyers, said:

And it was anciently holden, That the causing of an Abortion by giving a Potion to, or striking, a Woman big with child, was Murder: But at this Day, it is said to be a great Misprision [misdemeanor] only, and not Murder, unless the Child be born alive, and die thereof, in which case it seems clearly to be murder, notwithstanding some Opinions to the contrary.

Hawkins's view was based in part on the authority of the Old Testament.

And in this Respect also, the Common Law seems to be agreeable to the Mosaical, which as to the Purpose is thus expressed, *If Men Strive and hurt a Woman with Child so that her Fruit depart from her and yet no Mischief follow, he shall be surely punished according as the Woman's Husband will lay upon him, and he shall pay as the Judges determine; And if any Mischief follow, then thou shalt give Life for Life.*[2]

As Justice Blackmun was to conclude in his opinion in *Roe v. Wade*, it is doubtful that abortion performed to prevent live birth was ever established as a common law crime, even where a quick fetus was concerned.[3] The law had little to say about abortions performed before quickening. In part, the law's lack of concern for this act was due to the generally held belief that the fetus was not alive before quickening, or at least not independently alive, but was rather a part of the mother's body. As a practical matter, it would have been difficult to detect abortions performed before quickening. In the early weeks of pregnancy, it was very difficult to be sure that a woman was pregnant, and it would have been hard to distinguish between miscarriages and intentional abortions. A few criminal charges of abortion were tried in the American courts, but to convict on charges of abortion, it was necessary to prove not only that the woman was pregnant, but that the child was quick.[4] It was very difficult, if not impossible, to prove either situation in court.

Although the law was largely indifferent to abortion, it was widely used in early America as a method of family limitation. According to historian James C. Mohr, women used a variety of home remedies and potions to cause miscarriage. When folk remedies failed, physicians were capable of terminating unwanted pregnancies and successfully used techniques that were not unduly dangerous by eighteenth- and nineteenth-century standards. Pregnancy and abortion were both dangerous.[5] Throughout the period before the Civil War, abortion was advertised freely in newspapers, especially in the larger cities. Government was not particularly concerned about the practice.[6]

Although the British Parliament passed a statute forbidding

abortion in 1803, at that time America had no legislation what-
soever on the subject of abortion. A few state legislatures passed
abortion statutes between 1821 and 1841; Connecticut passed the
first such statute in 1821, followed by Missouri in 1825, Illinois
in 1827, and New York in 1828.[7] The early statutes were not
primarily designed to make abortion a crime; they were aimed at
unsafe practices, poisonous remedies, and criminally incompetent
practitioners. A legal scholar investigating New York's early law
found, for example, that the lawmakers had originally written the
antiabortion provisions as part of a section of the criminal code
dealing with the regulation of surgery, designed to prevent reckless and unnecessary operations.[8] Legislation of this sort was pushed
by the better trained, "regular" physicians, who hoped to drive
untrained, careless quacks out of medical practice. "Regulars" were
often reluctant to perform abortions for a variety of reasons. Many
had moral and ethical objections and subscribed to the Hippocratic oath and its proscription of abortion. Others were aware of
the continuity and unity of fetal development and objected to the
quickening doctrine with its assumption that the embryo, in early
stages of development, was a nonbeing. But some motives were
also practical and economic. The practice of medicine in the middle
years of the nineteenth century was open to all comers, and many
of those offering cures and medical care were untrained. Those
doctors who had had formal medical training resented having to
compete with abortionists and herb doctors for patients and wanted
to see the practice of medicine become respectable, professional,
and scientific.[9]

Concern of the medical profession for regularization, improved
professional standards, and elimination of substandard practitioners
lay behind the earliest antiabortion legislation; these concerns still
informed laws introduced after 1840. But after 1840 the laws were
broader and more restrictive, designed to go beyond the regulation
of medical practice and change the older lax attitudes toward
abortion. Some of the new laws, like the one passed in New York
in 1845-46, discarded the quickening doctrine and made abortion at
any time during pregnancy punishable. In some states, women were
now to be responsible legally if they sought or underwent abortions. In the follow-the-leader pattern that often characterizes the
state legislative process, other states revising their criminal codes

or passing abortion statutes for the first time learned from the New York model. By 1860 twenty of the thirty-three states in the union had abortion statutes.[10]

After 1857 leaders, mostly physicians, took charge of the campaign for abortion law reform, mounting what became almost a medical crusade on the subject. The number of abortions was soaring. Doctors who saw many women patients were aware of the frequency of abortion attempts, some performed by the women themselves, but many the product of professional as well as amateur abortionists. Advances in the sciences of biology and physiology, as the nineteenth century progressed, made physicians aware that the fetus develops gradually and that no stage can be conveniently labelled as "quickening," that no magic moment occurs when an inanimate growth suddenly becomes a human being. Some doctors were indignant that women could or would interfere with life in its early stages and were not particularly sympathetic to the views of the women involved, whom they saw as ignorant of the facts, anxious to conceal the "fruits of illicit pleasure," or selfishly determined to put their own interests ahead of those of the unborn child. Dr. Hugh L. Hodge, an early proponent of restriction, regularly lectured against abortion to medical students studying obstetrics at the University of Pennsylvania. In a published lecture, he declaimed that

physicians, medical men, must be regarded as the guardians of the rights of infants. They alone can rectify public opinion; they alone can present the subject in such a manner that legislators can exercise their powers aright in the preparation of suitable laws; that moralists and theologians can be furnished with facts to enforce the truth of this subject upon the moral sense of the community, so that not only may the crime of infanticide be abolished, but that criminal abortion be properly reprehended, and that women in every rank and condition of life may be sensible of the value of the embryo and foetus, and of the high responsibility which rests on the parents of every unborn infant.[11]

Some evidence shows that, by the middle of the century, the social character of abortion had changed and that it was being used by the women of the upper and middle classes to limit family size.[12] In the eyes of many contemporary physicians, the acts of these upper-class women were inexcusable. They not only did not appreciate the seriousness of what they were doing, but by failing to have the proper number of native American offspring, they were allowing immigrants from Ireland and Eastern Europe to populate the country with their teeming families. The shiftless breeding of the immigrant classes, physicians warned, would soon cause the older stock to be outnumbered, if American women looked to their pleasure and convenience by having abortions.[13] Many of these doctors also opposed contraception. In addition to these considerations, undoubtedly, the middle-class Protestant zeal for reform in this period, as well as opposition to the changing status of women, must have been partly responsible for the growing demand for antiabortion statutes.

Physicians like Boston's Horatio R. Storer saw in abortion not only a compelling moral issue but also the means for uniting doctors on an issue of medical ethics and a means of strengthening professional societies by giving a coherent goal to the new medical associations. The medical associations, led by activist physicians, pushed the state legislatures, lobbied and campaigned against abortion in the medical society meetings, and helped legislators to write statutes. As a highly motivated and well-organized pressure group, the physicians were extraordinarily successful. Between 1860 and 1880, forty antiabortion statutes were passed. Thirteen states or territories outlawed abortion for the first time, and twenty-one strengthened and broadened their older statutes. The pattern of legislation was now almost complete, with laws on the books in almost all states.[14]

Connecticut's 1860 law was tougher than most, but typical of the restrictive mood. The first section announced the state's opposition to abortion generally and ignored the quickening distinction. It made the crime a felony, punishable by a fine of one thousand dollars or imprisonment up to five years. The second section made it a felony to assist at an abortion. The third section made the woman herself guilty of a felony for soliciting an abortion, permitting one, or even attempting one on herself. The fourth section forbade the advertisement of any abortifacient materials or substances.

After 1880 abortion was illegal everywhere. All states except Kentucky had criminalized it by statute and had imposed penalties of fines and imprisonment for the abortionist and, in some states, for the woman. This was the legislation that, with only a few changes, would govern abortion until the 1960s and 1970s.[15]

In these laws, the old quickening doctrine no longer immunized early abortions, although penalties might be stricter for abortions performed in later stages of pregnancy. Most states would eventually allow some abortions to be performed in exceptional circumstances —for instance, to save the life of the mother. Four state statutes forbade it under any circumstances.[16] Many states, like Connecticut, also prohibited the advertising of abortion-producing drugs and devices.

This state legislation had been passed in response to active, vocal, visible, well-organized pressure from the medical profession rather than as a result of any grass-roots demand based on moral or religious scruples. In that these new laws prevented operations that were dangerous and drove incompetent practitioners off the streets, they were indeed reform laws. But from the point of view of women, who had always had access to abortion as an emergency measure, they were repressive and restrictive. Contraception was never reliable and was widely believed to be just as reprehensible as abortion.[17] By outlawing abortions, women's control over their reproductive functions was further decreased.

Some evidence indicates that by the 1880s and 1890s, public opinion had begun to follow the law. Prosecutors were finding that judges and juries were willing to convict in abortion cases; this had not been true before 1880. The influence of the medical profession had grown with the increasing professionalization of medicine, and many physicians strongly opposed abortion and refused to perform the operation. Contemporary comment indicates that abortion was used less freely as a method of family planning by upper- and middle-class women—a change from the situation in the 1860s and 1870s.[18]

The new laws themselves became a factor in changing public opinion from its traditional lack of concern about abortion, especially before quickening. The existence of laws on the statute books did not, however, keep women from having abortions. The perennial pressures were still present. Women have always wanted to avoid illegitimate births. Family size and spacing, health, freedom from annual pregnancies, inability to support additional children, have always been reasons for resort to contraception and abortion.

Older women whose families have grown often do not want new families or fear the impact of late pregnancies. As women began to join the work force, unintentional pregnancies meant loss of jobs and seniority rights. Equal rights, as feminists have often pointed out, are dependent on the ability to control reproduction.[19]

Even though illegal, abortion was still seen as a last-resort remedy. If the pressures were intense enough, a woman either tried to convince a physician that he should perform a therapeutic abortion or sought out an illegal abortionist. Since illegal abortionists were often untrained or operated in unsanitary and primitive conditions, these women risked death and serious injury.

In spite of the extremely repressive legislation on the books, illegal abortions were performed by the thousands or hundreds of thousands each year, and the toll in pain and suffering was high. Home remedies, self-abortion, and back-alley abortionists were still available and difficult for the law to control. Estimates of the total number of illegal abortions were not accurate and varied considerably, ranging from two hundred thousand to 1.2 millon a year. An influential article in the *Southern California Law Review* estimated that they numbered 1.0 million a year by 1962, with perhaps five thousand a year ending in death.[20] Another estimate, made in 1967, was that ten to twenty criminal abortions were performed every fifteen minutes, that twenty-five hundred a day was not an unrealistic figure, but that no one really knew the full extent of the problem.[21]

Yet in spite of the social costs in human pain and unhappiness, abortion was not a subject on which women could speak out openly. Abortions were had secretly and were rarely discussed. Because the operation was associated with sexual misbehavior and immorality, it carried overtones of shame and guilt, in spite of the fact that most persons seeking abortions were married women, worried about the size of their families, the costs of raising additional children, or their own health.

The Abortion Reform Movement: 1950-1960

As a public issue, the abortion question began to surface again in the 1950s. Many of the critics of existing antiabortion legislation were doctors, who had to turn away women seeking abortions and who saw the tragic results of incompetent and untrained abortionists. These physicians were beginning to realize that the overrigid laws written at the insistence of their predecessors made it illegal for them to give their patients the highest level of medical care. They believed that the doctor and not the law should dictate medical treatment and that physicians should decide when abortion was in the best interest of the patient.[22]

A few scattered conferences and a few books and articles during the 1950s discussed the problem and suggested that changes be made in the law.[23] Planned Parenthood and the New York Academy of Medicine sponsored a conference in 1954. An anthology of articles on many aspects of abortion was published by Harold Rosen, a psychiatrist, in 1954, and data on abortion collected by pioneer sex researcher Alfred Kinsey was published in 1958.

Another professional group, the lawyers, also began to study the problem of abortion. Glanville Williams's *The Sanctity of Life and the Criminal Law* (1957)[24] discussed ethical-legal problems. Lawyers also were becoming concerned about the widespread disregard for the law. Although criminal prosecutions were not numerous, since most abortions were done surreptitiously and the women who had them did not ordinarily come to the attention of the authorities unless they were injured or killed, it was obvious that the law was being widely ignored. Also, abortion is a consentual crime, or a victimless crime; women rarely could be found who were willing to start criminal proceedings with a complaint. It was up to the state to investigate, collect evidence, and prosecute, and prosecutors often had more troublesome crimes to occupy their attention. Occasionally, police raids on the offices of abortionists turned up evidence to be used in criminal cases, although by and large, the law worked principally to inhibit the performance of abortions by legitimate physicians.

Although in 1959 the American Law Institute (ALI), a lawyers' organization that proposes changes and revisions of state law, published the draft of a model state abortion law (which would have allowed abortion under certain conditions), little attention was paid to the subject in legal writings until the late 1960s. The *Index to Legal Periodicals*, which lists articles in all of the law reviews, shows that no more than one or two articles a year were published throughout the 1950s, mostly on criminal law or torts. The 1958-61 volume, however, lists ten entries, several on therapeutic abortion. Twelve are listed in 1961-64, twenty-five in 1964-67, and two full columns of entries, single spaced, in 1967-70.

By the late 1960s, the mass-circulation magazines had begun to publish articles on the subject of abortion, and a number of books designed for general readership were beginning to appear in the bookstores.[25]

To understand why an issue that had remained hidden during the first fifty to sixty years of the twentieth century suddenly emerged on center stage, we must look at a number of changes taking place in society. Population growth, concern for the environment, fears that the world's resources were being depleted, began to trouble people everywhere in the world. New techniques of birth control, the pill, IUDs, and other contraceptive devices were being introduced; more frankness and openness about sex, marital problems, and contraception were evident. Abortion, which had become a simple and safe operation if performed early enough, was seen as an alternative method of population control, in fact the only means of limiting families available to women in some parts of the world. In every country, people were asking whether the world would be able to accommodate ever-increasing additions to its population.

Abortion laws in the United States were far stricter than in most non-Catholic countries. In 1967 the most liberal group, Japan and Eastern Europe, allowed abortion virtually on demand. A more moderate group, including the Scandinavian countries and Great Britain, permitted abortions to protect the mother's health. Only the Catholic countries prohibited the practice as completely as the United States, although in those countries, illegal abortions were extremely numerous as they were here.[26] Women, not only in America but in all parts of the world, were beginning to press for recognition of their rights and improvement of their status.[27] Many of the women in the United States had been learning the art of confrontation politics, first in the civil rights movement and later in radical student and antiwar groups. The stage was being set for changes in the law.

The Beginnings of Legislative Reform

It is hard to pinpoint the exact moment at which a generalized desire for change began to filter into the political process. Changing the law is ordinarily a long, drawn-out process, especially when desirable changes conflict with long-standing habit and custom or run into opposition by powerful supporters of the status quo. But when support for existing rules of law has eroded because of shifts in attitudes and changes in conditions in society, reformers will approach the various rule-making institutions for the modification and reform of the law.

Polls taken in the decade following 1960 seemed to indicate that a strict antiabortion policy was no longer in line with public preference; that, in fact, only about 10 to 16 percent of the population disapproved of abortions done to protect the mother's life or health. If one assumes that the polls accurately reflected public opinion, state abortion statutes that did not allow therapeutic abortions were considerably out of phase with contemporary views. It was only a matter of time until proposals for revision would be introduced into some of the state legislatures. It might have been predicted that California and New York would be among the first states to introduce reform proposals, since the polls in this period showed that the far West and the East led in public support for abortion reform.[28]

Demands that the rigid and strict criminal provisions governing abortions be revised came first in state legislatures. Later, when the result of state legislative change seemed too slow and too marginal, supporters of a general decriminalization of abortion turned to the courts.

The study of a number of instances of legislative change seems to indicate a pattern of stages or steps by which reform ideas are eventually enacted into statute law. Different matters go through these states at different rates—some quickly, some very slowly. But the basic steps are as follows:

1. A problem emerges and attracts attention. New laws are sought, or changes have taken place that require adjustment of existing law.
2. Concern about the problem is heightened by individual reformers and

publicists who begin speaking out, writing, and agitating for change and suggesting solutions.

3. Reform groups and organizations appear. Group activity increases the tempo of publicity propagandizing and agitation for change. There is more writing, lecturing, and organizing, and the numbers of supporters for the new programs increase.

4. Litigation may take place if the problem is one that can be translated into a lawsuit; indeed, important adjustments in the law often can be accomplished by reinterpreting laws and redefining rights. Judicial decisions also can create pressures on legislatures.

5. Organized opposition to the changes develops. Persons and organizations who object to change speak out and begin to develop counteroffensives. Sometimes this tends to heighten controversy, develop interest, and increase publicity. It may also defeat early moves for change.

6. The legislative phase begins. A legislator is found in a state legislature or in Congress who is willing to introduce a bill proposing some degree of change. Usually, these bills die in committee for the first few legislative sessions.

7. A period of inaction sets in. There may be a long period when the balance in favor of the status quo persists. But during this period, there also may be gradual acceptance of reform ideas by the public and increasing familiarity with reform proposals in the legislature. A period of growth and acceptance, increased awareness by the public, and increased activity by supporters and opponents takes place.

8. A law is passed. Often the first changes are minor. But they may lead to further changes in succeeding statutes (e.g., the Civil Rights Act of 1957 was disappointingly weak, but it paved the way for stronger legislation).

9. Feedback or reaction. The changes may produce new problems and new proposals for change. Or the reaction of opponents may result in the revision of the changes and a lessening of their impact. But even marginal changes may also open the doors to greater change and further reforms.

Robert H. Walker, in his volume *Reform in America*, conceptualizes the reform process as a five-step sequence.[29] The first, or "random negative" stage, begins with a range of spontaneous responses to a problem. Individuals organize to spread awareness of the problem in the second, or "structured negative" phase, a period when complaints are voiced and the need for change is verbalized and publicized; many reform movements get no further than this stage. Proposals for reform and for solutions to problems lead into the third, or "random positive" level. When reformers begin to focus on specific solutions, aims, and priorities, Walker finds reform entering a fourth, "structured positive" condition. Success brings institutionalization of the reform movement by the passage of legislation, by executive action, or by court decisions. The abortion reform movement followed this pattern closely.

Often a specific act, disaster, personality, or event can supply the spark that moves reform from its negative to its positive phase. In the abortion controversy, several specific events focused public opinion on the need for change, dramatized the issue, and aggregated support for new policies. One such event was the completion of the draft for a Model State Abortion Law by the American Law Institute. A bill based on this model law was introduced in the California legislature in 1961 and again in 1963, but made no progress. But several events were to take place that moved similar laws through the legislatures in Colorado, California, and North Carolina and then through an additional group of state legislatures.

One of the activating incidents was the discovery that a new tranquilizer, Thalidomide, much marketed in Europe, caused terrible birth defects when taken by pregnant women. Many European women who had taken the drug sought abortions. Luckily, the Food and Drug Administration had not licensed the drug for sale in the United States, and few American women were affected; however, Sherri Finkbine, an American TV actress, had obtained the tranquilizer in Europe. She was refused an abortion in her home state of Arizona. She then went to court to test the law but was unsuccessful. Her court fight and subsequent trip to Sweden for an abortion was much publicized in the press.

This incident was followed by an epidemic of German measles (rubella) that swept across the United States in 1962-65. German measles is an extremely dangerous disease for pregnant women; since 1941 virologists have known that the disease can cause serious fetal damage—heart disease, blindness, deafness, and mental retardation—if a woman is exposed to it early in pregnancy. The risks of deformity, according to one estimate, run as high as 50 percent.[30]

In the 1962-65 epidemic in this country, about 82,000 pregnant women contracted German measles, and many of them sought abortions and were turned down. An estimated 15,000 defective babies were born.[31] Many hospitals will perform abortions when an expectant mother has had German measles; in 1964-65 California hospitals, in spite of a restrictive state law, were responding to the demands from frightened mothers and evading the law. Disturbed by this lawbreaking, a member of the state medical board who was a Roman Catholic physician (and opposed to abortion) brought political pressure against state officials to stop the practice. An investigation of hospitals in the San Francisco area led to charges of unprofessional conduct against nine local doctors. It was rumored that another thirty-nine would soon be called to account.[32]

Although the charges brought against these doctors served to stop further abortions from being performed in California hospitals, there was a public furor over the incident. Physicians across the nation came to their support. A Citizens Defense Fund on Therapeutic Abortions was launched in California and other states to raise money for the defense of the "San Francisco Nine."[33] Medical school deans and medical society leaders signed a brief in their defense. California State Senator Anthony C. Beilenson introduced a new reform bill in the legislature. This bill had the support of Episcopal and Jewish religious organizations, women's groups, abortion counselling services, medical societies, and individual doctors, all of whom lobbied for the bill in Sacramento.[34] The Catholic clergy hired a public relations firm to fight for the old law, but the legislature thought there was popular support for change, and the reform bill was passed and signed, reluctantly, by Governor Reagan in 1967. Colorado, with a smaller Catholic population, went on the record as passing the first reform bill in the nation, although California's struggle, not yet concluded, had led the way. North Carolina joined the other two states in 1967, and Delaware, Maryland, Georgia, Oklahoma, Florida, New York, New Jersey, and Pennsylvania saw similar bills introduced in their states legislatures. Twenty-eight state legislatures considered bills in the 1967 session.[35] Between 1967 and 1970, twelve states adopted some type of reform legislation, usually following the abortion provisions of the American Law Institute's Model Penal Code.[36]

In some states, the reform forces were vanquished; Connecticut and Maine considered new abortion bills, but rejected change. New

York, Alaska, and Hawaii eventually went further than the model law, rejecting reform in favor of outright repeal, with the only restriction on abortions being the requirement that they be performed before the twentieth week (in New York, the twenty-fourth week).

The fight in the New York legislature was particularly bitter.[37] Like California, New York had experienced earlier skirmishes, with both proabortion and antiabortion forces strong, emotional, and well organized. After a wrenching battle, New York's eighty-five-year-old antiabortion statute was replaced by a liberalizing law in 1970, although this was by no means final victory for the reformers. New York's battles were marked, however, by a new factor—the emergence of activist, highly visible women's groups, ready to take to the streets in support of abortion reform.

Women's Groups and Other Organizations

The early organizations interested in abortion law reform coalesced behind particular reformers. Patricia Maginnis, one of the first advocates of repeal rather than reform, founded the Society for Humane Abortion in California and used civil disobedience and confrontation tactics to publicize her cause. William Baird's Parents Aid Society in Hempstead, Long Island, began as a contraceptive service and was enlarged to include abortion referrals. The Clergy Consultation Service on Abortion was also formed as a referral service, that is, as an organization willing to help women find competent doctors who were willing to perform abortions. This group increased the active involvement of clergymen in the problems of women and the cause of abortion law revision. Some of the doctors performing abortions became active reformers, and a number of them served time in prison for disobeying the laws against abortion.[38]

The New York Association for the Study of Abortion (ASA) was a different kind of group, primarily an educational organization of lawyers and doctors. Later, some of the church groups and lay organizations were coordinated into various coalitions, such as the Coalition of Organizations for Abortion Law Reform and NARAL, the National Association for Repeal of Abortion Laws (1969 and after). These coalitions brought a greater range of supporters and more resources into the movement.[39]

With the organization of the National Organization of Women (NOW) in 1966, a group appeared that would have a much broader impact than any of these single-issue and ad hoc groups. At first NOW was afraid to touch the abortion issue, fearing, as had earlier women's organizations, that its broader goals of legal and economic equality for women would be obscured by commotion over sexual taboos and the emotional issues involved in any question of sex and procreation. Even Betty Friedan,[40] who was an important catalyst in the growth of the women's movement, did not initially see the importance of the abortion issue as a rallying point for women. But in 1967, a year after its founding, NOW included as one of the rights in its women's Bill of Rights the "Right of Women to Control their Reproductive Lives." A walkout by dissidents at its second convention indicated that this was a divisive issue that might split moderate from radical women. The younger and more radical feminists, indeed, were uncompromising on abortion, seeing the issue as one of "right" and not a matter for political compromise.

Radical women's groups that began to break away from the more moderate NOW—organizations like the Woman's Radical Action Project and the Westside Project in Chicago, and New York Radical Women, Redstockings, WITCH, and the Feminists—saw abortion as one of the key issues in the women's liberation movement.[41] They saw abortion as a matter of social justice rather than a private personal problem and encouraged women to speak out about their own experiences to publicize the humiliations and horrors of the old system. Actresses told of their abortions in news conferences and magazine articles. Women appeared whenever there was a public discussion of abortion to protest the domination of panels by male experts. NOW charged that a prestigious conference on abortion cosponsored by the Kennedy Foundation and the Harvard Theological School was controlled by academicians and Roman Catholics and included only three women.[42] Women also took to the streets, marching and picketing. The Redstockings stormed a New York legislative hearing in which fifteen experts (fourteen men and one woman, a nun) were testifying, shouting, "We are the experts!" To prove it, they held an open meeting in which women got up before the audience to tell of their own abortions.[43] Later in 1970, when the New York legislature was considering a reform bill, women's groups demonstrated near

Bellevue Hospital, St. Patrick's Cathedral, and Union Square in New York City; held a guerrilla theatre performance in the streets; and handed out wire coat hangers lacquered blood red to symbolize the way that restrictive laws forced women to undertake self-abortion.

Such activities dramatized the abortion issue and helped bring it out into the open for public discussion. The aura of guilt and shame that had prevented frank consideration of abortion legislation as a public issue began to dissipate. The women's groups now also began to use much more effective techniques of publicizing their cause. The period of ladylike lobbying in white gloves before legislative committees was over, and a period of confrontation politics and pressure tactics had begun.

The entrance of the women into the political arena also changed the nature of the issue from one of social reform to one of women's rights. Women have a right to control their bodies, these women insisted, and antiabortion laws are in essence "compulsory pregnancy" laws, forcing women to bear children against their wills on orders from the state. Women should no longer be compelled to go hat in hand to doctors and hospital boards to beg for help; a woman who needed a legal abortion had a right to one. In fact, the woman's ability to control her reproductive capacity was essential to her ability to compete on a basis of equality in the market-place for jobs. A woman who had to leave a good job or career to give birth to a child or who did not have a reliable place to leave children could not compete on the same level with male workers. Lucinda Cisler, an activist in the birth control movement, emphasized the importance of the capacity of women to limit their reproduction.

Without the full capacity to limit her own reproduction, a woman's other "freedoms" are tantalizing mockeries that cannot be exercised. With it, others cannot be long denied, since the chief rationale for denial disappears.[44]

The women's organizations all agreed: abortion laws must be repealed rather than reformed.

Repeal is based on the quaint idea of *justice*: that abortion is a woman's right and that no one can veto her decision and compel her to bear a child against her will.[45]

Indeed, in some of the legal briefs later submitted in court challenges to abortion laws, the argument was made that the Thirteenth Amendment to the Constitution forbids slavery, and this includes compulsory pregnancy.[46]

In the early struggles for abortion law revision, women's groups had not played an active part, and in some cases, women's interests were not as well represented as those of lawyers, doctors, and public health personnel. Examples of this may be found in two case studies of the campaign for reform bills; in North Carolina (1967) and later in Georgia (1968), the legislation passed, but in both cases, the reforms resulted in very little real change.

In North Carolina the success of the reform bill seems to have been in part due to the fact that the legislature was busy with other matters and considered abortion reform a peripheral issue. The legislative maneuvering was handled in a very skillful, low-key, and nonabrasive fashion, designed not to attract too much attention to what most legislators perceived as a relatively unimportant issue. The Roman Catholic clergy did not become involved directly in the legislative hearings, probably fearful of stirring up anti-Catholic sentiment and of gaining little support in a state where only about 1 percent of the population was Catholic. Roman Catholics testifying on the bill were mainly physicians. The legislators seem to have seen the bill as progressive (i.e., good, forward looking), as promoting good medical practice, and as having a generally useful purpose in reducing the number of deformed and retarded children being supported in state institutions. Many legislators had recently visited these institutions, and the solons had been shocked at some of the children ("vegetables," "basket cases") they saw.[47]

Women did not play a part in the bill's passage. No women's organizations lobbied, and only one woman, a physician specializing in obstetrics and gynecology, testified in the committee hearings. She did not think her testimony helped the bill, partly because she criticized it as being too limited and pointed out that 90 percent of all abortions are for socioeconomic reasons and not for the purpose of protecting the mother's life or health. No one else represented the female point of view, either for or against the legislation, although the bill's chief sponsor, State Representative Arthur Jones, remarked in debate that one of its purposes would be "to reduce the resentment of women to legislators who, for the most part are men and who never run the risks of pregnancy, but who deprive women of their right to abortion when such is justified and medically sound."[48]

A case study of the Georgia law's passage, the law that was later challenged in a companion case to *Roe v. Wade*, showed that the Georgia legislature was concerned, primarily, with two very narrow aspects of the abortion picture: the protection of doctors from prosecution for performing abortions, and a desire that any abortion laws on the books be so hedged with restrictions that out-of-staters would not flock to Georgia hospitals and thus turn that state into an "abortion mill." These limited reform laws did not make much change in the status quo.[49]

It did not take long for those who had had such high hopes that the ALI reform laws would improve existing conditions to be disillusioned. A Colorado doctor commented on his state's experience after a year's operation under the new law: "All the new law did was to put a medical problem into politics, and make doctors and hospitals so nervous that in 1967 we did fewer abortions on medical grounds than we did before the new law." The sponsor of the North Carolina law attacked his state's new law after watching it in operation for two years, saying that it only perpetuated "a system that will continue to send 95 out of every 100 women to illegal abortionists or to self-terminations." He came out for complete repeal.[50]

Experience with the reform laws in states that had passed them seemed to indicate that they would have very little positive impact. It was becoming clear that the reform bills on the ALI model would allow legal abortions only in a very narrow range of cases, and that it would be difficult, if not impossible, for any great number of women to qualify for legal abortions. Fred P. Graham, writing for the *New York Times* in 1967, foresaw the problem, predicting that, "Even if abortion reform proceeds at an accelerated pace as predicted, the changes will be so minor that this nation's laws will remain among the most restrictive in the world."[51] Not only did the laws allow abortion only in an extremely narrow set of circumstances, but they would probably help only fairly well-educated, middle-class women. The bureaucratic routines required by hospital abortion committees, the statements by doctors and psychiatrists, and, if all of this was successful, the fees would keep all but persistent and knowledgeable women from using the new laws. "Where will the ghetto-dweller find a psychiatrist to testify that she runs a grave risk of emotional impairment if she is forced to give birth to her nth baby?"[52] Even when cases seemed clearly within the limits allowable for legal abortions, women were often turned down or turned away from hospitals; it was much safer to resolve any doubt against the woman suppliant.

So it became clear to the women's groups that repeal of existing abortion laws would be much more beneficial to their cause than further efforts in favor of "reform," which they began actively to oppose. Repeal the laws and leave the subject to the woman and her physician; remove the state and its coercive powers from the picture entirely. Lucinda Cisler summed up disillusionment with these reform tactics.

Great things were expected of "reform": the illegal abortion racket would die, only wanted, healthy children would be born, and we would all be happy. Of course it didn't turn out like that: "reform" states were afraid of becoming "abortion mills" and their hospitals began, probably unconstitutionally, to refuse help to anyone who didn't come from their state or even from their city; the more prosperous women who used to fly to foreign parts or to New York City for illegal abortions could now stay closer to home and be attended by the family doctor, while poor women often didn't even know the new law existed, much less how to stretch it for their own purposes; city women tended to get more legal abortions than women served only by the smaller, more conservative town or rural hospitals; and we were hardly much happier.[53]

Into the Courts: Litigation
for Social Change

2

If the changes in abortion law made by the legislatures were unsatisfactory, another route was open to reformers—litigation.[1] If a ruling could be had that the state laws violated either the federal or state constitutions, the abortion laws could be overturned without legislative action; a ruling by the Supreme Court on constitutional grounds could overturn abortion laws in all of the states. Declaring these laws invalid on legal grounds would have the same effect as repealing them completely and would be a great coup for women's groups favoring that goal. Two difficulties would be getting the cases into court and finding a constitutional basis for challenging the laws.

Because courts are open to individuals and small organizations, they are often the political agencies that first feel the pressure to make changes in existing law. Legislatures, it is true, are open to views of all kinds, but some groups have better and more varied opportunities to influence the legislative branch than others do. Legislative bodies represent, by design, majority views and established interests. Legislatures like to "let sleeping dogs lie" and resist becoming involved in unpopular battles (such as repeal of the abortion laws) that lose votes without winning any. New ideas and changes in the law may find the status quo extremely resistant to change. Minorities, reformers, nonconformists, all must do long, hard spadework, cultivating public opinion, informing and convincing individual legislators, testifying before legislative committees —all of the preliminary work of the legislative process—before they can get consideration for reform and new policies.

Access to the courts is easier. An individual, no matter how far out of step with majority views, who has a good legal claim, a lawyer, and enough money to pay the various filing fees, can take his claim to court, and if he meets the technical requirements and conditions for filing suit, and is in the proper court, will have his claim heard and adjudicated. Winning a suit may do more than protect his own rights and interests. The court's decision becomes precedent that other courts will read and follow, perhaps applying the same rule of law to similar cases. A carefully planned series of cases, resulting in favorable decisions, may result in a series of precedents substantial enough to undermine a challenged doctrine or legal principle. The NAACP Legal Defense Fund's persistent attack on the racial inequalities in public education under the separate but equal doctrine resulted in the overturning of that doctrine in 1954, in *Brown v. Board of Education*. Following a blueprint for an attack on segregated education written by Nathan Margold for the NAACP in 1930, Fund lawyers brought a series of cases designed to lay the groundwork for the eventual overturning of the separate but equal doctrine. Attorneys for the Fund, Charles H. Houston, William Hastie, and Thurgood Marshall, were successful first in opening graduate and professional schools to blacks.[2] With each success, they increased their own courtroom expertise and refined their tactics, created publicity for their cause, and educated lawyers and judges to the facts of life under segregation.[3] The dramatic victory in *Brown* made it apparent to other minorities and special-interest groups with good causes that litigation might offer benefits and a chance of success denied them by the legislative process. Even a small group can sponsor a lawsuit, although money and legal resources are necessary to win more than an isolated victory. Litigation can put pressure on majority institutions, publicize causes, and educate the legal community, and each court victory can become the focal point for further organizing and fund

raising. It can become part of a process of changing and channelling public opinion that may later result in general revision of the
law by legislation. The litigation campaign for school desegregation
became the model for the later efforts to use the courts to abolish
the death penalty, to establish welfare rights, and to end gender
discrimination.

But although the courts offer an alternative route to policy
change, they have their shortcomings. A victory in court may
advance a cause, but a defeat can be devasting. *Plessy v. Ferguson*,[4]
the decision in which the separate but equal doctrine was devised,
was the result of a test case that was decided the wrong way. So
was *Bradwell v. Illinois*,[5] one of the first challenges brought
against state statutes discriminating against women. The timing of
a lawsuit may determine its success or failure; indeed, a single
victory may not be broadly influential, and it may be necessary to
bring a series of cases to have much impact on policy. But sustained
litigation demands money and legal talent. Cases that stretch over
weeks and months need organizational backing and the money to
pay lawyers or at least the organization to find and use volunteers.
The women's rights campaign, of which the quest for reproductive
rights was an early part, was more formidable after it had made
an organizational connection with the American Civil Liberties
Union.[6] This liaison with an older organization, experienced in
civil rights suits, gave the women's rights proponents financial
backing and access to organizational and legal resources that they
had not achieved on their own. With staff and a nationwide
organization, it was possible to plan overall legal strategy, coordinate litigation in different parts of the country, and bring a
sequence of cases designed to establish key principles.

Although courts offer an alternative route to policy change,
they have their own institutional peculiarities and idiosyncracies.
The mechanics of the judicial process is very different from that
of the legislative process, and the approach to judicial institutions
must be made in the traditional framework of the lawsuit. Two
traditional requirements for using the courts are that the dispute
must be justiciable, and that the court whose authority is invoked
must have jurisdiction.

Justiciability is a term of art and includes a number of elements, all of which must be present before a court will accept a case for decision.[7] For federal courts, the basic qualification is that a dispute must present a "real case or controversy." Authority is given to the federal courts by Article III of the Constitution to decide "cases and controversies" and nothing else. The courts have interpreted this limitation as allowing them to act only in real disputes, concrete and definite, neither hypothetical nor abstract, neither academic nor moot, where there are real problems and real parties with adverse legal interests. Various justifications for this requirement exist, but its principal rationalization has been that it keeps the judiciary tied to its traditional function of deciding disputes under optimum conditions and limits and discourages its exercise of general lawmaking powers.

Not unconnected with this requirement and one of the elements of justiciability is the requirement that a complaining party have *standing*, the right to stand before the court to assert his claims. To have standing, a litigant must have "such a personal stake in the outcome of the controversy as to assure that concrete adverseness which sharpens the presentation of issues upon which the court so largely depends for illumination of difficult issues."[8]

The reasoning behind this requirement is that *true adversaries*, persons having direct financial or personal interests in the outcome of a case, will present the court with the strongest and sharpest arguments for each side, facilitating the finding of the best legal solutions. Although some recent thinking is in favor of modifying this requirement, recognizing that persons with strong ideological claims have as much incentive to present issues strongly and sharply as persons with financial or personal claims, the courts have not yet fully accepted such a departure from tradition.[9]

Standing presented a real problem to parties trying to get the first cases challenging abortion laws into the courts. Although access is theoretically available to anyone meeting the traditional requirements of a lawsuit, in some cases, the conservative nature of the judicial branch leads it to read the threshold requirements narrowly and technically and to resist opening its doors to novel challenges. The Supreme Court, with its tradition of deference to the political branches and its arsenal of self-limiting and self-denying techniques, is often very cautious about entertaining unfamiliar legal problems. The birth control cases, brought between 1942 and 1965, in the hopes of getting a court ruling on laws restricting the distribution of contraceptives, were treated very inhospitably. Not until 1965 was the Supreme Court ready to override legislative decisions in this area. Caution was also the rule in the initial stages of the abortion controversy.

To get challenges to the various state abortion statutes into court, a number of technical barriers had to be overcome, especially problems of standing. First, who was to bring the suits? Most abortion laws penalized the performance of abortions and were thus aimed at abortionists. Some laws made the woman an accomplice, penalized her for soliciting an abortion, or made self-abortion criminal. But the primary impact of abortion legislation was on the medical profession. Doctors and hospitals were afraid to perform abortions because of the criminal penalties involved, and they were even reluctant to perform abortions justifiable under state law for fear of becoming involved in criminal prosecutions.

A physician indicted under an abortion statute thus would have standing in a real case to raise questions of the constitutionality of an abortion law as part of his defense. But few doctors wanted to risk criminal prosecution to test the laws, and some of those who were prosecuted were more interested in avoiding conviction than in raising constitutional issues. Even if they did, they were not ordinarily able to raise, on behalf of patients needing abortions, questions concerning a woman's possible right to this form of medical procedure. There are limits to the types of situations in which third parties are allowed to raise questions concerning the constitutional rights of others.[10] Physicians were not the ideal persons to make broad claims of abortion rights; yet it was difficult for women to raise these claims themselves.

Since women were rarely prosecuted under those state statutes that made them accessories to abortion or made self-abortion criminal, the option of raising challenges as part of a defense in a criminal case was rarely possible. Declaratory judgment statutes, state and federal, do supply an alternate route allowing persons to challenge the constitutionality of law outside of the framework of a

criminal prosecution.* But although the declaratory judgment procedure allows a person to test a law without acting "at his peril"
by breaking or ignoring it, the use of this device has technical
limitations.[11] The case and controversy limitation controls declaratory judgment actions. Persons bringing actions for declaratory
judgments must do it in the contest of real cases and controversies
and must have standing to bring the suits. In addition, courts have
been very reluctant to use this procedure where state criminal
prosecutions are pending, since this would violate the principles of
federalism by interference with state judicial systems.

It was theoretically possible to bring declaratory judgment actions
for rulings on abortion statutes, but in the 1965-72 period, the
courts were reluctant to entertain them and quite willing to dismiss
them because of technical defects. Pregnant women trying to use
this device to test abortion laws were unsuccessful. In a state
case in 1962, an Arizona woman who feared that she would give
birth to a deformed child because she had taken Thalidomide during
pregnancy brought suit seeking a declaratory judgment that her
physician could terminate her pregnancy without violating Arizona's
abortion laws.[12] When Arizona authorities denied any intention of
prosecuting anyone under the state statute, her petition for declaratory relief was dismissed as presenting no legal controversy. Thus
no way remained for her to challenge the Arizona law, although
it effectively denied her legal access to an abortion.

Pregnant women were reluctant to bring abortion suits, even
pseudonomously, in their own behalf.[13] Indeed, one of the key
elements provided by feminist organizations in this kind of litigation
was the finding of women who were willing to act as plaintiffs and
the providing of support and reinforcement. But psychological
inhibitions were not the only obstacles to women's cases; the
judicial process might move so slowly that the pregnancy would
be over and the case declared moot before a court could decide.

---

*Declaratory judgment is a procedure that allows a court to declare the rights of
parties or the court's opinion on a question of law, without ordering anything to be
done. It can be used before an actual wrong, giving rise to an action for damages,
has been threatened or completed. Both the states and the federal government
have declaratory judgment statutes that govern this procedure.

In addition to declaratory judgment suits and criminal prose-cutions, a few alternate ways of testing abortion laws were, for example, by a civil suit for damages against a hospital or doctor following the birth of a malformed child or possibly by a mal-practice suit.[14] However, the best chance of getting a test of abortion law seemed likely to be in connection with the criminal prose-cution of a doctor.

Technical obstacles to abortion suits abounded. But the nature of the issue itself hardly invited judicial consideration. Abortion was an explosive issue on which there was no consensus. It involved a variety of religious and moral issues of the kind that courts are eager to avoid, and very little established doctrine or precedent was available to guide decision. In addition, between 1967 and 1972, state legislatures were trying to rewrite their laws along more permissive lines, and it could have been predicted that the Supreme Court would exercise the passive virtue of self-restraint until the results were in on legislative reform. Even if the court could be persuaded to hear a case, available legal doctrine favored a decision leaving abortion to be controlled by state legislation. It had long been taken for granted that the states had the right to control abortion practices within their boundaries under the police power. State law regulated marriage, divorce, and legitimacy, forbade various kinds of sexual activity, and controlled the distribution and sale of contraceptives. About the only Supreme Court cases that could be found in the reproductive area were two sterilization cases.[15]

Until *Griswold v. Connecticut* was decided in 1965, little prece-dent existed that could be exploited in a test case, although some of the laws might be susceptible to attack on the ground of vagueness or because they improperly shifted the burden of proof from the state to the defendant. But no long-term benefits would result from overturning abortion laws on grounds of procedural due process. Proabortion forces wanted the courts to go beyond the technical defects of such laws and establish that the woman herself had interests that the law must not completely ignore. They wanted to establish that the women seeking abortions had rights that were violated by blanket state laws prohibiting them in all but the most exigent circumstances. One claim that might be made was that the laws violated the woman's right to privacy, in the sense of her right to make decisions about her family and reproductive life without interference by the government. A right to privacy had been asserted in other legal contexts, primarily in Fourth Amendment cases. It was to be developed, in a form that could be applied to abortion statutes, in court cases challenging state birth control laws.

The Justices Search for a Doctrine

For many years, a number of states had laws forbidding the sale, prescription, or even the use of contraceptives. These laws were passed during the last quarter of the nineteenth century but fell gradually into disuse as the population's attitudes about birth control changed.[16] By 1960 most of the laws were rarely enforced, but a few remained on the books simply because state legislatures wanted to avoid the inevitable confrontations that would result if they tried to repeal them. Segments of the community, especially the Roman Catholic church, were adamant in their opposition to birth control. Connecticut had a law, passed in 1879, as a result of Anthony Comstock's antivice campaign that was particularly offensive; rather than prohibiting the prescription or sale of contraceptives, it made their *use* a criminal act. Married couples and single persons alike were forbidden to use contraceptives. Planned Parenthood and other birth control proponents had been trying for many years to overturn this law; although it was rarely enforced, it was effective in keeping social workers from setting up birth control clinics or teaching birth control methods openly. The courts had had a series of test cases, several of them reaching the Supreme Court, but each had run aground on some technical or procedural shoal and had been turned back without a ruling on the merits.[17]

Poe v. Ullman, brought in 1961, with the support of the Planned Parenthood Federation and the American Civil Liberties Union, was not decided on the merits, but did elicit two dissents that developed in detail constitutional arguments for a right to privacy.

Justices Douglas and Harlan wrote lengthy dissenting opinions. Douglas's opinion anticipated the majority opinion he would write four years later in *Griswold v. Connecticut*. In arguing that Connecticut law prohibiting the use of contraceptives was unconstitutional, he raised four points, all of which would be developed and refined in his later opinion: First, the Constitution protects more than the rights specifically listed therein; second, "liberty" includes rights that "emanate" from specific guarantees, but also protects the essential conditions for life in a free society; third, one of the requirements of a free society is freedom from government intrusion on home, family, and marital relations; fourth, a right to privacy exists and is protected in part by the Fifth and Fourteenth amendments, but also because it is required by the "totality of the constitutional scheme under which we live."[18]

Justice Harlan covered the same points, although his dissenting opinion reflected his differing views on the nature of due process. Due process, he wrote, protects not a series of specific rights, but a "rational continuum" that includes "a freedom from arbitrary impositions and purposeless restraints."[19] Intrusion on the intimacies of marital life by the novel and obnoxious means provided by Connecticut's statute went beyond the limits of legislative authority.

Thus although the Court refused to decide the constitutional questions, the *Poe* case made it clear that two Justices were prepared to protect, whatever the exact constitutional location of its guarantee, a right against state interference with the private family-planning decisions of married couples. The *Poe* dissents produced two detailed sets of constitutional arguments available to lawyers who might succeed in getting another test case into court.

In 1965 such a case was docketed for argument.[20] Estelle Griswold, the wife of a Yale University professor and executive director of the Planned Parenthood League of Connecticut, and Dr. C. Lee Buxton, a prominent New Haven physician connected with the Yale Medical School, who was director of the New Haven Planned Parenthood League and had been one of the plaintiffs in *Poe v. Ullman*, were arrested for giving contraceptive advice to a married couple. Unlike the two earlier test cases, which were declaratory judgment actions, the *Griswold* case involved an actual criminal prosecution, albeit one that had been carefully invited and staged.[21] The defendants were convicted and fined one hundred dollars each, under Section 54-196, General Statutes of Connecticut (1958 rev.),

the same provision at issue in *Tileston* and *Poe*. The statute provided that:

Any person who assists, abets, counsels, causes, hires or commands another
to commit any offense may be prosecuted and punished as if he were
the principal offender.

Their convictions under this section were affirmed in the state
courts, and the *Griswold* case was argued in the United States
Supreme Court in March, 1965.

As they planned their appeal, lawyers for the appellants found
five possible constitutional arguments to use against Connecticut's
law; it could be seen as denying equal protection, freedom of
speech, due process, a right to privacy, or reserved rights protected by the Ninth Amendment.[22]

Since anyone except the very poor had access to contraceptives,
they could urge that the law denied equal protection (since the
poor were those chiefly affected by the unavailability of birth
control clinics). However, the Court might not be ready to hold
that a law that denied services to the poor, which those who were
better off financially could provide for themselves in other ways,
denied equal protection.

An argument from the First Amendment also might be weak.
Freedom of speech was indeed limited by the act, which made
counselling persons about contraception illegal. But the counselling
was closely tied to the activity of running a clinic, and the Court
might find that the restriction on speech was incidental to a
legitimate regulation of conduct.

Substantive due process seemed the best approach, but here
again there were pitfalls. It would be easy to argue that the law
was unreasonable, arbitrary, capricious, and not related to a proper
legislative purpose. Yet since the 1930s, the Court had been reluctant to substitute its views of reasonableness for those of the
legislature—at least where business and property rights were concerned. The legal team would have to convince the Court that
such supervision was legitimate in this case, because Connecticut's
law infringed basic human rights. They would have to argue also

that the legislature could not justify its regulation on ground of morality, unless there were some showing of an objective relationship between the regulation of morals and the public welfare. Without objective standards, "promotion of morality" could be used as a justification for almost any law.

The Ninth Amendment reads, "The enumeration in the Constitution of certain rights shall not be construed to deny or disparage others retained by the people." One of these unenumerated rights could arguably be a right to control one's own reproductive life free from coercion by the state. This Ninth Amendment claim was not raised at trial, but was urged before the Supreme Court as one basis for a right to privacy.

The right to privacy argument was risky "[s]ince no constitutional right of privacy had previously been recognized, at least as an independent doctrine; in order to dispose of the case on that ground it was necessary to establish a new constitutional concept."[23] The Court would have to find an anchor for this claim in the Constitution. It could be justified in two ways: first, aspects of privacy were protected by many parts of the Constitution; second, it could be argued that the concept of privacy was an essential element in a "scheme of ordered liberty." Different Justices would find the different approaches appealing.

In a surprising decision, the Supreme Court overturned the Connecticut law, holding that it abridged its citizens' rights to privacy. Six Justices found that a right to privacy existed, reading this concept for the first time into the Constitution.

Justice Douglas wrote the opinion of the Court, although only Justice Clark supported his reasoning without qualification. Douglas's opinion rested on a combination of grounds, some advanced in his *Poe* dissent and some suggested by the appellant's brief. Although he denied that the Court had the responsibility or authority to sit as a superlegislature, checking the wisdom, need, or propriety of economic and social legislation, Douglas indicated that closer scrutiny of laws restricting personal liberty was needed. This point, however, was not developed, and he expressly disclaimed any authority in the Court to substitute its prejudices for those of the legislature. The main thrust of his opinion was that the

Court had in the past protected rights not specifically mentioned in the Constitution and listed such peripheral rights as the right to free association, the right to educate one's children, and the right to distribute, receive, and read printed material—all rights that could be derived from the First Amendment. In such a fashion, a right to privacy, although not formally mentioned anywhere, could also be derived, not just from the First Amendment, but from the Third, Fourth, and Fifth amendments, all of which create zones of privacy by their provisions. The Ninth Amendment, with its statement that the listing of rights in the Bill of Rights is not exclusive, supports this interpretation. Douglas thus tied the concept of a right to privacy to several specific provisions of the Constitution, but based it broadly enough so that it would protect more than physical intrusions under the Fourth Amendment or the compelled testimony of the Fifth Amendment. In his closing peroration, he also tied the right to privacy to the tradition of individual freedom in private affairs that has been generally part of the American tradition.

We deal with a right of privacy older than the Bill of Rights—older than our political parties, older than our school system. Marriage is a coming together for better or for worse, hopefully enduring, and intimate to the degree of being sacred. It is an association that promotes a way of life, not causes; a harmony in living, not political faiths; a bilateral loyalty, not commercial or social projects. Yet it is an association for as noble a purpose as any involved in our prior decisions.[24]

Douglas's statement did not satisfy all members of the Court, and concurring opinions advanced both narrower and broader rationales for the holding. Yet six Justices accepted a right to privacy in some form, and seven voted to reverse the convictions.

The importance of *Griswold* was that it picked up and articulated a widespread concern for privacy, gave it constitutional grounding, and tied it to precedent and traditional political theory. For the first time, the Court acknowledged that such a right, implicit in our tradition of individualism and limited government, was basic enough to our society to be given constitutional dimensions. The time was ripe for the court to assert such a right. Throughout society, concern was widespread about government intrusions, inquisitions, and regulations: eavesdropping, wiretapping, record-keeping and data banks, surveillance of political dissidents, sexual deviants and criminal suspects, warrantless searches, and many other invasions of individual privacy. Many of the Court's own recent decisions in First and Fourth Amendment cases had upheld aspects of a right to privacy.[25] The skillful work of the attorneys in *Griswold*, especially Professor Thomas I. Emerson of the Yale Law School and Catherine Roraback, authors of the primary brief, put the constitutional arguments in a persuasive form and tied them to accepted precedent and doctrine. By design, the brief was a legal document, with nonlegal data subordinated to the legal argument or left to the *amicus* brief.[26] The legal team had carefully surveyed the due process positions of the sitting Justices, and their argument offered the Court options in several directions, all of which would allow the Court to create a right to privacy out of traditional materials and weave it into the fabric of familiar constitutional law.

Although the right established in this case was limited to marital privacy, a basis was laid for the elaboration and refinement of a more general right. But even the relatively narrow protection of marital privacy could have a broad impact on existing laws. Writing about the case after it was over, Professor Emerson predicted that the decision might be used to require stricter standards of relevance and public purpose in many areas where the state interfered with private sexual and marital conduct. It might even, he ventured, supply the basis for an attack on state abortion laws.

A Flood of Litigation in the Lower Courts

If *Griswold* established the constitutional grounds for such a challenge, a germinal article by Roy Lucas supplied the blueprint for a successful lawsuit in the abortion area.[27] Lucas, a professor of law at the University of Alabama School of Law, further outlined possibilities for an attack on state abortion statutes. When Lucas's article was published in 1968 in the *North Carolina Law Review*, no test case or other litigation had yet carefully explored constitutional issues underlying abortion legislation. Lucas was interested in the possibility of abortion reform through judicial interpretation and thought that established constitutional concepts were available on which such a challenge could be made. First, such statutes could be seen as abridging a "fundamental right of marital privacy, human dignity, and personal autonomy reserved to the pregnant woman acting on the advice of a licensed physician." *Griswold v. Connecticut* seemed to be a precedent reasonably applicable to abortion legislation insofar as it protected marital privacy and the woman's strong interests in protecting her right to decide for herself questions affecting her health and well-being. Her claim could be based on individual liberty under the due process clause of the Fourteenth Amendment, as well as on penumbral rights "emanating from values embodied in the express provisions of the Bill of Rights themselves."[28]

Lucas's article laid a foundation for much of the later constitutional argument in lower court challenges and indirectly for Justice Blackmun's opinion in *Roe v. Wade*, which drew heavily on ideas developed in lower-court arguments and opinions. He not only isolated and discussed the various interests affected by state abortion laws—the woman's, the fetus's, the physician's, society's —but also pointed out some of the defects in state laws that might be attacked and exploited. He saw a variety of problems with these laws. Their scope was uncertain and their standards vague; they were unevenly and unfairly enforced and thus were discriminatory in effect; they were at odds with current medical standards; they put criminal sanctions behind subjective religious values; and they failed to assert clear, contemporary governmental interests that justified restrictions on abortion. In many ways, this article supplied a master plan for an extended litigation campaign.

Even as Lucas's article appeared, a criminal prosecution was taking place in California that would result in the first important judicial ruling on abortion. In 1967, shortly before California revised its old 1850 abortion law, Dr. Leon Belous, a California doctor, was convicted in a jury trial of criminal abortion and conspiracy to commit abortion and fined five thousand dollars. He had referred a distraught girl, who was threatening to go to Mexico for an illegal abortion if she could not get one in California, to a Los Angeles doctor. Dr. Belous was afraid that a Mexican abortion would be dangerous, and knew that the Los Angeles physician was well trained and reliable. Both Dr. Belous and the other physician were arrested. Since the old California statute made abortions criminal except where "necessary to preserve the life" of the mother, the California Supreme Court was asked to construe this phrase and decide whether it was too ambiguous to support a criminal conviction. The California Supreme Court held that the standard was, indeed, too vague; a doctor must make a decision about whether the woman's life is in danger, but he decides at his peril. If his guesses wrong—if the state prosecutor disagrees with his decision—he may be prosecuted and convicted. The law was held to be unconstitutional. In the written opinion of the California Supreme Court, the Justices went beyond the question of vagueness and held that a woman has "a fundamental right" to choose whether to bear children.

The fundamental right of a woman to choose whether to bear children follows from the Supreme Court's and this court's repeated acknowledgment of a "right to privacy" or "liberty" in matters relating to marriage, family, and sex.[29]

The *Belous* case was a landmark decision for abortion law reformers. As the first case holding that women had rights that were abridged by at least some aspects of abortion legislation, it would be a revolutionary precedent for other abortion cases, and persons prosecuted for performing abortions would now raise these constitutional claims.

While Dr. Belous was being tried, a surgeon involved in abortion referral services on the East Coast was arrested in his office in Washington, D.C. Dr. Milan Vuitch, a Yugoslavian immigrant, believed that abortion was a standard medical service and that abortion laws were irrational. Since 1966 hundreds of women had been referred to him by referral services in the New York-Washington area. Taking advantage of the District of Columbia statute, which allowed abortion for the "preservation of the woman's life or health," he regularly performed abortions that he thought were perfectly legal.[30]

After Dr. Vuitch's arrest, his attorneys decided to use the occasion for a broad attack on the District of Columbia law. Their brief attacked the law not only as unconstitutionally vague, but as abridging the physician's right to carry out his professional responsibilities and as interfering with the woman's right to avoid childbirth. But before the trial began, Judge Gesell of the District Court of the District of Columbia dismissed the indictments on the grounds that the abortion statute was unconstitutionally vague. The United States appealed.

Although the validity of a direct appeal to the Supreme Court was questionable, the Court accepted the case for argument.[31] A fragmented Court held that the appeal was properly before it (Justices Black, Stewart, Douglas, and White and the Chief Justice), but that the law was not invalid (Justices Black, Harlan, Blackmun, and White and the Chief Justice). Writing for a majority of five on the question of constitutionality, Justice Black argued that the preservation of the mother's health and life are not terms so vague that they invalidate the statute. Physicians regularly make decisions to treat patients to preserve health and life. However, he also held that the law had been improperly construed to require that the physician himself prove that an abortion was necessary. Under the District's law, some abortions were legal—those performed to preserve a woman's health or life. But to require the physician to justify each abortion before a judge or jury would be to shift the burden of proof from the state to the defendant contrary to established criminal procedure. Thus for the government to convict a physician of improper abortion, it should be obliged to prove that the abortion was *not* necessary to preserve the recipient's health or life. The Supreme Court, therefore, reversed and remanded the case to the District Court, where presumably the government would be free, if it so chose, to try Dr. Vuitch under the proper procedure.

Justice Black, in ruling as he did, was following traditional practice in reading a statute to "save" it from a charge of unconstitutionality, one of the devices commonly used by courts to reduce conflicts with legislatures. The Court had handled the first abortion case to reach it very gingerly, deciding on the narrowest possible basis. It upheld the statute, but it did not reach constitutional claims based on the *Griswold* case. This decision indicated that the Court would be deeply divided on the broader issues. Only two Justices, Douglas and Stewart, indicated that they would have serious doubts about the constitutionality of abortion statutes.

But the process of educating the Court had barely begun. Before 1973 the Justices would learn a great deal about abortion from the lower court cases, from *amicus curiae* briefs,* and from argument and reargument before the Court itself. When *Vuitch* was decided, the issue had not been fully briefed and argued, although two cases were set for oral argument in December, 1971. At that time, presumably, the Justices would also read some of the opinions in lower court cases beginning to pile up below. Many of the opinions in these cases were full of information and analyzed the problem from many angles. Law reviews would also help educate the Court. Some law review articles had already appeared, the Lucas article in 1968, one by former Justice Tom Clark in 1969,[32] and an article by C. C. Means, a lawyer active in the reform cause, that was said to have been written especially to influence the Supreme Court.[33]

As one of the women's issues reaching the courts in these years, abortion was not a subject on which the largely masculine legal profession had much information or experience. One of the overt aims of the women bringing litigation was that of informing and educating the courts. In an interview in the spring of 1973, Nancy Stearns and Janice Goodman reviewed this aspect of the abortion litigation.

NANCY: Looking back from three years ago to where we are now, with the ROE and DOE decisions, I don't think we can possibly underesti-

---

Amicus curiae is literally "friend of the court." *Amicus curiae* briefs are briefs from nonparties who are interested in the outcome of the case. They may be filed upon written consent of the parties or by permission of the court. They often present arguments and information not included in the main briefs. The filing of amicus briefs is a subtle form of lobbying, a method by which organizations can indicate their support of a certain policy perspective.

mate how much women have taught judges, lawyers and the public generally on the women's rights issues, particularly on what an unwanted pregnancy and child mean to a woman. When we came into court three years ago with all this, the judges didn't have the foggiest notion of what we were talking about and many male lawyers treated us as unwanted interlopers. I mean they really did not understand women's rights claims and they certainly did not understand how serious it was to a woman to have an unwanted child. The degree of progression of the opinions was extraordinary in a period which I consider fairly short, given the novelty of the fundamental rights that we are talking about here. I think that that was extremely impressive. But again I must stress that I think that this progression was largely due to the strategy of bringing women's rights cases. I don't think we could have educated the judges the same way in purely doctors' lawsuits.

When we talked about women's rights, we presented the judges with live testimony on exactly what the abortion experience meant to women themselves. The lawsuit provided the best educational device we could think of.

JAN: But not all judges wanted to learn. In the New York case we had to take women's testimony by deposition. In Rhode Island two of the judges walked out of the courtroom.

NANCY: One of them was stuck there alone. He was very kind and decent to us. The others had listened to us women lawyers, but they didn't want to hear the testimony of women talking about their lives. They understood the concept of the testimony of experts, of doctors, embryologists. . . . But who ever heard of a woman walking into the court room talking about something so personal and emotional as a backstreet abortion. . . . None of the judges wanted to hear about that. They all felt it was irrelevant.[34]

In 1969 and 1970, the trickle of cases into lower federal and state courts became a flood of litigation. The *Congressional Quarterly* reported that legal actions, civil and criminal, were pending in thirteen states by 1970.[35]

Four cases brought in 1969 in New York are typical of many

of the abortion cases filed in these years. Many of the cases were movement cases, brought as part of a political strategy by local, activist women's groups, and were designed as much to educate the community and publicize women's issues as to invalidate abortion statutes. Dozens of cases were brought, across the country, by women who saw abortion rights as the key to women's liberation. These cases were brought more or less independently of each other, although the groups exchanged information and often hired the same lawyers. The women's movement, at this stage in its development, did not have the resources to mount an organized and coordinated effort to build a body of precedent favorable to their views and aims. Nor did it have a cadre of volunteer lawyers or money to pay them.[36] Rather, it had to rely on individual and local initiative to bring cases and to find whatever supporting resources were available in the community.

The four New York cases, consolidated for trial, were brought by different kinds of community organizations. The first, *Abramowicz v. Lefkowitz*,[37] had 314 plaintiffs, mostly women. The Women's Health Collective, a group organized by women involved in various ways in the health care system, had been discussing a legal attack on the state abortion law for some months. This group got in touch with women's liberation activists and other groups concerned with women's issues; a coalition of women's groups called Women's Abortion Project was formed to coordinate the effort. Lists of plaintiffs were drawn up and a press conference held in which representatives from legal groups, health groups, media women, and women's liberation people came. Lawyers from several community and public interest organizations prepared the necessary legal papers. Much of the work was volunteered and expenses were defrayed by fund-raising activities of all kinds. Two lawyers involved in the New York cases wrote:

As usual, when there is need in a "movement" for litigation, affirmative of defensive, there was no money for legal fees or expenses. Again, as is usual when oppressed people need money to go to court, there was considerable discussion of various fund-raising projects. There was no money for the facilities of the Law Center for Constitutional Rights, out of which

Nancy Stearns practices, and the Law Commune, where Carol Lefcourt and Ann Garfinkle were partners. All legal, clerical, and secretarial work were on a volunteer basis.[38]

The *Abramowicz* case was designed to assert women's claims that the New York law abridged their constitutional rights. It and the three companion cases sought a declaratory judgment that the law was unconstitutional and an injunction prohibiting its further enforcement. *Hall v. Lefkowitz* presented the claims of physicians who believed their right to practice medicine was inhibited by the law. *Doe v. Lefkowitz* presented the claims of poor people and persons on welfare and was brought by the Community Action Legal Services Office. The *Doe* plaintiffs were poor people—one palsied couple had been denied a therapeutic abortion even though they were unable to care for a child, and three plaintiffs were women with unwanted children, two on welfare. *Lyons v. Lefkowitz* presented claims against the law by a minister, Reverend Jesse Lyons, involved in abortion referral services. The defendants included the attorney general of New York, Louis J. Lefkowitz, and the district attorneys of various boroughs. A group of Catholic doctors was allowed to join the case as intervenors on the side of the defendants. Various organizations prepared *amicus curiae* briefs.[39]

Influenced by tactics developed in civil rights litigation, the lawyers who organized the *Abramowicz* case tried, first, to use direct testimony by witnesses to establish the oppressive nature of New York's abortion statutes. They selected a number of women who were prepared to testify about their own illegal abortions, the circumstances under which they had been obtained, the reasons for resorting to abortion, and the stresses, pain, and indignity forced on them by the existing system.

The busy federal court before which this and the other three cases were to be tried refused to set aside time to hear lengthy testimony, but agreed to let witnesses submit written depositions. The strategists decided that it would be effective to have these witnesses depose in meetings open to the public and to invite the press. The case could thus be used as an educational device, not only for the lawyers and judges who would read the depositions, but for the general public.

The constitutional arguments that were developed in the cases followed the suggestions set forth two years earlier in Roy Lucas's *North Carolina Law Review* article. Lucas, now a member of the James Madison Constitutional Law Institute, was an attorney for the plaintiffs in the physicians' case.

The principal case, the woman's case, raised challenges to the New York law under the First, Fourth, Fifth, Sixth, Ninth, Tenth, and Fourteenth amendments, claiming invasions of a number of constitutional rights. As set forth in Paragraph 13 of the Complaint:

13. The challenged statutes are unconstitutional on their face and as applied in that they:

   (a) invade plaintiff's right of privacy or liberty in matters related to marriage, family, and sex; the sacred right of every individual to the possession and control of her own person; and the right to be left alone as guaranteed by the First, Fourth, Fifth, Ninth, and Fourteenth Amendments to the Constitution;

   (b) chill and deter plaintiffs in the exercise of their rights of association, privacy, and sexual and family relations, as guaranteed by the First, Fourth, Fifth, Ninth, and Fourteenth Amendments;

   (c) deprive plaintiffs of the fundamental right of a woman to choose whether to bear children, as guaranteed by the Fourth, Fifth, Eighth, Ninth, and Fourteenth Amendments;

   (d) deprive plaintiffs of the right to safe, speedy, and adequate medical care on the basis of wealth in violation of the constitutional guarantee of equal protection of the laws;

   (e) deny plaintiffs life and liberty without due process of law, despite a lack of compelling State interest and despite the fact that "Childbirth involves risk of death," *People v. Belous*, in that they force them to expose themselves to the hazards and risks of illegal abortion in order to terminate an unwanted pregnancy;

   (f) deprive plaintiffs of safe and adequate medical care on the basis of the religious beliefs of others in violation of the First Amendment guarantee against the establishment of religion;

(g) deny plaintiffs access to information concerning their health, safety and welfare, and the availability of safe, speedy and adequate medical care in violation of the guarantees of the First Amendment;

(h) deprive plaintiffs of guarantees of due process of law in that the only criterion for a legal abortion is the preservation of the life of the mother which is unconstitutionally vague and without standards;

(i) deprive plaintiffs of what little access they might have to a legal abortion without due process in violation of the Fourteenth Amendment in that they chill and deter doctors and hospitals from performing such medical procedures because of fear of prosecution under the unconstitutionally vague statutes;

(j) constitute cruel and unusual punishment in violation of the Eighth Amendment in that they force plaintiffs to bear and raise unwanted children;

(k) deny plaintiffs their right to pursue a career in violation of their rights of liberty and property as guaranteed by the Fifth and Fourteenth Amendments by forcing them to give birth to a child when they do not wish to;

(l) deprive plaintiffs, most of whom are taxpayers, of equal access to both public and private medical facilities which on information and belief receive substantial Federal and State funding, such equal access guaranteed by the Fifth and Fourteenth Amendments to the Constitution.[40]

Plaintiff's brief, which ran to eighty-eight pages, was written by Nancy Stearns and emphasized the discriminatory effects of abortion laws on women, drawing heavily on the California *Belous* decision and its recognition of a fundamental right to choose whether or not to bear children. Stearns developed arguments that denials of both life and liberty existed, tying these arguments to a woman's right to pursue common callings and develop all of her faculties.[41] By forcing a woman to remain pregnant against her wishes, restrictive abortion laws limited her right to work and hold a job, ended educational opportunities, in some cases barred her from public housing, and forced her into marriage or onto welfare to pay for her child's upkeep.

Thus, having been forced to bear a child she did not want, she may be deprived of her right and ability to provide for herself and her child, either because of employer policies or because of her inability to leave the child. Surviving on at least marginal income when she is obviously in need of public housing, she is then deprived of decent shelter because of the existence of that very same child.[42]

Although the main emphasis of the brief was on loss of liberty, it also developed claims to equal protection, right to privacy, cruel and unusual punishment, and religious freedom. None of these infringements, the brief argued, was justified by any compelling state interest.

An *amicus curiae* brief written by Emily Goodman added the additional argument that compulsory pregnancy was a violation of the Thirteenth Amendment's prohibition of slavery and involuntary servitude.

Where a woman is under the compulsion of the abortion laws to retain the status of unwanted pregnancy, there is a punitive, tragic denial of self; that human female is a slave to an embryo, in as compelling and torturous a way as Dred Scott was to his master. The state is now in the position of master to the individual, dictating *individual* breeding habits and patterns. . . .

Slavery implies involuntary servitude—a state of bondage; the ownership of mankind as a chattel, or at least the control of the labor and services of one man for the benefit of another, and the absence of a legal right to the disposal of his own person, property and services.[43]

This argument was made in the *amicus curiae* brief rather than in the main brief. It is likely that some of the attorneys recognized that it would have been too extravagant for the District Court and might have antagonized conservative judges.

Abramowicz v. Lefkowitz and the other three cases never came to trial. On July 1, 1970, the New York legislature passed a reform statute that legalized abortion, if performed by a doctor before the twenty-fourth week of pregnancy. Judge Henry J. Friendly of the United States Court of Appeals, 2nd circuit, who was the senior judge on the three-judge statutory District Court designated to hear this case, dismissed the proceeding as moot on the same day that the law was passed.

Although this case was never tried, lawyers involved in both this and the companion cases found their experience in preparing it valuable; they acted as counsel in a number of the abortion cases filed in courts across the county. Although a well-organized litigation campaign on the model of the NAACP-Legal Defense Fund campaigns for school desegregation and the abolition of captial punishment never developed, an informal network of communication resulted, and groups bringing suits in different cities exchanged ideas and legal strategies. Several lawyers worked in a number of these suits.[44]

Nancy Stearns and Janice Goodman worked in New Jersey[45] and Rhode Island,[46] helped the lawyers in Massachusetts,[47] and worked in Florida[48] and Connecticut.[49] They also gave advice and sent papers to women all over the country who wanted to start lawsuits in their own communities. Rhonda Copelon Schoenbrod represented the defendants in *Byrn v. New York City Health and Hospitals Corporation*.[50] After *Roe* and *Doe*, these lawyers were involved with Medicaid and other problems rising out of new state laws.[51] Nancy Stearns and Roy Lucas also appeared as counsel in *Y.W.C.A of Princeton New Jersey v. Kugler*, and *Abramowicz v. Kugler*.[52] This suit was very much like the New York case. It was a class action on behalf of twelve hundred women plaintiffs and resulted in a declaratory judgment holding that New Jersey's abortion statute abridged fundamental individual and family rights and that a woman had the right to determine whether to bear a child or terminate an early pregnancy.

A number of different contentions were examined in the lower court decisions. In *Babbitz v. McCann*,[53] the first federal court decision overturning a state abortion law, attorneys for the defendant doctor decided to argue the unconstitutionality of the statute as well as defending against the criminal charges. They called in Joseph Nellis of Washington, D.C., who had represented Dr. Vuitch, and filed a declaratory judgment action in federal District Court. The District Court found that the Ninth Amendment and various decisions protecting the right to privacy in home, sex, and marriage forbade the state from depriving the woman of her private decision on childbearing.

Another lower court opinion explored the rights of the fetus. In *Abele v. Markle*,[54] a class action representing hundreds of Connecticut women, the District Court invalidated a newly enacted statute that forbade all abortions except to preserve the life of the mother and protected the fetus from the moment of conception. The court refused to hold that the fetus was a person protected by the Fourteenth Amendment, but agreed that the fetus could have rights conferred on it by law. The state could not, however, strike a balance that abridged all of the mother's rights, including her constitutional rights to privacy and personal choice. Especially in a situation where sharp public disagreement occurred over the status of the fetus, one group must not be allowed to use the criminal law to enforce its views on others, asserting the rights of the fetus at the expense of the woman.

As abortion challenges were decided in the lower courts, state and federal, the Supreme Court was bombarded with appeals and petitions for *certiorari*.*[55] Appeals came both from procedural decisions and decisions on the merits. Some decisions declared laws invalid; some upheld them; some granted declaratory judgments or granted or denied injunctions for the enforcement of the statutes. Clearly, the situation indicated a need for a definitive decision by the Supreme Court. At first the Supreme Court was in no hurry to take a case and seemed to be avoiding decision by deciding cases on jurisdictional and procedural bases.[56] Appeals from six cases were dismissed or dismissals by the lower courts affirmed. Six more cases, including the two that would eventually be decided in 1973, were before the Court at the end of the 1970 term, and another was filed that summer. *Roe v. Wade* and *Doe v. Bolton* were accepted for hearing on May 31, 1971.

In view of the importance of the issue and the uncertainty produced by failure to decide it, it was clear that the Supreme Court

---

* A petition for *certiorari*, if granted, brings a case before the Supreme Court for review.

would not be able to avoid the issue indefinitely. However, it was by no means clear that the ultimate decision would favor the reformers. The *Vuitch* decision, the one case accepted and decided by the Court, gave some indication of the positions of the Justices in 1971. At least five Justices (the Chief Justice and Justices Black, White, Harlan, and Blackmun) had all voted to uphold the law or at least refused to find it unconstitutional. Justices Douglas and Stewart, as their votes in *Vuitch* indicated, would probably vote to overturn an abortion law, and it was possible (although by no means certain) that Justices Brennan and Marshall, once a case was accepted for review, would vote with them. Both had taken a strong "right to privacy" stance in the *Griswold* case. But these figures indicated that even if the Supreme Court agreed to hear an abortion case and decide it on the merits, the chances of its being resolved in favor of proreform litigants was unlikely.

Other factors were present that must have made the Court cautious on this subject at this time. The political climate of 1971 and 1972 was inauspicious for a revolutionary decision that would overturn old social patterns and blaze new legal trails. President Nixon had campaigned in 1968 against an activist Court and had already succeeded in placing two appointees on what would soon be the Nixon Court. Justice Fortas's resignation and the confirmation fight over his replacement had rocked the Court and perhaps made it aware of political threats to it as an institution. There can have been little appetite at this time for a struggle with the controversial subject of abortion. Justice Douglas had seen the dangers of the abortion issue in his dissent in *Vuitch*, where he wrote (although he was referring to difficulties that such cases presented to juries):

Abortion statutes deal with conduct which is heavily weighted with religious teachings and ethical concepts. . . . Mr. Justice Jackson once spoke of the treacherous grounds we tread when we undertake to translate ethical concepts into legal ones, case by case. The difficulty and danger are compounded when religion adds another layer of prejudice.

The subject of abortions—like cases involving obscenity—is one of the most inflammatory ones to reach the Court.[57]

In 1971 Justices Harlan and Black retired and died. They were replaced, after another battle between the President and the Senate, with Lewis F. Powell of Virginia and William Rehnquist of Arizona. Appointed as conservatives, both Justices might have been expected to favor a ruling leaving the regulation of abortion to the states.

Appeals from District Court decisions invalidating abortion laws in Texas and Georgia finally brought the issue back into the Supreme Court. The two cases involved both the older type (Texas law was passed before the Civil War) and a reform version (Georgia's ALI type statute was passed in 1968) of state abortion laws. The cases were set for oral argument on December 13, 1971.

In the Supreme Court

Courts and Public Policy

The decision in *Roe v. Wade* was an activist decision, one with enormous potential impact on public policy. Justice White, in dissent, characterized it as "an exercise in raw judicial power" that, "with no constitutional or legal justification, overrode the decisions made for people in the states by their state legislatures." It invalidated traditional state power to make abortion a criminal offense and forced a shift from an older set of accepted state policies on abortion to a legal position more in line with newer currents of public opinion.

Although the decision was framed in terms of traditional principles and precedents, these principles and precedents were clearly being used to make new law. Behind the legal formulae lay issues such as the need for population control, the depletion of natural resources, the changing status of women, and concern about illegitimacy, welfare costs, and child care, which were not openly discussed. Yet the Court was clearly not indifferent to the underlying policy considerations, although it seemed to avoid their discussion as a matter of conscious strategy. Part of the Court's enormous power has always come from the fact that it can change the law in the process of interpreting and applying it, legitimatizing changes by invoking the authority of the Constitution. Such a shifting of the grounds of debate from the underlying policy considerations to legal principles is nothing new. The translation of social and political issues into constitutional questions so that a solution can be attempted in the cooler language of the law and the quieter atmosphere of the courtroom is a classic exercise of the Supreme Court and is certainly typical of the Court's handling of controversial issues during its most powerful and effective periods of operation. Alexis de Tocqueville's much quoted statement that "scarcely any political question arises in the United States that is not resolved sooner or later into a judicial question" was made not in 1973 but in 1835.

But in spite of the fact that judicial policymaking is nothing new, the Justices in dissent in *Roe* and *Doe v. Bolton* pointed out, as dissenters have always done, that the Court was making law and that decisions that are not directed by the words of the Constitution but are in fact legislative in nature ought to be left to the legislative bodies. Legislatures not only represent the people but are better equipped to weigh policy alternatives and balance interests. As Justice White explained, where no clear constitutional command exists, the courts should defer "to the people and to the political processes the people have devised to govern their affairs."[1]

Although this is the traditional dogma of separation of powers, realists are aware that some of its assumptions are doubtful. Legislatures are not always representative and do not always do a more conscientious job than the courts in making policy. Archibald Cox, former Solicitor General and Watergate Special Prosecutor, discussed in a recent lecture some of the shortcomings of the traditional view. He described a classroom session in which he was trying to illustrate the differences between the responsibilites of legislatures and courts to his students. He painted a picture of the careful, detached, and wise legislator weighing proposals and finally coming up with a good bill. What was the function of a judge in a situation where such a law was before the courts for evaluation of its constitutionality; should he go over the same ground again in assessing the legislature's performance, acting as a superlegislator? One of Cox's students pointed out that balanced and detached legislation is not what goes on in legislative bodies.

The student replied that my question was based on a false hypothesis because no legislature acted or was even expected to act in the manner I had described; what I had described was the process of decision followed by the Court.[2]

Cox said that although he disagreed with the student's analysis, it hit near a different truth.

The political branches are the forums where group interests are served, coalitions are built, loyalties are formed, and obligations respected.

The court's decisions are legitimate only when it tries to disassociate itself from individual and group interests and apply objective standards.[3] But although courts try to rule in terms of legal principles instead of group demands, their decisionmaking (especially that done by the Supreme Court in interpreting and applying the Constitution) is often legislative in that it is prospective and affirmative, rather than historical and negative.[4]

Federal courts have been moving toward greater *affirmative* involvement with public policy since the desegregation cases were decided in 1954. Where earlier courts controlled policy by negation, imposing constitutional limitations and nullifying legislative proposals, in more recent years, the judiciary has been ignoring many of the classic limitations of the judicial process and becoming directly involved in "controversial programs of affirmative action requiring detailed administration for protracted periods under constant judicial supervision."[5] They have been evading restrictions stemming from the adversary system itself that have in the past kept courts from ranging too broadly through the wonderland of social experimentation. Instead of deciding particular disputes between clearly identified parties, they have opened their doors to class action and group suits involving large numbers of litigants.

Litigation is no longer clearly defined or tied to specific remedies for private wrongs committed in the past. The lawsuits are often sprawling and amorphous and require the judge to predict future developments and devise plans that will control future events.[6] For example, federal District Court judges have issued orders restructuring entire school systems of 750,000 or more students[7] and implemented a broad range of reforms in state prisons, covering minute details such as how many and what types of toilets must be provided for each cell block.[8]

In many of the newer cases, the courts have come to act more like legislative bodies in that they respond not to the claims of individuals seeking settlement of particular disputes, but to the demands of interest groups using the courts to promote their policy goals. The assumptions of the traditional lawsuit are now reversed. Instead of a carefully limited dispute, tied to the claims of two contending parties arguing about private rights, many of the newer suits are disputes over the proper policy that should be adopted, are brought by organized groups, and seek to influence a broad range of future behavior in conditions they predict may take place at some later time. The judge is no longer a passive umpire, evaluating the implications of past conflict; he now becomes a philosopher king, deciding what will be a good program for the future.[9]

Roe v. Wade had many of the characteristics of the newer kind of public law case coming into the Supreme Court. It was a class action suit and represented the interests of many women, not just those of the principal parties.* It used declaratory judgment procedures that allowed challenges to a criminal law without the risk of criminal penalties for the challengers and sought court orders enjoining the further enforcement of such laws, should they be held unconstitutional. A variety of interests and groups were represented both in the cases themselves and by *amici curiae*. In *Roe v. Wade* three parties represented the interests involved—a pregnant woman, a couple wanting to prevent pregnancy but wanting access to abortion as a last resort, and a physician being prosecuted for performing abortions. The list of *amici* included thirty-six reform

---

* Class action suits permit people "similarly situated" to litigate a single case on behalf of all members of the class, rather than requiring each individual to bring a separate lawsuit.

organizations—church, medical, university, public health, legal, welfare, women's and population-control groups. The antiabortion side included seven groups, a number of individuals, and attorneys general of five states.

The companion case, *Doe v. Bolton*, presented the claims of Mary Doe and twenty-three others, including nine physicians, seven nurses, five clergymen, two social workers, Planned Parenthood, and Georgia Citizens for Hospital Abortion. Briefs were filed for eleven organizations and groups in *Doe v. Bolton*. The cases were not concerned primarily with the indiv:dual litigants, who were in a sense symbolic rather than real parties—Jane Roe and Mary Doe were no longer even pregnant by the time the decision was handed down—but with major public policy issues. The decision was framed in legal terms and carefully tied into the legal and constitutional traditions of the country, but was in many ways legislative. In addition to negating the existing laws in thirty or more states, it laid out guidelines for future state legislation.

This careful working out of rules to guide other agencies of government reminds one of the 1966 *Miranda* decision with its prescription of "prophylactic" procedures to be followed by law enforcement officers in obtaining admissible confessions.[10] The Court was criticized for its basically legislative approach and for deciding the case too broadly and addressing issues not before the Court.[11] Nevertheless, the Court was probably wise in trying to set forth as precisely as possible the limits within which new state abortion legislation should stay; any other course of action would have invited additional litigation, and the Court may have felt that with such an explosive issue, it would be better to try to short-circuit other appeals, to avoid overemphasizing and overpublicizing the issue until the nation had had a chance to adjust to the central ruling. Granted that the decision was, as it is, one of major policy, it was good tactics to state the policy as clearly as possible and not leave its limits undefined and its central questions unanswered. Women's rights lawyers were pleased with the legislative approach.

JAN: It seems to me that they really wanted to lay down a policy and let the states know how far they could go, with restrictive abortion laws. This was clearly different from BROWN v. BOARD OF EDUCA-

TION. There, folks were stuck with a decision which said "with all deliberate speed" and little more than that. Here, the Court said, "We're telling you right off the bat what you can and cannot do. . . . [t]he majority did go out of its way to spell out the ground rules very clearly. It should prevent years of litigation.[12]

Archibald Cox also noted the legislative qualtiy of this decision and criticized it for "not articulating a precept of sufficient abstractness to lift the ruling above the level of a political judgment based on the evidence currently available from medical, physical and social sciences."[13] But Justice Douglas had tried to articulate such a precept, in his concurring opinion, setting out the structure for a broad right to privacy that would protect (1) "autonomous control over the development and expression of one's intellect, interests, tastes, and personality," (2) "freedom of choice in the basic decisions of one's life respecting marriage, divorce, procreation, contraception, and the education and upbringing of children," and (3) "the freedom to care for one's health and person, freedom from bodily restraint or compulsion, freedom to walk, stroll, or loaf."[14] The Supreme Court had not been ready to accept this articulation of a broad and striking new protection of privacy. It settled instead for a carefully limited right, balanced against the claims of a number of the other interests involved.

The *Roe* and *Doe* decisions involved a major adjustment of the law to the changing requirements of society. When the abortion laws had been written in the 1860s and 1870s, they reflected the concerns, the outlook, and the state of scientific knowledge of those times. The physicians crusade against abortion, which began before the Civil War, succeeded in changing public perceptions and public opinion and replacing tolerance of abortion with a demand for rigid control. In the 1960s and 1970s, the rigidity of the nineteenth-century laws was under attack by interests that had not existed at the time of the original accommodation, and public opinion was shifting back toward tolerance and acceptance.

The Decisions: *Roe v. Wade* and *Doe v. Bolton*

First argued in December, 1971, and reargued in October, 1972, the cases had been before the Court for over a year. According to some sources, the long wait had reflected disagreement within the Court about how the cases should be handled. In conference, after the initial argument in 1971, the vote seems to have been five to two to strike down the abortion laws; at this time, Justices Hugo Black and John Marshall Harlan had left the Court, and their replacements had not yet been sworn in.

According to a report in *Time* magazine, Chief Justice Burger had taken the unprecedented step of assigning the majority opinion, although he was on the dissenting side in conference.[15] This report was later confirmed in the account printed in *The Brethren*, a 1979 expose of the inner workings of the Burger Court.[16] Traditionally, the Chief Justice assigns the opinion of the Court when he is voting with the majority, but leaves this duty to the senior Associate Justice on the winning side when he is in the minority. Justice Douglas was convinced that the Chief Justice was trying to influence the substance of the Court's decision by keeping control of the assignment of opinions. Insiders suggested several reasons why the Chief Justice might have preferred that Justice Blackmun write the abortion opinion. Blackmun was experienced in handling medical-legal problems; he had served as counsel to the Mayo Clinic, the big medical complex in Rochester, Minnesota, before ascending the federal bench. But he was also a very slow, deliberate worker and might not, predictably, be able to finish his opinion before the 1972 presidential election; for obvious reasons, Nixon's new Chief Justice might have wanted to keep the Court from handing down a proabortion decision during the reelection campaign. There was also gossip[17] that the Chief Justice wanted Blackmun to take this opinion because he might be influenced and persuaded to limit and soften the decision. On the other hand, as senior Associate Justice voting with the majority, Justice Douglas might assign the opinion to himself and might produce a broadly written, right-to-privacy opinion along the lines of his opinion in *Griswold v. Connecticut*.

In any event, Blackmun's draft opinion, circulated at the end of the year, did not satisfy other members of the majority, and he withdrew it, asking that the case be set for reargument in the fall. By this time, the two newest Nixon appointees, Justices Powell and Rehnquist, had taken their seats, and it was a possibility that their votes could affect the outcome of the case. Justice Douglas was so infuriated by what he saw as unjustified interference and maneuvering for political purposes with the Court's procedures that he wrote a scathing memorandum accusing the Chief Justice of manipulating assignments and delaying the publication of opinions in order to suppress the majority view.[18] This could only lead to erosion of goodwill among the Justices and damage the Court as an institution. Douglas circulated his memorandum to other members of the Court and appeared to be ready to publish it, even after being urged by Justices Brennan, Marshall, and Stewart to reconsider. He eventually decided not to publish the memorandum, and the cases were put over until the next term for reargument.

As it turned out, the majority's vote after reargument was enhanced rather than diminished, and the final vote was seven to two. Newly appointed Justice Powell joined the majority, and then the Chief Justice himself, possibly to help form a more unified Court on such a controversial issue, changed his vote and supported Justice Blackmun's rewritten opinion. Justices Byron R. White and William H. Rehnquist dissented.

Only three members of the Court supported Justice Blackmun's opinion without qualification—Justices Brennan, Marshall, and Powell. Even before *The Brethren* revealed the extent to which other Justices had suggested changes, modifications, additions, and subtractions, it was clear that this was a compromise opinion. It is too loose-jointed, too clearly an attempt to stitch together a variety of diverse approaches to be the composition of a single Justice. Blackmun himself worked through several drafts, as did his law clerk. Justice Brennan sent him a list of thoughts and suggestions that totalled forty-eight pages. Important suggestions by Justice Marshall were incorporated into the opinion, and Justice Stewart insisted that certain points be included.[19] It is not unusual for an opinion to change and develop after consultation with other Justices, since standard procedure involves circulating the majority opinion (as well as concurrences and dissents) to other members of the Court.[20] The other Justices make notes and comments in the margins of their copies and return them to the author, and a certain amount of discreet bargaining takes place. But with Blackmun's opinion, the law clerks were surprised at the amount of open negotiation, "surprised to see the Justices, particularly Blackmun, so openly brokering their decisions like a group of legislators."[21]

The opinions in the two cases were announced on January 22, 1973. The first case, *Roe v. Wade*, involved a challenge to a Texas law passed in 1857 that made the procuring of an abortion a crime except where the act was done to save the life of the mother. Jane Roe, a pregnant woman, sought a declaratory judgment that the Texas law was unconstitutional because it denied her access to a safe, legal abortion, performed by a competent physician. She challenged it under the First, Fourth, Fifth, Ninth, and Fourteenth amendments, maintaining that it infringed her rights and personal liberty. Two other cases were argued with the *Roe* case. Dr. Hallford, a physician, claimed that Texas law injured him, since he had been arrested for violating the abortion statute that, he claimed, kept him from prescribing the proper treatment for many of his patients. In the third case, a married couple challenged the law on the grounds that the wife had a medical condition that would endanger her life if she became pregnant, and the law would not allow her a legal abortion under safe conditions. The three cases were heard together in a federal District Court in Texas. The suits presented three facets of the abortion problem: the Texas law was being challenged by a pregnant single woman, a childless couple where the wife's health would be threatened by a pregnancy, and a licensed, practicing physician.

A case from Georgia presented still another variation. *Doe v. Bolton* attacked a Georgia statute of the ALI type, although the Georgia law was more complicated than the model law, and any woman seeking an abortion under it was faced with a formidable amount of red tape. Unlike Texas, Georgia permitted some abortions in addition to those necessary to save the mother's life. A woman could apply for an abortion when the fetus was likely to be born with serious defects, when the pregnancy had resulted from rape or incest, or when the pregnancy endangered her life or health. But the statute made it very difficult to qualify for an abortion even when these conditions were present. It set up an apparatus of restrictive regulations, consultations, abortion review boards, court actions, and requirements that abortions be performed only in accredited hospitals. As a practical matter, such a restrictive law would allow very few abortions.

Mary Doe had applied for an abortion at the Grady Memorial

Hospital in Atlanta, claiming that she was a pregnant woman who had been advised that her health would be endangered if she gave birth. She was denied an abortion by the hospital's Abortion Committee. She sought a declaratory judgment holding that the Georgia statute was unconstitutional; she also sought an injunction against its continued enforcement.

The cases, together, presented a wide range of abortion issues. Both could have been rejected on procedural grounds, but the decision on the jurisdictional problems was postponed until the hearing on the merits. Both cases presented unique problems of standing and justiciability.[22]

Jane Roe's initial suit was filed in March, 1970, and Mary Doe's in April, 1970. The pregnancy of neither litigant would have lasted past December, 1970, but the cases did not reach the Supreme Court until 1971 and were not finally resolved until 1973. The women in both cases had by then either terminated their pregnancies or delivered their children, and their cases were clearly moot. However, by this time, it seemed important to have a definitive Supreme Court ruling on abortion, and the Court ruled that abortion cases could be treated as an exception to the general rule that "an actual controversy must exist at the appellate stages of a case, and not simply at the date the action was initiated." Although a particular pregnancy may be over by the time the case reaches the appellate courts, pregnancy is a condition likely to be repeated. Some additional questions presented further opportunities for avoidance, but the Supreme Court finally agreed that in spite of its difficulty, a decision on abortion should be made.

The historic decision was handed down on Monday, January 22, 1973. It made the following key points:

1. A survey of American history and American law established that abortion had not always been a crime and was, in fact, tolerated or treated leniently until the second half of the nineteenth century.
2. The constitutional concept of "liberty" as well as the right to privacy protects a woman's right to choose to terminate a pregnancy, at least in the early weeks of pregnancy. This right is fundamental and may not be abridged, except when a state interest is "compelling" enough to override it.

3. One has no absolute right to control one's own body, or to have an abortion, but a limited right to be balanced against competing interests.
4. The state's interest in protecting fetal life and its right to regulate health care have to be balanced against the woman's rights.
5. In the early part of pregnancy, the woman's claims are much stronger than the competing claims. But the balance changes as pregnancy progresses. After the first trimester of pregnancy, the state may regulate abortion; after the second, it may forbid it (except when it is necessary to preserve the life or health of the mother).
6. States may not impose procedural requirements that unduly burden the performance of first trimester abortions.
7. Constitutional law has no basis for holding that the fetus is a person.

In spite of its revolutionary holding legalizing first trimester abortions, the decision took a middle of the road course. It was indeed a victory for reformers, who were pleased with it but dissatisfied with its limitations on abortion; it displeased and shocked opponents of abortion, who had hoped for a decision outlawing most abortions or at least allowing states to regulate as they chose. But Justice Blackmun's opinion was a compromise opinion that sought a middle ground between conflicting interests. Sarah Weddington, who had argued the *Roe* case before the Supreme Court, later testified before the Bayh subcommittee of the Senate Committee on the Judiciary that:

I am told that Justice Blackmun, in trying to write the opinion for *Roe v. Wade*, spent the entire summer prior to the time the decision was released doing research. He had been medical counsel to the Mayo Clinic for many years. It is my understanding that it was really Justice Blackmun who formulated from his own research the trimester approach that was later reflected in the Court's decision.[23]

Options and Strategies

As he approached the writing of the opinion, Justice Blackmun must have reviewed the various options open to the Court. There were, in fact, four. The Court could have avoided the issue on jurisdictional grounds or postponed its consideration. This option may have been rejected because of the number of cases in the lower courts awaiting review and the conflicting decisions on the subject by state and federal courts. It might also have been seen as an unconscionable avoidance of a difficult duty.[24]

The Court could also have agreed with the position Justices Rehnquist and White expressed strongly in dissent, that the regulation of abortion is a matter that should be left to state legislative judgment. Although this was a thoroughly legitimate position, by adopting this stance, the Court would have said, in effect, that a woman had no reproductive rights that a state legislature was bound to respect. In 1972 Connecticut's legislature had responded to a federal court decision outlawing its ancient abortion statute by passing one that was even more restrictive. The new law allowed abortions only to save the physical life of the mother. It also set out the state's interest in detail as that of "protecting and preserving human life from the moment of conception."[25] Such a statute would be constitutional under the Rehnquist-White approach.

A decision leaving the determination of the allowability of abortion to the states would be the equivalent of a decision holding that women had no rights to terminate pregnancies, except under conditions specified by state law. Some states might, presumably, try to forbid all abortions, absolutely. If the Court had held that abortion is a matter for the states to control, or that the fetus is a person from the moment of conception, there would be no reason why the state need countenance any abortions.

The third possibility was one urged by plaintiffs in many of these abortion cases: a holding that everyone has a right of privacy or liberty in matters related to marriage, family and sex; that everyone has a sacred right to control her (his) body; that everyone has a right to be let alone guaranteed by the First, Fourth, Fifth, Ninth, and Fourteenth amendments. So broad a holding could have affected many matters besides abortion, outlawing state regulations of things such as suicide, the wearing of motorcycle helmets, the use of narcotics, sexual practices between consenting adults, and many victimless crimes.

When the Court's options are set out in this fashion, it becomes obvious that the most desirable, least objectionable course for the Court to follow would be a compromise of some kind that balanced the interests of the fetus, the interests of the state in regulating health and medical practice, and the rights of the woman. Justice Blackmun appears to have worked out the basis for such a compromise in terms of the "viability" of the fetus. The train of thought that brought him to this point must have started from the old common law idea that abortion was not a crime until the fetus had quickened. *Quickening* was the term used to denote the time (sixteenth to eighteenth week) when movements of the fetus were first recognized. It is an old word, based on the superstition that life suddenly rushes into the unborn child at a certain time.[26] The problem with the quickening concept was that although it was of legal and historical importance, it was considered more of a clinical sign of pregnancy than a scientific standard. It was imprecise, and it was closely tied to the religious idea of "ensoulment." Blackmun evidently thought that viability was not only a more precise but a biologically and logically defensible distinction. The fetus, when it was capable of independent life, might logically be given legal protection as an independent being. Here, then, was the basis for a balancing of rights. As long as the fetus was incapable of independent life, the mother's rights could be held to prevail; after viability the balance would shift, and the states might prohibit abortion.

As for the regulation of abortion, here also was a changing situation as pregnancy progressed. Early abortions, done by competent personnel in sanitary surroundings, are not dangerous. As the pregnancy progresses, the operation becomes more complicated and more dangerous. Blackmun thus decided, at some point in the process of working out his compromise, that he would argue that pregnancy is divided into three trimesters. In the first, the woman's rights prevail; in the second, the state may regulate, although not prohibit abortion; in the third, the fetus's interest may be found by the state legislature to predominate over the woman's desires to terminate her pregnancy. This delicate balancing of interests avoided a decision supporting any of the extreme claims, yet recognized the validity of some aspects of all of them.

But the viability compromise did not please any of the parties to the case. The states and their supporters sought confirmation of their authority to prohibit abortion completely. The Roman Catholic church insisted that the fetus at all stages of its development was a human being and denied the morality of taking any human life.[27] The women's groups and some others declared that governmental manipulation of the individual's reproductive life was totally reprehensible, and that both "compulsory pregnancy" and compulsory sterilization laws involved state interference in what should be completely a matter for private decision. Since they saw no justification for state regulation of any kind, Justice Blackmun's division of the pregnancy into trimesters, with the state's interest becoming significant when the fetus became viable, was unacceptable. Among other things, they charged that Blackmun's distinction involved a doctrine of contingent constitutionality, making the woman's right dependent on the state of her pregnancy. The woman is free to choose until a certain point in time; after that "the woman and her fetus revert to state ownership." The viability distinction, they complained, also has the objectionable result of tying the woman's rights to the current state of science and medicine; the woman's right to choose will disappear when scientists are able to keep all fetuses alive in the laboratory. Indeed, they maintain, with the breathtaking advances in medical technique that now allow test-tube fertilization, the removal of a fertilized egg from one woman to another (perhaps even to a man), fetal surgery, ovary and testes transplants, and the possibilities of cloning and genetic manipulation, rights cannot be made dependent on the latest developments in bioengineering. A whole new jurisprudence may be needed to deal with man's ability to alter the human reproductive process at will, but until it is developed and accepted, human rights should attach, as they always have, only to those persons already born. Birth is a clear, recognizable fact; "all else is mystique and conjecture."[28]

This is approximately what Chief Justice Burger said, in another context, in *Eisenstadt v. Baird*, namely, that "The commands of the Constitution cannot fluctuate with the shifting tides of scientific opinion."[29]

The Court had been unwilling to hold that a blanket protection of human life exists from the moment of conception, but it had also been unprepared to hold that the states have no power to protect fetal life. If it was unwilling to say when life begins, still it was willing to hold that where life is present, and can survive, it may be protected.

With the outline of his compromise in mind, Justice Blackmun must have considered the strategies needed to present it in acceptable terms. A number of issues had to be addressed, but a number of others, equally clearly, should be avoided. First, it was necessary to explain exactly what history, especially American history, said about traditional attitudes toward abortion and its past regulation by law; second, it might be a good tactic to emphasize the idea that the Court was approving abortion for medical purposes and not for socioeconomic reasons; third, it would be wise to evade discussion of philosophical and religious doctrines on which there was no agreement and no hope of finding consensus, and which might involve the Court in church-state complications; fourth, it would be a good strategy to resist using social science or medical data extensively and to emphasize the constitutional grounding of the decision; and fifth, it was clear that without some general guidelines to state legislatures, the Court would be involved for years in case-by-case determinations of constitutionally acceptable and unacceptable legislative schemes.[30]

The first question to answer concerned the historical background of the abortion question. By this time, Justice Blackmun was aware that history gave no clear directions on the issue, that no venerable and consistent legal tradition could be found behind state statutes, and that even the attitude of Western European cultures on the subject had been inconsistent. The first section of his opinion was used to examine the medical-legal history of abortion. His search began back in the pre-Christian era, with the ancient Greeks, for it was claimed that the tradition represented by the Hippocratic oath showed a centuries-old belief that abortion was contrary to natural law. The Hippocratic oath, taken in classical times by young men entering the practice of medicine, is still taken by young doctors graduating from medical school. The oath begins with the words, "I swear by Apollo, the physician, by Aesculapius, by Hygieia, Panacea, and all the gods and goddesses . . ." and goes on to pledge the young doctor to act only for the benefit of his patients. It includes among things he should *not* do the vow, "I will not give a woman a pessary to produce abortion," or in another translation, "I will not give a woman an abortive remedy."[31] Surely, it was argued, a legal or historical tradition this old must reflect basic principles. Justice Blackmun found, however, that the oath represented only one strain of thinking about abortion. The ancient world, he learned, practiced abortion freely, and although some opposed it, it was a common practice and not universally considered a crime against nature. The Hippocratic oath reflected only one of the ancient attitudes on the subject, that of the Pythagorean school of philosophy, the ethical teachings of which later appealed strongly to the Christian church.

He found little more guidance from his researches on the common law, the body of legal principles built up by early English and American courts. Writings that remain treated abortion inconsistently, some as a misdemeanor, and some did not see it as a problem with which the courts were concerned. Justice Blackmun was forced to conclude that "whether abortion of a *quick* fetus was a felony at common law, or even a lesser crime, is still disputed." As for American courts, the few reported cases indicate that it is doubtful "that abortion was ever firmly established as a common law crime even with respect to the destruction of a quick fetus."[32] Justice Blackmun was forced, after this survey, to conclude that "At common law, at the time of the adoption of the Constitution, and throughout the major portion of the 19th century, abortion was viewed with less disfavor than under most American statutes currently in effect." At the time the Constitution was written, he found, women "enjoyed a substantially broader right to terminate a pregnancy" than they had in most states in 1973.[33]

Attitudes toward abortion began to change significantly, Justice Blackmun discovered, in the nineteenth century. The American Medical Association probably helped bring about the change to a more restrictive treatment of abortion. From 1857 to 1871, various reports and conferences and resolutions railed against the destruction of fetal life and urged changes in the laws to protect it. Legislatures responded to medical pressure, at first tentatively but with increasing zeal, by tightening the laws regulating and prohibiting abortion. In 1972, when the opinion was being written, a full-length, careful study of the origins of state abortion legislation, like that done in 1978 by historian James C. Mohr, had not yet appeared. Justice Blackmun, reading through the resolutions and reports of the medical societies, sensed the importance of the medical profession's role in promoting legislation, but he probably did not fully understand the motives for this sudden interest in abortion or the general relationship of the movement to regulate it to the institutional needs and philosophical concerns of the medical profession of the time. He did, however, find that whatever the causes, public opinion had crystalized against abortion by 1880 or 1890, and state legislatures in almost all states had enacted clear prohibitions against it. The law was no longer neutral in the matter; in a majority of states abortion, except to save the life of the mother, was now a crime. Showing as it did that American attitudes had shifted and changed over the years, the Court's historical survey dispelled the idea that a change of policy on abortion would be un-American.

A second point to be emphasized in the opinion was the medical nature of the justification for abortion. A decision supporting abortions for nonmedical reasons, unrelated to the woman's own health and survival, would be open to attack for undervaluing the life of the fetus. Why, after all, should a woman be allowed to destroy life in order to take a trip abroad or buy a new car? The abortions authorized by the decision were those undertaken by women after consultation with their physicians. Underscoring the idea that abortions were to be for medical reasons, Justice Blackmun wrote:

The decision vindicates the right of the physician to administer medical treatment according to his professional judgment up to the points where important state interests provide compelling justification for intervention. Up to those points the abortion decision in all its aspects is inherently, and *primarily a medical decision and basic responsibility for it must rest with the physician.*[34]

Throughout the opinion, the emphasis was on medical factors. Even the viability distinction, which supplied the dividing line between permissible and impermissible abortions, was based on medical knowledge and technique. In some ways, he seemed almost to be appealing to the medical profession to supply the authority he could not find in the law books. An unusually large number of references were to physicians and medical matters in the two opinions. The discussion of the Hippocratic oath, although interesting, was probably unnecessary to the opinion. Sections of *Roe v. Wade* canvassed the views of the American Medical Association and the American Public Health Association on abortion.

In *Doe v. Bolton* the state tried to limit the number of abortions by requiring doctors and hospitals to go through a stiff list of bureaucratic routines before giving its approval, and the appellants contested some of these procedures. They were afraid the physicians would decide not to allow abortions because they disapproved of premarital sex or on other subjective grounds. Justice Blackmun thought that this was an unfair criticism of the medical profession, and he wrote a strong defense of the objectivity, good judgment, high principles, love of humanity, and integrity of medical men. The conscientious physician, particularly the obstetrician

is concerned with the physical and mental welfare, the woes, the emotions, and the concern of his female patients. He, perhaps more than anyone else, is knowledgeable in this area of patient care, and he is aware of human frailty, so-called "error" and needs. The good physician—despite the presence of rascals in the medical profession, as in all others, we trust that most physicians are "good"—will have a sympathy and an understanding for the pregnant patient that probably is not exceeded by those who participate in other areas of professional counseling.[35]

It is hard to see what the function of this outburst of praise might be except perhaps to substitute some of the authority on medical matters that physicians command for the legal authority the opinion lacked—"Doctors do" . . . "doctors recommend" . . . "five out of six doctors use." However, this strategy of emphasizing the integrity of doctors and the medical nature of abortion had the practical result of appearing to supply some kind of objective standards to govern the abortion decision. Doctors make many decisions involving life and death without the help of government. It would be appropriate to defer to the expertise of the medical profession and let individual doctors decide when abortion is in the best interests of the patient.

The conflicting moral and religious attitudes on abortion provided the most difficult problem for Justice Blackmun to handle. The life of the fetus, reverence for life, and the beginning of life all presented philosophical questions. The answers to these questions varied enormously, some groups holding that the fetus is a person from the moment of conception and that all abortion is murder and other groups equally convinced that life begins at birth and that it is an immoral act to bring unwanted children into the world, many of whom would have the additional handicaps of poverty, disease, and mental or physical defects. Religious issues also presented problems, since the doctrines of various churches determined their stands on abortion. Many persons and groups in society believed, however, that the Constitution incorporated their own religious and moral principles. Since the Constitution protects life as well as liberty and property, they concluded that it must safeguard life as soon as it exists. For those who were convinced that human life exists in the embryo, it followed that the constitutional protection of life must include the embryo. But for the Court to have adopted a position so clearly identified with a constellation of religious and philosophical views that is strongly endorsed by Roman Catholics and other identifiable religious groups would have come perilously close to preferring one religion to another. The Constitution forbids this. For the Court to have supported Texas's decision that the developing embryo was "life," and that the existence and value of this life was to be valued over the mother's life, health, or other needs, might have involved the Court in "establishment" or "freedom of religion" problems. Although the Court is careful to avoid a direct statement of this issue, it does say that:

In view of all this, we do not agree that, by adopting one theory of life, Texas may override the rights of the pregnant woman that are at stake.[36]

Epperson v. Arkansas, decided in 1968, had held that a state might not adopt one theologically based view of the evolution of man and prohibit the teaching of other views in its public schools. Government must be neutral in matters of religious doctrine. The First Amendment, it held in *Epperson*,

forbids alike the preference of a religious doctrine or the prohibition of theory which is deemed antagonistic to a particular dogma. As Mr. Justice Clark stated in Joseph Burstyn, Inc. v. Wilson, "the state has no legitimate interest in protecting any or all religions from views distasteful to them."[37]

The reasoning in *Roe*, not spelled out explicitly, seems to be that for the state to decide that immediately after conception the embryo constitutes actual human life, and to protect it absolutely, would in effect be to adopt a theologically based ethical standard. As in the Arkansas case, where the only state reason for forbidding the teaching of evolution in the schools was religious, and no substantial state interest other than this was advanced, the law here is open to challenge on grounds of religious partiality. Although this is not dealt with overtly, the Roman Catholic church's insistent support of the sanctity of early fetal life and its heavy lobbying efforts in state legislatures may have made the Court wary of upholding a Right-to-Life view not supported by either history, precedent, or a strong statement of tangible state interests.[38]

The Court concluded that it must decide on constitutional rather than philosophical or religious principles. A number of years later, addressing a National Law Day audience, Justice Blackmun noted the "long struggle" the Justices had with this case. But the Court, he explained, had decided on constitutional rather than philosophical principles. "All of us have our personal ideas about abortion [but] the fact that I happened to write that opinion . . . doesn't mean that I am a pro-abortionist." Most people

forget that the Court functions only on constitutional principles. All we were deciding was a constitutional issue, not a philosophical one. . . . What we tried to do was face the issue in the light that the Constitution demanded, and I hope that the moral issue is a greater and far more reaching and ranging one. This I think is where the responsibility of the clergy of the church, of the family, of the school, comes in. The Court can't solve everything.[39]

If it was wise to avoid moral issues, it would be equally wise to refrain from arriving at a decision in terms of pressing social problems with which the question of abortion was clearly intertwined. Relevant as these considerations were, the Court's authority does not lie in this direction, but rather requires decision in terms of the provision of the Constitution and constitutional precedent. Early in his opinion, Justice Blackmun acknowledged the difficulty of adjudicating questions so tied into both moral and social issues.

We forthwith acknowledge our awareness of the sensitive and emotional nature of the abortion controversy, of the vigorous opposing view, even among physicians and of the deep and seemingly absolute convictions that the subject inspires. One's philosophy, one's experiences, one's exposure to the raw edges of human existence, one's religious training, one's attitutde toward life and family and their values, and the moral standards one establishes and seeks to observe, are all likely to influence and to color one's thinking and conclusions about abortion.

In addition, population growth, pollution, poverty, and racial overtones tend to complicate the not to simplify the problem.

Our task, of course, is to resolve the issue by constitutional measurement free of emotion and predilection.[40]

Constitutional Alternatives

The crucial question, of course, was whether constitutional measurement sustained the proposed solution. Did the Constitution protect a right to privacy or liberty that required freedom to choose an abortion, if necessary, in the first months of pregnancy? The majority thought it did. The source of the right was either the right to privacy, set forth in *Griswold*, or liberty, protected from unwarranted state restriction by the due process clause. The

Justices differed on the source of the protected right, some preferring the concept of a right to privacy and others preferring a right to make private decisions about private life seen as an essential element of liberty in a free society. The Ninth Amendment's generalities could be seen as supporting either view.

Precedent existed for both concepts, in *Griswold v. Connecticut* and in a more recently decided contraceptive case that further elaborated the privacy concept—"If the right to privacy means anything, it is the right of the *individual*, married or single, to be free from unwarranted governmental intrusion into matters so fundamentally affecting a person as a decision whether to bear or beget a child."[41]

The liberty approach had an older heritage. Cases cited in both *Griswold* and *Eisenstadt* upheld various aspects of a right to freedom of private choice in various matters affecting the family, the home, the private individual—schooling, education, childraising, and bodily integrity. The *Griswold* decision had emphasized marital privacy. The *Eisenstadt* case dealing with unmarried persons, broadened the right of private decisionmaking about reproduction, holding that it would deny equal protection to withhold this right from unmarried persons.

The right to choose to avoid conception, protected in *Griswold*, could have been distinguished from the right to choose an abortion claimed in *Roe*. Abortion and contraception are not the same, although some contraceptive methods, may, in fact, dislodge a fertilized egg, causing abortion, rather than prevent conception. The difficulty of drawing a line between the two would have presented problems in making this distinction. The Court evidently thought that a refusal to extend *Griswold* to a matter so clearly related to it would be a repudiation of the right to privacy so recently established and of the two contraceptive cases so recently decided. These cases did offer a clear, relevant line of precedent.

In addition to a constitutional rationale and clear, if recent precedents, a well-defined strain of respect for the individual and his privacy can be seen in American law and political theory.[42] Locke's political theory, in particular, so major a source of our thinking, emphasizes the "moral primacy of the private over the public sphere of society." Private behavior, belief, religious practice, private property, individual liberty, and individual legal rights were all assumptions implicitly behind the Constitution, and this tradition provides a source of authority for preserving the private sphere. The Constitution's checks on government, ideas of limited government, and the rule of law all grow from the assumption that government should intrude as little as possible on private behavior.

In his 1967 volume, *Privacy and Freedom*, Alan Westin concluded that the notion that privacy is a modern legal right is bad history and bad law.[43] Early American law protected privacy in many ways. It protected against trespasses, private searches by creditors, warrantless searches, and eavesdropping. The law of nuisance protected the individual right to enjoyment of private property. Law forbade compelled testimony, and limited discovery in civil cases. The law was slow, however, to develop beyond propertied privacy to individual privacy. Before *Griswold*, extended discussions of a right to personal privacy had come mostly in dissents and concurrences—Justice Brandeis's classic statement in *Olmstead v. United States*[44] and dissents by Justices Douglas and Harlan in *Poe v. Ullman*.[45] Although the articulation of this right was clearest in search and seizure cases, it was also mentioned in other contexts: the noise pollution of sound trucks[46] and broadcasts of advertising on public transportation,[47] forcible pumping of a suspect's stomach,[48] health inspections,[49] and an attempt by a state investigating committee to get organizational membership lists.[50] Justice Douglas had always been solicitous of this right, and his early opinion in *Skinner v. Oklahoma*,[51] protesting the sterilization of criminals, foreshadowed in language and sentiment his later *Griswold* opinion.

Between the decision of *Griswold* in 1965 and *Roe* in 1973 there were a number of privacy-related decisions, marking a gradual shift from emphasis on physical intrusions on person and property to more subtle invasions of psychological privacy and personal space.[52] The *Roe* court continued this trend, moving beyond physical intrusions on person and property to a view of privacy that included the right to make individual, uncoerced decisions about matters deeply affecting the individual, especially highly personal decisions involving the family and reproduction.

By 1972 world population had exploded, and some governments began to take positive action to discourage childbearing. It then became clear that the right to make reproductive decisions free from compulsion might cut both ways and might involve the right to have children as well as the right not to breed. Once only an imagining of science fiction writers, drastic intervention of government into the business of population control is no longer speculative.[53] When one notes the kind of population-control program undertaken by India in 1976—a massive state effort to reduce the size of families, backed up by penalties and in some cases the seizure on the streets and forcible sterilization of males—one sees the advantage of an ideology that allows people to limit population by voluntary, individual decisions. The *Washington Post* reported in November, 1976, that:

More than 2 million Indians have been sterilized since April, the government claims, under a vast national program intended to limit families to three children.

Each patient gets a cash reward of up to $16, but "disincentives," or penalties, are a much more potent factor. Pressured to meet tough targets and deadlines set by New Delhi, the 22 states are using a variety of bureaucratic armholds to force ordinary citizens into undergoing sterilization and to motivate state employees to push the program.[54]

The *Roe* decision, insofar as it tried to insulate decisions on family planning from government control, may have involved a certain amount of wishful thinking on the part of the Court, a laissez-faire optimism that the implementation of population control could be left to the automatic workings of the natural order. It is possible that the Justices instinctively supported a view of individual liberty that rejects state control of family size, in this instance laws forbidding abortion. If the state can control procreation, future laws might limit family size, or, like India, require sterilization after a certain number of children have been born. In some respects, the protection of a right to make private decisions about the family reinforces old-fashioned libertarian values traditional in our legal system, which the Justices could have been expected to support. If private choice (for contraception, sterilization, or abortion), dictated by individual self-interest, helped to reduce the rate of population growth, the Court might never have to face the question of whether laws making sterilization or family planning compulsory were invasions of privacy justified by a compelling state interest.

The *Griswold* privacy-liberty approach was not the only possible source of decision. As the dissenters in *Roe* and *Doe* made clear, a strong argument existed for leaving the abortion decision to the state legislatures. They had controlled this subject by legislation for over one hundred years without challenge. No clear constitutional command forbade the restriction of abortion, and it seemed, therefore, appropriate to let the people of the states decide how to handle this controversial subject. The protection of life, even the rudimentary life of the unborn, was surely a sufficient justification for legislative action inhibiting freedom of individual choice.

Deference to legislative choice in policy areas where the Constitution's commands were vague, and the temptation to judges to read their own policy preferences into the document was great, was a respected exercise of self-restraint. The right to privacy is not an express right guaranteed by the Constitution of the United States. Although some rights to privacy exist and are exempt from unwarranted state intrusion, the legislature is justified in intruding on those rights where the competing values are greater. The protection of life is, if anything else, a compelling state interest justifying the exercise of state authority, and the rights of the unborn child can be given precedence over the less drastic intrusions on the privacy of the mother.

Problems were evident with both of these constitutional positions. The strongest objection to the Griswold privacy-liberty approach was, as the Attorney General of Texas had argued, that no express right to privacy, especially privacy to choose an abortion, is guaranteed under the Constitution; but even if such a right exists, it does not take precedence over the fetus's right to life. For the Supreme Court to overturn state regulatory statutes that reflect this judgment involves unwarranted judicial policymaking. Decisions such as this are best made by the state legislatures that reflect the wishes of the people.

On the other hand, the deference argument also had its flaws. The right to privacy, while not expressly stated, is readily inferrable from the Constitution and is in harmony with the American individualist tradition. No consistent legal tradition of protection of the unborn exists, and no evidence that the law has ever regarded them as persons until after birth can be found. Indeed, the Texas and Georgia statutes did not even have legislative histories supporting the alleged intention of protecting life. Texas seems to have had the mixed purpose, when its statute was passed, of checking the number of abortions, promoting morality, and protecting the mother's life and health. Its first antiabortion statute did not place an unqualified value on potential life, since it did not forbid abortions before quickening.[55] The impulse behind Georgia's statute seemed to have been limitation of the legal risks run by physicians.[56] Neither of these cases presented a clear instance of a state legislature balancing the life of the unborn against the rights of women wanting or needing abortions and coming up with a considered judgment in favor of the former. Abortion, because of its position at the intersection of cross-pressures of so many kinds, was, in fact, a subject on which the state legislatures have had a particularly difficult time doing a careful and objective job of weighing and balancing values. Full of emotional dynamite and closely tied to religious beliefs, abortion was the kind of "bullet" issue that legislators have avoided when possible. Their decisions, when unavoidable, may be a response to the most vocal and politically potent organized interests, often well-financed minorities, rather than a reflection of judgment and balance. Sarah Weddington, counsel for Jane Roe, later testified to this before the Senate subcommittee considering an antiabortion amendment to the Constitution. She had been a member of the Texas legislature and knew how it felt, after 1973, about addressing the abortion issue anew. She believed that overall, the state legislators do not have the strongest feelings about any supposed need for abortion legislation . . . they would prefer that the Court's decision simply remain standing, and that they not be forced to vote on the issue.[57]

In deciding the constitutional questions, the Supreme Court was aided by the fact that several of the District Courts had already worked through the issues and arguments carefully. For a strong stand in support of state legislation, the Court had a model in *Rosen v. Louisiana State Board of Medical Examiners*,[58] a 1970 decision. There, a three-judge District Court divided on the issue but upheld a state statute that forbade all abortions (although prescribing punishment only for persons performing abortions for reasons not connected with saving the mother's life). Circuit Judge Ainsworth, for a divided court, tried to construct a general defense of the "protection of life" position. His main argument was basically that the legislature has the right to determine the public interest, that there is no excuse for federal court interference with the legislative ordering of priorities in promoting the public welfare, that the State of Louisiana intended to protect embryos, and that such protection does not invade any constitutional right. The Louisiana court refused to follow the decisions given by District Courts in Wisconsin and Texas, in *Babbitz v. McCann*[59] and *Roe v. Wade*,[60] ruling that "As an ethical, moral or religious matter, a woman's refusal to carry an embryo or fetus to term both historically and today, has been condemned as wrong by a substantial if not a dominant body of opinion, except in very limited circumstances." He had some difficulty basing his decision more directly on the rights of the fetus or on an asserted right to life, because of the absence of court decisions equating a fetus and a person already born. His arguments rested on biology (after conception, the fetus is genetically a full human being), morality (the dominant moral view of the nation), and the proper role of courts (federal courts have no authority to interfere with this type of legislative decision).

The dissenting judge in *Rosen* raised a variety of objections to this analysis. One of these objections was the fact that Louisiana's statute, like those in Texas and Georgia, did not show a clear legislative intention to protect fetal life. This argument was presented clearly in a later case coming from Connecticut.

The Connecticut legislature had faced this issue squarely and passed a law declaring that the fetus was a person from the moment of conception, that the state's intention was to protect and preserve such life, and that abortions would be allowed only to save the physical life of the mother. A Connecticut District Court invalidated this law on the grounds that a legislature may not strike a balance between fetal life and maternal rights, which completely overrides the latter. Although the state may protect the fetus to some extent, it may not adopt a controversial theory and use it to deny the rights of other claimants. Judge Newman, speaking for the court, wrote:

But where a state interest subject to such a variety of viewpoints is asserted on behalf of a fetus which lacks constitutional rights, and where the assertion of such an interest would accomplish the virtually total abridgment of a constitutional right of special significance, in these circumstances such a state interest cannot prevail.[61]

The lower courts had done a lot of groundwork in exploring the legal problems involved in abortion before the controversy reached the Supreme Court. Undoubtedly, the careful assessment of the issues by men such as Judges Ainsworth and Newman, as well as by dissenting judges, helped the Supreme Court by working through the issues with great care and pinpointing the theoretical problems that had to be addressed. It was clear during oral argument that the Justices had read all the lower court decisions thoroughly.[62] Justice Blackmun's final opinion echoed a number of these opinions.

The fact that legitimate alternatives to select existed meant, however, that the Court would eventually have to choose, and the choice would probably be made in terms of the policy implications of each course of action. Neither doctrinal option was neutral; the consequence of either would be far-reaching. When the Court decided to uphold a right to legal abortions, it chose a course in harmony with worldwide efforts at population control and international improvements in the status of women.[63] A decision to defer to state legislatures would have allowed at least some states to move counter to these trends. Not all states would have reimposed controls on abortion, but the pressures on the state legislatures would have been enormous, especially once the threat of having their laws declared unconstitutional was removed.[64] By permitting the reinstitution of excessively restrictive rules on abortion, the Court would also have made a highly symbolic move to check further gains by the women's rights movement. In 1972 it had only recently shown signs of taking a harder stand against sex discrimination in state law, overturning an Idaho law that gave automatic preference to males as the administrators of estates.[65] Oral argument had already been set for January, 1973, in a case where the Court would be urged to hold that sex was always a "suspect classification."[66] State legislatures were themselves removing some legal incapacities from women, and Congress had not only passed several statutes forbidding sex discrimination, but had approved the Equal Rights Amendment. An antiabortion decision would have run counter to these feminist gains. It might also have been a backward step as far as the reduction of illegal abortions was concerned, if it encouraged any states to reimpose restrictive laws. But far from satisfying extreme Right-to-Life forces, a decision deferring to state legislatures would have been unacceptable to them insofar as it allowed states to authorize abortions. Battles over abortion at the state level surely would have continued, as would the demands for an amendment to the federal Constitution banning all abortions. It must have been clear to the Justices that no matter how the Court decided, it would not be able to avoid an outburst of condemnation and the bitter charge that it was making policy and not finding the law.

Abortion had many of the characteristics of the issues that had caused problems of compliance and acceptance for several of the historic Warren Court decisions. It pitted the forces of tradition and the forces of change against each other in a subject-matter area where social mores were in transition and public values were changing. In this way, it bore some semblance to *Brown v. Board of Education* and the reapportionment decisions, all of which were greeted with anger and criticism. Like *Brown*, it brought to court demands from a group that had not been heard from before in court, but that had long-term grievances with the substance of the law. In an interview after the decision, women lawyers who had been involved in many of the abortion cases found a close parallel with the desegregation decision.

> JAN: I see parallels between BROWN and the abortion decision even more so than between BROWN and REED because the abortion decision goes to the guts of the women's struggle and also of society's view of women just like the right to equal and integrated education did for Blacks.[67]

Like the school prayer decisions, it raised religious and moral questions, some of the most difficult on which to gain acceptance. Like *Miranda*, it imposed restrictions on an area traditionally controlled by state law.

In confronting a highly controversial subject, where prevailing views were in the process of change but where those holding traditional beliefs could be expected to react strongly, the Justices should have expected to find themselves again in the storm's center. Lulled by Justice Blackmun's carefully constructed and seductive compromise opinion, the Court may not have expected the degree of reaction that followed. Even the proponents of legalized abortion were stunned by the decision, which many of them clearly did not expect. Lawrence Lader, associated with abortion reform since 1966, whose new book on abortion was just going to press, wrote that:

> It came like a thunderbolt—a decision from the United States Supreme Court so sweeping that it seemed to assure the triumph of the abortion movement. . . .

> the Court went far beyond any of the eighteen new state laws the movement had won since 1967, with only New York's law approaching its scope. It climaxed a social revolution whose magnitude and speed were probably unequaled in United States history.[68]

Now it remained to be seen what the practical results of this landmark decision would be.

The Politicization of Abortion

4

The first signs of reaction came quickly. The Court's decision was greeted with elation by women's organizations that had been fighting a generally unsuccessful battle to get restrictive state abortion laws repealed. They thought this was the most far-reaching constitutional and legal advance for women's rights since women had gained the right to vote.[1] Women congratulated themselves on having had a great deal to do with producing this favorable decision. Teach-ins, speak-outs, picket lines, demonstrations, lobbying, and class action suits had paid off handsomely. The secret to success, they believed, had been the change from the futility of ladylike lobbying efforts in legislative committee rooms to dramatic, direct-action tactics that demonstrated the strength of public opinion in favor of legal change and also helped give women, singly and in groups, the courage to bring the problem out into the open.[2] Women's rights advocates realized that the victory would not be complete until abortions were freely available for poor women as well as for rich women. They also predicted that ingenious maneuverings would be tried to forestall compliance with the Court's ruling.[3] More litigation would probably be necessary to require hospitals to perform abortions, to bring

abortions under Medicaid, and to keep some of the state legislatures from using their power to "regulate" abortions during the
second trimester, to close off access completely to these later
abortions. Women did not have the right to abortions on demand,
but the Court's decision had been a major change in the right
direction.

Predictably, the Roman Catholic reaction to the decision was
strong. In a pastoral message issued February 13, 1973, Roman
Catholic bishops called for civil disobedience of any law requiring
abortion. In no other situation in recent times has the hierarchy
felt that other moral issues outweighed the obligation to obey the
law.[4] There was concern that this decision might lead to laws
requiring Catholic doctors or hospitals to perform abortions.[5]
According to *Commonweal*, a Catholic publication, a bill in the
Oregon legislature would require all hospitals to admit patients
for abortions, and a bill in Wisconsin threatened loss of license
to individual doctors who refused to perform abortions. Of course,
legislators often put forward plans that are never enacted into law,
but these prospects frightened Catholics. In Congress, Senator
Frank Church of Idaho moved to protect Catholic hospitals
against loss of funds under the Hill-Burton Act by introducing a
resolution that would protect hospitals from performing operations
that violated their religious beliefs.[6]

The Catholic hierarchy reaffirmed its position that any person
who underwent an abortion would be subject to excommunication.[7]
The bishops also urged Catholics to use all means possible to
reverse the decision. A citizens group in Virginia suggested that
Justice William Brennan, the Court's only Catholic Justice and a
member of the majority, be excommunicated.[8] Two publications of
the Catholic Right—*The Wanderer* and *Triumph*—also called for
Justice Brennan's excommunication. Archbishop Francis J. Furey
of Texas characterized the Justices voting for the ruling as "fetal
muggers," and John Cardinal Krol, president of the National
Catholic Conference, accused the Court of opening the doors "to
the greatest slaughter of innocent life in the history of mankind."
Catholic and Right-to-Life forces that had been active in opposing
the modernization of abortion laws in state legislatures now urged
the states to block the Court's decision in any way possible.[9]

Opponents of abortion immediately initiated countermeasures. Not all were Catholics, not all right-wingers politically, but a great many were both. The National Right to Life Committee, a Washington-based coalition, claimed affiliates in all fifty states—four hundred to five hundred groups, with many locally based smaller groups.[10] The director of one large group, the National Youth Pro-Life Coalition, denied charges by proabortionists that he was getting money from the Catholic church, insisting that his group's activities were financed by volunteer fund-raising affairs like bake sales and raffles. But evidence was available that the church, through the National Conference of Catholic Bishops, had already been spending heavily—$4 million in 1973 alone—to finance antiabortion activities.[11]

All of these groups saw abortion as a human rights issue. They compared abortions to the killings in Hitler's Germany and in Vietnam and declared themselves willing to use whatever tactics were necessary, at any level of government, to stop them.[12]

One method was to identify congressmen as for or against abortion and to take steps to defeat them in their home districts. The first such attempt in the congressional elections of 1974 backfired badly when Representatives James W. Symington (D., Mo.) and Don Edwards (D., Calif.), both identified as supporters of the Supreme Court's decision, won landslide victories.[13] Admittedly, the post-Watergate year of 1974 was not a good year for Republicans, but it was a blow to the antiabortion strategy when Congressmen Lawrence J. Hogan (R., Md.), Harold V. Froelich (R., Wis.), and Angelo Roncallo (R., N.Y.), the leaders of the antiabortion forces in the House of Representatives, were all defeated. A gubernatorial candidate, running on an antiabortion plank in the 1974 Democratic primary, lost every county in Pennsylvania.[14]

At first the antiabortion (now styled "pro-Life") forces concentrated their fire on state legislatures, introducing dozens of bills trying to limit abortion within the limits of the Supreme Court's ruling. A number of these bills were passed; some were quickly overturned by the courts. Congress was the arena for several contests over legislation, on the relatively few subjects where federal health programs were related to abortion in some fashion —abortions in federal health programs or facilities, aid programs overseas, and the like. A campaign to pass a constitutional amendment reversing the Court's stand stalled in Congress. Although many proposed amendments were introduced, all were buried in committee with no immediate likelihood that public hearings would be held on any of them.

Possibly because the results of the first two years of opposition had been so unspectacular, the leadership of the American Catholic church decided, in 1975, to take its opposition to abortion into electoral politics.[15] This "big plunge" into political activism was made public at the National Conference of Catholic Bishops, which announced a Pastoral Plan for Pro-Life Activities. This was to be a well-organized and sophisticated political effort. It would involve every parish in the country in a program of prayer, education, and political action designed to educate the public about abortion, counsel women with problems involving pregnancy and abortion, mount an effort in all three branches of government to protect the right to life, and defeat proabortion policies of any kind.

Grass-roots political organization was to be the key to this political effort, with Catholic organizations at the parish and diocesan levels as the core cadres. Each parish would be encouraged to set up a pro-Life committee. Diocesan committees would coordinate local groups, and committees in state and congressional districts would monitor "political trends in the state and their implications for the abortion effort."[16] These groups would keep an eye on state and local officials and congressmen, identify their stands on abortion, and urge the passage of a constitutional amendment to reverse the Supreme Court decision and provide a legal basis for the protection of the unborn. Not only congressmen but presidential candidates were to come under scrutiny and would feel the heat of pro-Life pressure.

In this new campaign, techniques of professional political organization would be followed and a file kept on every elected official and potential candidate. A telephone network was to be readied for mobilizing pressure. Once the abortion stands of candidates were identified, the pro-Life groups would work for all candidates who were willing to promise to support a constitutional amendment. The pro-Life organizations were not, however, to be organized as agencies of the church, but rather as public interest groups or citizens lobbies. Connections between these organizations and the hierarchy of the church were to be minimized and de-emphasized, lest they create problems of tax exemption for the church.[17] To avoid direct involvement in politics, the Bishops' Conference set up its own lobbying arm, the National Committee for a Human Life Amendment. The bishops hoped that in addition to identifying the candidates' stands on abortion and influencing the choice of elective officials favorable to their point of view, the pro-Life organizations would have an impact on the decisions by federal and state agencies on abortion programs—the funding of clinics, abortions for welfare recipients, or any other use of tax dollars for abortions or abortion-related facilities. Catholic lobbyists in Congress would resist any spending for foreign aid programs relating to abortions as well as opposing proposals by groups such as Planned Parenthood, the American Civil Liberties Union, Americans United, National Organization of Women, the American Jewish Congress, and the various proabortion (pro-Choice) groups.[18]

The bishops were taking a risk by proposing such a clearly political strategy rather than by using more indirect means of influencing politicians and voters through moral leadership. Especially if the campaign were perceived as being "run from a bishop's desk," it might activate latent anti-Catholic feeling and old fears of Catholic power. Liberal Catholics might be alienated by a campaign they saw as "reactionary," as the kind of "European-style church political maneuvering" whose time was past.[19] Many Catholics might also consider definition of a right to life in anti-abortion terms alone as one-dimensional; for many, a meaningful Right-to-Life program should include a much broader emphasis on the social programs that make life liveable. An overtly political campaign might also raise questions about the separation of church and state. In spite of these risks, the big organizational effort went ahead. If it were successful, its effects would be felt in the 1976 presidential election.

The move into electoral politics, however, politicized an issue that is exceptionally unsuitable for solution in the political process. Debate over the subject is divisive and emotional, full of rhetoric and symbolism. Extremists on either side show little restraint in their appeal to the emotions. Pro-Life campaigners show lurid films of abortions and display fetuses in jars—"Waving the bloody fetus," as one columnist described such inflammatory routines.[20] Pro-Choice activists use equally sensational images—a bloody coat-hanger represents the danger that desperate women will resort to self-abortion; pictures of the corpse of a dead woman on the floor of a motel room remind us of the victims of illegal abortion-ists.[21] Feminists also exploit some of the rich political symbolism of sex and class. Restrictive abortion laws discriminate against the poor woman, they argue, because rich women have always been able to finagle abortions. Abortion laws also reflect the biases of a male-dominated social order that uses "compulsory pregnancy laws" (laws regulating abortion and contraception) to deny women equality, liberty, and the right to control their bodies. Like war, slavery, liquor, and race relations, these issues have such a high emotional content that they make accommodation and compromise difficult. Each side believes it stands for morality and right against evil and sin, and in such a climate of high emotion, rational and temperate public debate cannot take place.

Although the abortion issue was highly charged, evidence showed that it was overridingly important only to a relatively small number of voters. A 1974 poll by the National Conference of Catholic Bishops showed that although only a small group saw abortion as our most important social issue, almost 13 percent of the persons polled said that they would vote against any candidate who supported abortion, no matter what stands he took on other issues. Another 15 percent took the opposite position—that the right to abortion is so important that they would vote *against* a candidate who took a negative stand on this issue.[22]

As the presidential nominating races heated up in January and February of 1976, the political impact of the bishops' campaign began to be felt. Until this time, abortion had been a negligible issue in national politics. In 1971 President Nixon had come out against abortion in hopes of attracting antiabortion voters away from the Democratic party. Women's organizations had tried to write a proabortion plank into the Democratic party's platform in

1972 and failed. After the Supreme Court's decision in 1973, some lobbying had taken place in Congress, and some support for and opposition to individual candidates had resulted, based on their abortion stands, but a well-organized national campaign had not occurred. Much of the early lobbying may even have been counterproductive, because it lacked organization and because the methods of fervent antiabortionists were often crude. Male legislators were definitely "turned off" by their "preachy, pushy style —reading Bibles in the Capitol corridors, toting jars of dead fetuses into legislators' offices and shouting 'murder' with little awareness of the tedious and lengthy legislative process."[23]

The 1976 Campaign: Politics and Religion

The 1976 presidential primaries, however, offered pro-Life forces a national forum for testing their political power and a chance to influence the selection of presidential candidates in the nominating races of both parties. The first step would be to force various contenders to reveal their views. Two Republican hopefuls, President Ford and Ronald Reagan, had already taken positions, of sorts, on abortion. Ford, in the House of Representatives, had supported a constitutional amendment to turn the control of abortion over to the states, and Reagan, while governor of California, had fought against legislation liberalizing his state's abortion laws. The Democratic field was crowded with contenders from all parts of the political spectrum, and it was not clear how some of them stood on the abortion question. Sargent Shriver, a Roman Catholic, had already stated that although he opposed abortion, he was not in favor of a constitutional amendment to prohibit it. Right-to-Life forces thought Senator Henry Jackson favored their cause but were afraid that Senator Birch Bayh's position was too liberal. Other candidates had not taken a clear stand either way.

Jimmy Carter, the former Georgia governor, was pressed to define his views during the opening moments of the presidential race. Iowa makes its selection of delegates to the Democratic National Convention in a series of precinct and county caucuses held early in January. In Iowa pro-Life supporters quizzed Carter relentlessly on his stand, and he told them that he believed abortion was morally wrong, but did not support a constitutional amendment allowing state control. Then, according to some press reports, he hedged, adding that he might support, under some circumstances, a constitutional amendment limiting the conditions under which abortions might be performed. Another interviewer reported him as saying that he might support a "national statute" (whatever that might mean) limiting abortion.[24] To some Democrats, his stand seemed to be one of opposing all constitutional amendments, to others he seemed to have left the door open to some kind of restrictive program. Carter won a substantial victory in Iowa, getting about 27 percent of the vote, more than any other candidate.[25] But Carter was accused of waffling, trying to be all things to all people, and of winning delegates by deceit. Carter denied that he had vacillated and stated that he had consistently held the same position on abortion. He did not approve of abortion, but did not favor either a constitutional amendment to prohibit it or an authorization to return the problem to the states to handle. His program would be, instead, to try to limit resort to abortion by promoting other forms of birth control and family planning. In stating his views, he said, "I believe that positive action should be taken in better education, better family planning programs, the availability of contraceptive devices for those who believe in them, better adoption procedures."[26]

At the beginning of February, other candidates came out with statements of their views on abortion. George Wallace, challenging Reagan for conservative votes, was the next candidate to commit himself. He announced on February 3 that he opposed abortion and would support a constitutional amendment to "protect the lives of unborn children," although he did not indicate exactly what kind of amendment he had in mind.[27] Other candidates were no more eager than Carter to define their views on this subject. Constant questioning of President Ford by newsmen finally brought out a reluctant news release and television interview in which Ford said that he "opposed abortion on demand," but believed that in some cases, including situations of rape of where the mother's life was in danger, abortions should be permitted. If a constitutional

amendment should pass, he would prefer one that returned constitutional authority to the states, a position Ford had supported
earlier as a member of the House of Representatives.[28]

Some critics called this the "local option" plan. Ford emphasized
that as President he would enforce the Supreme Court's decision
as the law of the land. Mrs. Ford, however, who had stated earlier
that she approved of the Supreme Court's decision, reaffirmed her
support, saying, "I am glad to see that abortion has been taken out
of the backwoods and been put in the hospital where it belongs."[29]

As might have been expected, the President's stand pleased no
one. Roman Catholic Archbishop Joseph L. Bernardin denounced it.
Women's rights leaders said that it was regressive and that it
encouraged lawlessness. Sarah Weddington, a Texas lawyer who
had argued the abortion cases before the Supreme Court, said that
it was a step backward, and that Ford's solution would reintroduce
the situation in which abortions "would be denied to the poor,
uneducated and young, while women of wealth could travel to a
state where the law was more liberal."[30]

As other Democratic presidential candidates came into the race,
they had as little success as Carter in avoiding the issue. Governor
Milton Shapp of Pennsylvania was already on the Right-to-Life
blacklist for vetoing a law passed by the Pennsylvania legislature
in 1972 that was designed to restrict abortion. Senator Birch
Bayh of Indiana claimed that he was not personally in favor of
abortion, but as chairman of the subcommittee of the Senate
Judiciary Committee that holds hearings on constitutional amendments, he had become a target for the extremists on both sides
who considered abortion a nonnegotiable issue. Antiabortion forces,
resenting his failure to take any action to support their amendments, tried to disrupt his campaign appearances, throwing tacks
on the streets and sidewalks outside of meeting halls, yelling
that he was a murderer, beating on the walls of rooms where he
was speaking, and even hiring a boy to play taps on a bugle
during some of Bayh's speeches.[31] On the other hand, he also
received hate mail from feminists who resented the fact that he had
allowed the hearings to go forward on the proposed amendments.
One angry correspondent labelled him a "genocidal pro-spermist."[32]

Other Democratic candidates took the stands that might have been expected of them. Senator Henry M. Jackson said he was opposed to abortion, but he was unwilling to come out for a constitutional amendment forbidding it. Representatives Morris Udall and Fred Harris were also moderate, supporting the Court's decision and opposing an amendment, although Harris said that "there is no excuse to abrogate the civil right of a woman to control her body." Eugene McCarthy agreed that the Court's decision should stand, but commented with his usual acerbity that abortion was probably not a matter that could be controlled by the state anyhow. He might also have noted, but did not, that abortion is an odd issue to interject into a presidential campaign, since the President can do very little about it. As a *Washington Post* editorial remarked, to require candidates for the Presidency to take stands on abortion is "rather like making a position on Angola the litmus test of someone's fitness to serve on the City Council."[33] In spite of this, no presidential candidate felt that he could ignore the issue. Even that darkest of dark horses, Senator Robert Byrd of West Virginia, decided that he should speak out on abortion: he proposed an amendment that would allow abortions only in cases of rape or when the mother's life was in danger.[34]

Thus by the early spring of 1976, Right-to-Life forces had been successful in forcing candidates of both parties to identify their views on abortion. They had dogged the Democrats with embarrassing questions and had been unwilling to let the issue drop or to let any of the officeseekers gloss it over. They wanted a President who would support efforts to amend the Constitution to prevent abortion, or at the least, who would refuse to support federal programs making abortions accessible to more people. They hoped by focusing public opinion on abortion to increase its importance as a key issue in the polling booth and weld antiabortionists into a "swing vote" that might decide the election.

In addition to supporting candidates on the basis of their stands on abortion, however, another possible tactic was the fielding of a single-issue candidate who would run on a platform in which abortion was the central plank. To some extent, this strategy might conflict with the other, since such a candidate would attract almost all antiabortion votes, devaluing the issue as a bargaining point with candidates who were more likely to win. It would, however, demonstrate the strength of the pro-Life element, if any significant number of voters turned out in support. A New York housewife, Ellen McCormack, decided to take this course and enter the campaign for president directly as a pro-Life candidate. By February, 1976, running as a Democrat, she was on the ballot for both the New Hampshire and Massachusetts primaries and hoped to qualify for $140,000 in federal matching funds under the new Federal Campaign Act of 1974. This act allows presidential candidates to qualify for public funds by raising at least $5,000 in contributions of $250 or less in each of the twenty states. McCormack claimed to have done this, but some of her opponents charged that dollars contributed generally to the antiabortion cause and not specifically to her candidacy had been funnelled into her campaign. The National Abortion Rights Action League (NARAL) filed a complaint with the Federal Election Commission charging that the McCormack campaign used deceptive practices and violated federal election laws,[35] but the commission held that she had a right to public money. On February 24, McCormack polled 1 percent of the vote in the New Hampshire primary; and a few weeks later, less that 4 percent of the vote in Massachusetts.[36]

Although McCormack claimed not to be running a one-issue campaign, abortion was her main concern. "The fetus is a human life," she stated. "The Constitution guarantees equality to each and every person and abortion gives one generation the power of life and death over succeeding generations." Critics of her campaign charged that she was not a genuine candidate and that contributions to the Pro-Life Action Committee were not matchable contributions. Public funding was being used, they argued, to publicize the Right-to-Life position, attracting media attention, buying radio and TV spots, and using material prepared by professional advertising specialists for a pseudocandidacy that sometimes showed antiabortion ads without even mentioning the so-called candidate's name. The National Abortion Rights Action League vowed to challenge her right to funds in the courts.

In May the Federal Election Commission curtailed the funding of six presidential candidates, including McCormack—not on grounds of the genuineness or lack of it in her candidacy, but because she and the others had received less that 10.0 percent of the vote in primaries held on May 18 and May 25. The new ruling was that any candidate receiving less than 10.0 percent in two consecutive primaries would be ineligible for further matching funds. The commission also cut off funds to candidates campaigning in only one state. Such rulings also ended funding for Democrats Bayh, Shapp, Harris, and Shriver.[37] By the end of the primary campaign, McCormack had run in seventeen states, peaking at 7.2 percent of the vote in South Dakota. She received 2.02 percent of the total vote. (For official figures, see Table 1). Her campaign, said one election analyst, "partly funded by U.S. taxpayers, laid a giant egg and bombed out even in heavily Catholic areas."[38]

In February and March, as the primary campaign was gaining momentum, abortion had seemed like the "sleeper issue," and newspapers and newsmagazines were full of it as they tried to assess its importance. By the end of the primary campaign in July, however, its impact seemed less important. Some of the earlier analyses seemed to have been journalistic hyperbole. In spite of all of the press attention, it had never developed as a major influence on voting behavior.

In the party nominating conventions, the topic was to surface again, but was disposed of without undue emphasis, to the relief of the politicians and party functionaries. The Democrats, bowing to the insistent urging of women's groups, included a plank in their platform that stated, "We feel that it is undesirable to attempt to amend the U.S. Constitution to overturn the Supreme Court decision permitting abortion." This was not as strong as the plank that had been urged by the National Womens Political Caucus in 1972, and that narrowly failed of adoption, but that would have supported the *right* to abortion. The Republican convention, its platform committee dominated by supporters of Ronald Reagan, took a stand against abortion. Its plank stated that the "Republican Party favors a continuance of the public dialogue on abortion and supports the efforts of those who seek enactment of a constitutional amendment to restore protection of the right to life for unborn children."

Table 1
Ellen McCormack's Primary Support

State[1]	Date	Votes for McCormack	Total Democratic Votes	Percentage of Total
Calif.[2]	June 8	28,995	3,375,482	0.86
Fla.	Mar. 9	7,595	1,300,330	0.58
Ga.	May 4	635	502,471	0.13
Ind.	May 4	31,708	614,361	5.16
Ky.	May 25	17,061	306,006	5.58
Md.	May 18	7,907	591,746	1.34
Mass.	Mar. 2	25,772	747,634	3.45
Mich.	May 18	7,623	708,666	1.08
Neb.	May 11	6,033	181,910	3.32
N.H	Feb. 24	1,007	95,088	1.06
N.J.[2,3]	June 8	19,700	462,859	4.26
Pa.	Apr. 27	38,800	1,367,447	2.84
R.I.	June 1	2,468	60,348	4.09
S.D.[2]	June 1	4,227	58,726	7.20
Tenn.	May 25	1,782	331,921	0.54
Vt.	Mar. 2	3,324	38,714	8.59
Wis.	Apr. 6	26,982	740,528	3.64
Unofficial Totals		231,619	11,484,237	2.02

Source: Planned Parenthood—World Population, Washington Memo, June 18, 1976 (Washington, D.C.: The Alan Guttmacher Institute). Reprinted by permission of The Alan Guttmacher Institute.

1. States where McCormack's name appeared on statewide ballot. New York and Texas delegates sought votes in five (N.Y.) districts and one (Tex.) district only.
2. Unofficial totals.
3. Totals for delegate preference voting.

The Republican position was obviously more congenial to the anti-abortion forces and considerably to the right of that previously announced by President Ford, who had promised support only of an amendment to return the control of abortion to the states. It seemed designed to attract Catholic and conservative Protestant voters away from the Democrats. The platform also endorsed a constitutional amendment restoring prayer and religious exercises in public schools and tax credits for parents of children in parochial elementary and secondary schools.[39]

Beginning his general campaign, Jimmy Carter, the Democratic candidate, must have thought it was important to avoid a straight party division over abortion, with all antiabortion and many Roman Catholic votes shifting to the Republicans. If the abortion issue was as important to Catholics as the church hierarchy maintained, this vote would be jeopardized unless the issue could be defused. Accordingly, at the end of August, Carter sought a conciliatory meeting with the six bishops who make up the executive committee of the National Conference of Catholic Bishops to explain his views and to reassure them of his personal reluctance to use government funds or machinery to encourage abortions.[40] Democrats were perplexed by Carter's action and could only speculate that perhaps he had in mind the kind of meeting with the bishops that John F. Kennedy had had with the Protestant clergy in 1960, a meeting that many commentators believe helped defuse anti-Catholic sentiment by bringing religious prejudice and fear out into the open in a frank discussion.

If it had been Carter's hope that similar boldness in meeting the religious issue head on would reduce hostility and misunderstanding, he was to be disappointed. The bishops were neither charmed by the candidate nor impressed by his statement that he was personally opposed to abortion.[41] Abortion and aid to church schools were two topics on which the hierarchy would refuse to compromise. "We could have told them that," said an aide to Senator Edward M. Kennedy, long familiar with the church's unyielding position on these issues.[42] In spite of its failure, however, Carter's move to neutralize the church's hostility had been worth a try. The Democratic stakes in preventing an election split along religious lines were high.

Carter began the campaign with what some commentators called a Catholic problem, that is, very little appeal to Catholic voters, especially in the big cities of the Northeast. Both Carter and his running mate Walter Mondale, Democratic senator from Minnesota, had rural and small-town backgrounds. Senator Edmund Muskie of Maine, with his Polish Catholic origins, had been considered as a vice-presidential candidate but had been rejected, supposedly leaving the ticket with little appeal to the so-called ethnic voters. Some campaign advisers thought that without skilled advice, Carter might not only fail to excite these more cosmopolitan voters, but might actually be misunderstood by them. If the urban Catholic voters who had always formed the backbone of the Democratic party stayed home on voting day, the election would surely be lost.[43]

President Ford also suspected that Catholic votes might supply his needed margin of victory. In five of the six last elections, Catholics have favored the Democrats. But each time the Democrats' estimated percentage of the Catholic vote dipped below 60 percent the Democrats had lost. This was true in the 1952 and 1956 elections, when Eisenhower won, and in the 1968 and 1972 elections, when Richard Nixon was victorious. President Ford's research director, Robert Teeter, produced figures that showed the proportion of Catholics in the voting-age population of each state and designated eleven heavily Catholic areas as the targets for special campaign attention. Teeter figured that a sweep of all of them would give the President 238 of the 270 electoral votes needed to win the election. This list included many of the states with big electoral votes that could go to either Ford or Carter by a narrow margin, states such as California, New York, Pennsylvania, New Jersey, Illinois, and Wisconsin. California had the lowest percentage of Catholic voters in this group, with 21 percent; all of the others had more than 30 percent Catholic voters.[44]

Pursuing this strategy, President Ford determined to try to capitalize on what might be Carter's weak appeal to Catholic voters and even considered using the football stadium at the University of Notre Dame as the site for the Republican campaign kickoff (eventually this plan was discarded, and the campaign opener was held in the fieldhouse at the University of Michigan). The President also sought a meeting with the Catholic bishops, inviting them to the White House for a discussion of Catholic issues, hoping to find common ground where Carter had failed. The bishops emerged from their meeting with a statement that Catholic leaders were "encouraged that the President agrees on the need for a constitutional amendment dealing with abortion." Archbishop Joseph L. Bernardin of Cincinnati, president of the National Conference of Catholic Bishops, said that Ford's position, which included support for a constitutional amendment that would give the states greater power to limit abortion, was not entirely what the bishops wanted, but that it was preferable to that of the Democratic nominee.[45] Bernardin also said that the President had promised to try to restrain the use of federal funding of abortions and to look with interest on any ideas that "can meet the Constitutional issues" involved in giving federal and state aid to parochial schools. In September attacks by Catholic leaders on the Democrats were so continuous, and support for President Ford so open, that the church seemed to be endorsing the Ford candidacy. Someone inside the hierarchy must have decided that this was a dangerous tactic, because the Catholic bishops issued a public statement assuring voters of the church's neutrality.[46]

But both Democrats and Republicans were naive in believing that abortion was the single key issue for Catholic voters. Carter's own polls showed that problems of unemployment, crime, inflation, and housing were of greater concern to working-class Catholics than issues like abortion.[47] A new adviser from Senator Kennedy's staff, Jim King, suggested that Carter ignore the bishops and talk about economic issues. More sophistication about Catholic attitudes came with the addition of a Catholic "desk" to the campaign organization and the hiring of knowledgeable staffers; a Catholic nun was brought into the campaign organization in Atlanta.[48] The newer advisers pointed out that it was by no means certain that Catholics would vote as a bloc or follow the instructions of the church hierarchy. Even on abortion, polls seemed to show that the rank and file was more liberal than the church leaders, and that many Catholics who were personally opposed to abortion might be unwilling to impose their views on non-Catholics.[49]

The Catholic church was not the only religious group to react politically. Conservative Protestants, fundamentalists, and evangelicals also began to lambaste Democrats and liberals for their support of abortion. These groups were not concerned with the abortion issue alone, but saw it as one of a cluster of liberal social issues on which they had strong convictions: abortion, ERA, homo-sexual rights, prayer in the schools, and other "family issues." Fundamentalist ministers were to become increasingly active in the political campaigns of 1978 and 1980; in 1976 they were just beginning to see the possibility of organizing their memberships for a direct foray into electoral politics.

Although the legalization of abortion and many other social issues present serious moral questions to which religious leaders properly address their attention, direct intervention of churches in electoral politics has always been viewed as suspiciously close to the line separating church and state. Churches have usually been content to assert their "judgmental role" and have considered it beneficial to themselves and to society to stay somewhat apart from party politics.[50] Active clerical intervention in electoral politics in support of particular candidates has been rare and generally is considered politically naive. But individual Catholic clergymen occasionally endorse candidates from the pulpit.[51] Cardinal Krol and the Pennsylvania hierarchy attacked Governor Milton Shapp in 1974, after he had vetoed an abortion restriction bill, and Catholic newspapers urged state Catholics to vote in a bloc against him.[52] Right-wing Christian political groups often have actively supported ultraconservative political causes, using radio and television to disseminate their political views, but only occasionally have fielded candidates.[53]

The "Vote Christian" campaigns organized in a number of congressional districts dismayed more moderate religious leaders who were alarmed about "political religion" and afraid such campaigns would encourage bigotry.[54] Because of the intensity with which religious views are held, political contests over social views stated in religious terms were seen as likely to generate the kinds of explosions that cannot be worked out peacefully inside the constitutional framework and to threaten the stability of the political system itself. Columnist Clayton Fritchey saw abortion as the kind of issue that could polarize religious factions and divide the electorate along religious lines.[55] He and others feared a national religious battle that would destroy the religious detente that has prevailed in America for many years.

The entry of the Catholic bishops and the fundamentalist preachers into the 1976 campaign in turn generated an organizational response from the moderates and liberals. A Religious

Coalition for Abortion Rights, sponsored by Protestant and Jewish organizations, spoke out against the Catholic church's organizing moves, labelling the bishops' campaign as an attempt by the Catholic church to write its religious views into the Constitution.

As the campaign swung into full gear, emphasis on abortion as an issue receded, and foreign policy, amnesty, military preparedness, the state of the economy, and jobs all pushed abortion into the background. Carter ran into Right-to-Life demonstrations on the campaign trail, especially in urban Catholic areas like Scranton, Pittsburgh, and Philadelphia. The issue also reemerged occasionally, as it did in the televised debates, but it no longer seemed to be the key issue or even one that would affect the election in a significant fashion.

In the end, religion turned out to have played a relatively minor role in the election, and agitation over abortion probably influenced few votes. Concern about the Catholic vote had been unwarranted. Polls taken at this time showed that 60 percent of Catholics now approved of the Supreme Court's 1973 decision, with only 31 percent opposed. Polls taken after the election showed that Carter got 54 percent of the Catholic vote—10 percent more than McGovern received in 1972, but less than the 60 percent it had been said that he needed to win.[56]

Thus in spite of the predictions in early spring that abortion would be the "sleeper issue," it did not materialize as a campaign question of overwhelming importance. But it was a troublesome issue for the candidates as they were hooted at and harassed, dogged by questions on abortion at press conferences, and forced to devote more time than they wished to spend devising conciliatory strategies. Most candidates saw it as a no-win issue that would harm them but not help them at the polling booth. In general, the persistence of the antiabortion forces did not result in a clear choice for the voters, During the primaries, some candidates, often those with the least chance of winning the nomination in each party, took strong stands against abortion; moderates tried to avoid the issue or to find a neutral ground. In the general election, the voters could perceive very little difference in the stands of the two major party candidates. Both Ford and Carter opposed abortion personally. Ford wanted to let the states handle this matter; Carter opposed federal spending for Medicaid abortions, but wanted to set up federal programs to give poor women "alternatives." A *New York Times*-CBS poll taken in September found that voter preferences were not importantly related to the candidates' positions on abortion.[57]

If the campaign had any long-range effect, it was to push Candidate Carter into taking a campaign stand that he would later feel obliged to respect. His choice for Secretary of the Department of Health, Education and Welfare, the federal agency with the most responsibility for abortion policy, was Joseph A. Califano, a Catholic lawyer with a strong personal distaste for abortion. This appointment might not have been made by a president who had not already committed himself on the issue. In June, 1977, President Carter echoed his campaign talk of the previous spring by supporting, in a press conference, a recent Supreme Court decision allowing the state to refuse funding for many Medicaid abortions.

By and large, however, abortion is not a subject over which the federal government has major responsibilities. Its introduction into the presidential races as a political issue might have served in a close race between candidates with clearly divergent views to swing votes one way or the other. In a race between moderate candidates with similar views, it had little effect. It did offer antiabortion activists a chance to "go national," to air their opinions in the national media, and provided an opportunity to organize their strength for future battles.

But although the interjection of abortion into the 1976 campaign probably did not affect the outcome of the presidential race, it had provoked thought about several subsidiary matters; one of these matters was the effect of moral issues on the political dialogue; another, the limits of legitimate church involvement in electoral politics. The campaign that year also gave us a preview of the rising importance of single-issue groups on the political scene.

Single-Issue Politics in 1978 and 1980

During the 1970s, concern was growing about the proliferation of single-issue groups at a time that one writer has labelled the "era of strenuous clique and vociferous claque."[58] Small, vociferous, well-organized groups, fervently espousing narrow causes, seemed at times to dominate public discourse and to discourage, by provocative and emotional strategies, the search for consensus and majority rule. Single-issue groups differ from broader economic and social organizations like labor unions or consumer groups in that they build their campaigns around a single dominant cause, and regard loyalty to that cause as a moral litmus test that allows no compromises or bargains.[59] Determined and activist factions feel that their programs become too diluted and compromised when filtered through the party's mechanisms for reaching compromise and coalition. Since any attempt to sell the favored cause to one of the political parties creates a risk that the strength of the commitment will be watered down and lost in the broader agenda, these groups prefer to use direct lobbying to sell the cause to the public. New computerized, direct-mail techniques and television programs that target specific audiences lend themselves to such direct public appeals.

In part this change of tactics may be due to the increasing weakness of party authority and organization and the growing importance of issue-oriented voting. For many contemporary voters, allegiance to one of the major parties is no longer an important fact of life; these independent voters feel competent to make up their own minds both on issues and on candidates. Voters are more issue conscious and are willing to desert party guidelines on public matters that are important to them. Weak parties and strong interests have always been characteristics of the American political scene.[60] But with the coming of "flea-market politics," where maverick outsider candidates win elections without organization support, politicians in and out of office are also tempted to desert the parties and play the politics of personality and issue. Without the backing of supportive party organizations, politicians often find it difficult to withstand the assaults and threats of single-issue interest groups. Indeed, they may actively seek the support of such groups. Campaign-spending reforms, the rising costs of campaigns, and the agonizing need for funds may encourage candidates to take stands that will bring in money from special groups and their political action committees.

Right-to-Life activists soon decided that grass-roots organizing and direct pressure on candidates was the most effective method of fighting the liberalization of abortion. With the political experience gained in the 1976 campaign, they were ready for an all-out campaign in the 1978 congressional and gubernatorial elections. Now more professional at organizing, identifying voters, and getting out the vote, they made targets of a number of congressmen and supported those who favored limiting abortions.

Although by this time pro-Choice organizations were anxious to play down the abortion issue, they tried to counteract these efforts by quietly supporting candidates whom they thought favored reproductive rights. A NOW tally of Senate races, after the election, claimed that nine senators "favorable to reproductive rights" were elected, and eleven who were unfavorable were beaten. Not all of these contests were clear-cut, however, since in several races, incumbents and challengers held the same position on abortion. In House races, each side had gains and losses. According to the NOW tabulation, pro-Choice incumbents were victors in most cases, although many of these campaigns involved many issues and were not decided in terms of the candidate's stand on abortion.[61]

Abortion was also an issue in several gubernatorial races. In Michigan, Illinois, Colorado, Maine, and New York, the pro-Choice candidates won. In Connecticut, Massachusetts, Ohio, Oregon, Texas, and Wisconsin, the pro-Life candidates won. In Pennsylvania a single-issue candidate for lieutenant governor on the Democratic ticket was defeated. In New York the Right-to-Life party ran a candidate on its own ticket, to guarantee the party a place on the ballot in 1980; it won the ten thousand necessary votes. This race featured a sensational television advertisement that some stations refused to run. The film showed a fetus in a womb; then a probe was shown entering the womb and the picture dissolved into a bloody mass.[62] One of the races clearly influenced by Right-to-Life support was the senatorial contest in New Hampshire, where the New Right candidate Gordon Humphrey defeated Senator Thomas McIntire. The anitabortionists again used highly inflammatory campaign material. Leaflets circulated against McIntire accused him of supporting abortion and experimentation on unborn infants. One leaflet read, "If we truly respect God's Gift of Life, can we do less than vote for Gordon Humphrey for Senator. Seven million dead babies are enough. Humphrey—the choice we can all live with . . . unborn babies, too!"[63] Responsibility for conservative Democrat Edward J. King's gubernatorial victory in

Massachusetts was claimed by both antiabortion and antigun-control forces. On the other hand, although pro-Lifers claimed credit for the defeat of Iowa's Senator Dick Clark, some observers thought the real reason for his defeat was his support for liberal spending programs.[64]

Whether or not their influence was as great as they believed, foes of abortion believed the 1978 elections had established their credibility as a political force. "There is a pro-Life vote," said Paul Brown, director of one of the Political Action committees that were springing up for all kinds of issue groups. His group, the Life Amendment Political Action Committee (LAPAC), a Washington committee raising and spending money for antiabortion candidates, hoped to be able to swing a pro-Life vote of 5 to 8 percent, enough to make a difference in close elections. This group, which has close informal connections with the National Right to Life Committee, established a hit list of liberal senators and representatives, for 1980. Democratic Senators Birch Bayh, George McGovern, Frank Church, Patrick Leahy, and John Culver were grouped with Republican Senator Robert Packwood. Congressmen marked for defeat because of proabortion sentiments were Morris Udall (D., Ariz.), John Anderson (R., Ill.), Harold Hollenbeck (R., N.J.), Joseph Fisher (D., Va.), Robert Edgar (D., Pa.), and Robert Drinan (D., Mass.). Some of these targets were puzzled by their inclusion on the list. Representative Drinan was a Jesuit and opposed abortion, and Frank Church denied vehemently that he was proabortion.[65]

The head of the National Abortion Rights Action League, Karen Mulhauser, correctly saw this attack on liberal congressmen as evidence that antiabortion forces were moving into closer alliances with groups espousing other right-wing issues. The fund raiser for the American Conservative Union, Richard Viguerie, who has been called the undisputed champion of direct-mail money raising, obtained $30 million from computerized mailings for antiabortion, antigun-control, anti-ERA, and other conservative causes in 1977.[66] NOW noted that conservatives and antiabortion organizations, with only one exception, had endorsed the same candidates in the 1978 elections.[67]

There were also signs of an alliance between New Right leaders, fundamentalist and evangelical churches, and the stars of the popular religious programs on television and radio. About 1,300 "Christian owned and operated" TV and radio stations were now reaching 150 million listeners and viewers through programs such as the P.T.L. (Praise the Lord) Club and Christian Broadcast Network's 700 Club. Television and radio evangelists like Jerry Falwell, Jim Bakker, Oral Roberts, Billy Graham, Rex Humbard, and Robert Schuller were enormously popular.[68] Abortion was only one of the issues. Some of these broadcasters, dismayed by what they saw as a decline in the country's moral standards, also opposed ERA, feminism, homosexuality, and atheism in the public schools. In addition to national political organizations such as Christian Voice, Moral Majority, Religious Roundtable, and the National Christian Action Alliance, these leaders hoped to mobilize fundamentalists everywhere through grass-roots organizations led by fundamentalist preachers and Christian school administrators.[69] Christian schools now numbered somewhere around 15,000; their principals and administrators had been shocked into political awareness by the Internal Revenue Service's 1978 plan to drop tax-exempt status for private schools that did not push integration,[70] now these schools could be counted upon to bus students, teachers, and parents to political rallies and committee hearings as well as to antiabortion and anti-ERA demonstrations.[71]

Leaders like Howard Phillips, national director of Conservative Caucus, worked out a formidable blueprint for activating and focusing conservative, fundamentalist sentiment for political purposes.[72] In a plan that almost seemed to be modelled on the Catholic church's 1975 political organizing strategy, Phillips hoped to have a lead church in every congressional district in the nation with a pastor "who is plugged in to the political issues." Local organizations would monitor the performance of incumbent congressmen, and state leaders would conduct campaigns to unseat those who were wrong on moral issues.[73]

Trends barely discernible in 1976 and not fully developed in the congressional elections of 1978 were clearly established by the 1980 presidential campaign. Antiabortionists joined forces with fundamentalists and New Right organizations; radio and television evangelists urged their flocks to "vote Christian" and to vote against candidates supporting liberal causes; political action committees on all sides poured money into the campaigns of candidates with congenial political stands and financed media campaigns designed to pull down their political enemies. One political action committee, the National Conservative Political Action Committee (NCPAC) was unusually active and successful. The spokesman for a collection of Far Right groups, it specialized in negative attacks on liberal senators and congressmen and on President Carter. Fund raising through computerized mailing lists obtained from Richard Viguerie and Senator Helms of North Carolina identified persons opposing ERA, abortion, and gun control and the subscribers to *Human Events*, a conservative magazine. Between January, 1979, and June, 1980, according to Federal Election Commission reports, it received about $4 million.[74] Because of court rulings exempting spending by independent groups from federal election restraints, as long as they do not contribute directly to the campaigns of particular candidates, this committee was able to launch a two-year campaign against liberals in a number of states. The list of congressmen selected for elimination by NCPAC was identical to that of the Life Amendment Political Action Committee.

The well-heeled New Right attracted a whole spectrum of conservative, extremist, and single-issue forces to form a solid bloc behind the candidacy of Ronald Reagan. This group was influential enough in the Republican convention to force through planks against ERA, abortion, and even to pledge the nominee to appoint judges who "respect traditional family values and the sanctity of human life," a clear, if linguistically veiled, reference to abortion.

In the 1980 election, defecting Democrats, disillusioned on various grounds by their party, joined traditional Republicans and conservative activists in sufficient numbers to hand Reagan a decisive victory and to defeat a number of incumbent Democrats in the House and Senate. Among these Democrats were four on the Life Amendment PAC/NCPAC hit list. Senators McGovern, Church, Culver, and Bayh were all defeated, as was Representative Fisher (D., Va.). Pleased with its success, the NCPAC announced that it would flush out any remaining liberals in 1982.

As a political issue in its own right, abortion was not the decisive factor in any of these elections, but as one of a cluster of conservative issues, it had found a constituency on the Far Right. Catholic organizations were no longer the only source of organized opposition to abortion. The church had played an important role in the politicization of abortion, especially by its 1975 "plunge into politics." Its decision at that time to mount an all-out political drive to reimpose legal restrictions on abortion had supplied organization and leadership at a key moment to a movement that had been fragmented and leaderless. Church leaders were now repudiating single-issue bloc voting and calling for an evaluation of candidates on a wide range of economic, social, and philosophical issues.[75] The New Right, however, had seized upon abortion as one of the emotional issues that could attract those voters frightened by the accelerating pace of social change.

AFTERMATH: THE CONFLICT RESTRUCTURED

The State Legislative Response

5

After *Roe v. Wade* was handed down, the Court's decision itself, as has happened many times before, became the focus of political contention. People lined up for or against. It was either a wise decision whose recognition of constitutional rights was long overdue or an unwarranted judicial misreading of the Constitution. The furor was not only about the Constitution; it was not even about the fetus, even though much of the debate centered about the "right to life." In a larger sense the controversy was related to the complex of social issues that abortion seemed to symbolize: the disturbing impact on the American family of changing patterns of family organization, sex, reproductive rights, and the stresses on families caused by rapid social change and technological development. Reaction to the decision made it clear that many matters once considered nonpolitical and private had become charged with political significance.

By deciding the case as it did, the Supreme Court changed the structure of the conflict over abortion policy. As far as abortion was concerned, the quarrel, earlier, had been about the very existence of reproductive rights and whether or not states could constitutionally prohibit all resort to abortion. After *Roe v. Wade* one point at least was settled—within certain limits reproductive choice was a woman's right. But immediately after the case was decided, it was not certain where the boundaries to the new right were located. The next step would be to explore the meaning of the decision and its limits. The opinion of the Court would have to be studied and tested to see what the Court had actually required and where its ruling could be circumvented, narrowed, delayed, avoided, or ignored.[1]

A federal system encourages political debate and conflict over any problem at a number of different levels of the system in a variety of different political units and agencies of government. In the abortion dispute, most of the early activity took place at the state and local levels, and most of the initial moves came in state legislatures. In some states the immediate reaction to the *Roe* decision was minimal. In states that had already taken steps to liberalize their abortion laws, the decision did not appear to offer major conflicts with state policy. In states with different political geography, brushfire wars of opposition broke out immediately, and bills were introduced in the state legislatures to probe the possibilities of limiting the impact of the decision, to exploit its ambiguities, and to fill in the gaps the Court had left. Litigation over the constitutionality of the new statutes would shortly begin to mark out the limits of abortion rights. In a symposium on the abortion dispute held by the Brookings Institution in 1982, Lawrence M. Friedman spoke of the abortion conflict as a "complex ritual dance between the Court and the state legislatures," with the states "wiggling and squirming" to find ways around the *Roe* decision and the Court, alarmed at the intensity of the reaction to that decision, trying to decide where to bend or compromise and where to stand firm.[2]

There was also a stirring of activity on the national level. By putting political pressure on senators and representatives and introducing abortion as an issue in presidential campaigns, abortion opponents ensured that some action would be taken by federal officials. Here the primary target for antiabortion forces would be a constitutional amendment to reverse the Supreme Court's ruling. Congress has little constitutional authority to legislate directly on abortion, but there were peripheral matters on which legislation could be passed: the funding of various health and foreign aid programs, abortions in the military, and other programs related to reproductive rights. The lines were drawn for pitched battles in Congress over the funding of elective abortions under Medicaid.

Some abortion opponents nourished the hope that the Supreme Court might be influenced—if not by outright political pressure, at least by a change in personnel—to overrule its own decision. Even if a reversal was not forthcoming, new litigation could exploit ambiguities in the decision and might result in rulings confining and narrowing abortion rights. For the next decade and a half, the dispute would move back and forth between legislatures and courts, and the details of the contested territory would be mapped out in case-by-case decisions.

A number of generalities in Justice Blackmun's opinion could be read narrowly as well as broadly by lower courts and state legislatures. For example, was *any* regulation to be allowed in the first trimester of pregnancy? Certainly, the state could require that abortions be performed only by licensed practitioners. Could it also require that they be performed in hospitals rather than in clinics or doctors' offices? Since hospitals in many states are crowded, the requirement that abortions be performed in hospitals might make them more costly and difficult to obtain—only patients who could reserve beds and operating facilities would be served, and a hospital abortion could end up being as expensive as a normal delivery. It was not even certain that all states would have hospitals willing to perform abortions.

If clinics or doctors' offices could be used, what might the state require in the way of preoperative examinations and evaluations, emotional and contraceptive counselling, inspection, record keeping, reporting, and other procedures? Could clinics be required to have emergency backup services? Whatever conditions might be imposed on first trimester abortions, regulation during the second trimester was clearly allowable if it was reasonably related to the protection of the mother's health, and it was as yet unclear how far such regulation could go. All of these uncertainties could be exploited by opponents of abortion. Even within the framework of *Roe v. Wade*, state legislatures could limit, if they chose, freedom of choice and could burden women seeking abortions with a multitude of conditions and regulations.

Immediately after the decision, it was not surprising that some hospitals decided to wait until guidelines were more clearly marked

out before opening their doors to abortion patients. Doctors themselves would have a great deal to say about the manner in which a
given state would comply with the new ruling. When medical
leaders shared the views of antiabortion groups, they would
probably be able to delay the implementation of more lenient procedures. Even when they were not opposed to abortion, the
medical profession might act as a conservative force to keep change
from taking place very rapidly. Abortion counselling services in the
states, noting the reluctance of doctors and hospitals to change
their policies, were still sending their clients to well-established
contacts in New York and Washington.[3]

Eighty bills relating to abortion were introduced in state legislatures between January and April, 1973.[4] In October, 1973, seven
months after the decision, twenty-three states had enacted laws
dealing with abortion, and although most of these laws provided
for relatively unrestricted first trimester abortions, others had added
conditions that made the operation less accessible. These conditions included reporting and record-keeping procedures, requirements of written consent by the woman, consent of husband or
parents, waiting periods, counselling, and similar provisions.
Nebraska required notification of the grandparents! Many laws
contained provisions protecting persons and institutions with religious scruples from being forced to perform abortions.

Several weeks after its January 22 decision, the Court cleared its
docket of abortion cases; it sent eight state challenges back to the
lower courts for action along the lines it had marked out. These
cases were pending when the decision was handed down, and they
involved challenges to laws in Connecticut, Missouri, Illinois,
North Carolina, Utah, Kentucky, Ohio, and South Dakota. It also
dismissed without a hearing a suit arguing that the fetus has a right
to life on the grounds that it did not present a "substantial federal
question."[5] Most of the state laws involved in these cases were like
the Texas statute; North Carolina's, like Georgia's, permitted
abortion if a woman's life or health was endangered.[6] Some of the
lower federal courts and state appellate courts were beginning to
apply the Supreme Court's ruling. Abortion laws in Massachusetts,
Michigan, Nebraska, Ohio, Rhode Island, and Tennessee had been
invalidated by federal courts. Appellate courts in Minnesota and
Arizona had declared their state laws unconstitutional. All of these

states had laws similar to the Texas statute.[7] In April the Supreme Court denied rehearings to groups in New York and Connecticut who claimed they had found new evidence concerning the exact time when the life of a fetus begins.[8]

Throughout the remaining months of 1973, federal and state courts continued to overturn restrictive state laws on the basis of *Roe* and *Doe*, and state legislatures began to enact new abortion laws to replace those invalidated. Physicians and hospitals often found, in the interim period before new laws were passed, no state policy to guide them. They could choose to stall and delay, or they could begin implementation of the Court's decision on their own. Hospitals performing abortions for the first time did not always find that the new policy was greeted with unanimous approval. An incident in Boston was to highlight some of the questions that had not been resolved by the Court's decision.

The *Edelin* Case

The *Edelin* case, a much publicized trial for manslaughter of a doctor who had performed an abortion, demonstrated the way that ambiguities in the Court's decision might be exploited by hostile state officials. One of the incidents that precipitated the trial was an abortion performed in October, 1973, in the city hospital that served Boston's poorer citizens, on a teenaged unmarried woman of West Indian extraction.[9] A related incident was the publication of a report by four medical researchers on research being done on aborted fetuses.

Seven months after the *Roe* decision, Councilman Albert "Dapper" O'Neil launched an investigation into stories about research involving aborted fetuses at the Boston City Hospital. A team of researchers had been trying to find out the effects of antibiotic drugs on the unborn by giving antibiotics to women about to have therapeutic abortions and then testing the absorption of the drugs by the fetuses after the abortion was over. The experiments had been undertaken to study alternatives to penicillin, to which many pregnant women are allergic. Penicillin or some other drug must often be used when it is feared that the child in the uterus may contract an infection such as congenital syphilis. When the results of this research were published in the June 7, 1973, issue of the *New England Journal of Medicine,* a public uproar resulted, and pressure was put on the Boston City Council to investigate.[10] The investigation led to the indictment of the four doctors who were involved in the research and the chief resident in obstetrics, Dr. Kenneth C. Edelin, who had performed one of the abortions.

Although the inside story on the decision to bring criminal charges is not clear, contemporary press reports suggested that many Bostonians believed these indictments were "a politically motivated attempt to set up a test case against both the Supreme Court's decision on abortion and the equally emotional issue of experimentation with dead fetal tissue."[11] Under the Supreme Court's ruling in *Roe v. Wade,* the abortion performed at the Boston City Hospital was undoubtedly legal. Massachusetts had not yet replaced its antiabortion law, overturned by the decision, with a newer state statute, so Massachusetts had no law at all regulating abortions. If Edelin or the researchers were to be prosecuted, it would have to be for some other offense. The manslaughter charge against Edelin was based on the theory that the fetus had been delivered live and then killed. Phrased in traditional legal language, the indictment charged that "Kenneth Edelin, on the third day of October in the Year of Our Lord one thousand nine hundred seventy-three did assault and beat a certain person, to wit a male child described to the [Grand] jurors as 'baby boy,' and by such assault and beating did kill said person."[12]

The four doctors who had been conducting research on aborted fetuses were charged with illegal dissection under an 1814 state statute originally designed to prevent grave robbing, the carrying away of human bodies or remains for medical dissection. (Early students of anatomy, who could not study cadavers legally, as today's medical students do, were often guilty of robbing graves.)

By using laws against manslaughter and grave robbing to prosecute abortion and fetal research, the state was trying to do indirectly what it could not do directly. The four researchers were never tried. Edelin's trial took place during the following January and February in a state Superior Court before Judge James C. McGuire and a jury. The trial took six weeks and resulted in a jury verdict against Edelin. The key issue in the trial was whether or not manslaughter had occurred. The judge's charge to the jury made it clear that the jury could not convict for manslaughter unless it believed the evidence showed that the fetus or baby had been born alive and then either killed or negligently allowed to die. If the *subject* (since the use of the term *baby* or *fetus* more or less depended on one's attitude toward abortion, the term *subject* was used throughout the trial) had not been born alive, no person existed to be killed, and the manslaughter charge could not be sustained. On the question of live birth, conflicting evidence was presented, since several witnesses, including the chief prosecution witness, testified that the subject was lifeless when removed from the mother; it may well have been dead, since the mother had been injected with saline solution (saline amniocentesis) in earlier attempts at abortion that had failed. Other witnesses claimed that the subject had been born alive and had made an attempt to breathe. One witness contended that Edelin had smothered the fetus in the womb before delivering it. The evidence presented to the jury in most of these matters was conflicting in the extreme. Also conflicting was the evidence about both the age of the fetus (from twenty-three to twenty-six weeks) and its weight (between 600 and 700 grams).[13]

The jury found Edelin guilty, a verdict that was criticized by many participants in the trial. The defense thought it was contrary to the evidence and asked that it be set aside. Edelin's defense attorney, William P. Homans, Jr., saw the prosecution as a demonstration of dissatisfaction with the Supreme Court decision and the verdict a result of jury bias. Comments made by jurors and alternates left no doubt that the trial had been full of emotional crosscurrents. In an interview with the press after the trial, Edelin stated, "A lot came together for them (the prosecution) in my case. They got a black physician and they got a woman more than twenty weeks pregnant, and they got a fetus in the mortuary."[14] Edelin thought that the prosecution was primarily political, motivated by hostility to blacks and a product of the District Attorney's desire to promote his own personal and philosophical views of abortion, using public funds and his official status. As evidence that this was a trial to promote the antiabortion cause, Edelin submitted that the witnesses called against him were not experts in fetal development or in obstetrics and gynecology, but leaders in the antiabortion movement like Dr. Mildred Jefferson. Jefferson, the principal witness against him, Edelin said, was "a founding member of every anti-choice group in the state of Massachusetts" and was a general surgeon who never performed abortions.[15]

Assistant District Attorney Newman Flanagan, who prosecuted the case, insisted that this was an ordinary trial for manslaughter, not an antiabortion trial.

Whatever the motivations of the participants, Edelin's trial was a cause celebre and was followed with interest in all parts of the country. People on the pro-Choice side were afraid that the possibility of indictment and conviction for manslaughter when fetuses survived an abortion and then died would keep doctors from performing abortions and that the Massachusetts episode would have an adverse impact on medical research and practice. Church leaders hoped that this would indeed be the case. Cardinal Krol, Roman Catholic archbishop of Pennsylvania, commented, "Some have expressed concern that the decision may inhibit abortion. We pray to God it will."[16]

Scattered trials for manslaughter, murder, and even self-abortion did take place, sporadically, in the areas most opposed to the Court's ruling. A physician in North Dakota, known to perform elective abortions, was tried for manslaughter in 1977.[17] Dr. William B. Waddill, a California obstetrician and gynecologist, was tried in 1978 for murder.[18] Charges were brought against a South Carolina gynecologist for illegal abortion and murder for aborting a twenty-six- to thirty-week-old fetus, which lived for twenty days on a life-support system.[19] Marla Elaine Pitchford was tried in 1978 for performing an illegal abortion on herself, but was acquitted on grounds of temporary insanity.[20] In 1979, authorities in Omaha, Nebraska, brought charges against a doctor in a medical center, charging him with illegal abortion and failure to care for a live fetus. Like Edelin, he claimed that the charges were politically motivated.

In a way, the *Edelin* case can be said to be the result of incomplete answers given by the Supreme Court in its original decisions. The question of viability had been central to the Court's solution. Before viability, the decision to abort could be made by the woman and her doctor without considering the welfare of the unborn child; after viability, the state had grounds for intervening to protect the fetus. But exactly when is a fetus viable? Justice Blackmun had found some disagreement among members of the medical profession, but had relied on the generally accepted rule that viability "is usually placed at about seven months (28 weeks) but may occur earlier, even at 24 weeks."[21] It became clear in months following the decision that although there was a generally accepted gestational age at which the fetus had the ability to survive outside the mother, earlier fetuses occasionally did survive. A report made for a federal commission on the subject, the Behrman report, tied survival to birth weight, saying that no newborn under 600 grams has ever been known to survive, that the survival rate of babies weighing over 600 grams at birth is 3.6 in a million, but that babies weighing over 900 grams do have a small chance of survival. At the Supreme Court's twenty-eight-week figure, the average fetus would weigh 1,000 grams or about 2 pounds, 3 ounces.[22] Perhaps nine hundred babies a year (out of 3 million) could be born at this low weight and survive, although the number is probably less.

The Supreme Court had not addressed itself to the problems presented by an assumption that some children, even though a tiny fraction, might be viable before twenty-four weeks and that a few might survive the abortion.[23] So it had left unanswered the question about whether the states should be allowed to forbid or restrict abortions at this stage of pregnancy, perhaps pushing the date of allowable abortions back to eighteen to twenty weeks. A second question that now had to be answered was, what should be done when such fetuses did survive? Was the attending doctor responsible for trying to save such babies, even though the chance of survival for them was very slim? Who would pay for the incubators and specialized medical care required to save them? If they survived, who was responsible for them? What would the situation be for a woman who had entered the hospital to have an abortion, if she found that she was, after all, the mother of a very premature infant? Does the fact of abortion presume that the child will not survive?

State legislatures had already begun to consider these and other unanswered questions at the time of the Boston indictments, and some would incorporate provisions protecting viable fetuses, born during abortions, into their new state laws. The indictment and conviction of Edelin brought these questions to the attention of the general public. Edelin himself was exonerated after appeal. In 1976 the Supreme Judicial Court of Massachusetts reversed Edelin's conviction on the grounds that the evidence was insufficient to support a manslaughter charge (no wanton or reckless conduct). The Massachusetts court believed the trial judge should have directed a verdict of acquittal.[24]

The question of fetal research raised by the Boston cases was also considered elsewhere. Concern had already been voiced about the use of fetuses for medical research, and this concern was heightened by the prospect of a larger number of abortions. If more fetuses were available, they might be widely used in research projects, and many people feared that this would lead to gruesome experiments with live fetuses. Although fetuses from abortions performed in the United States have rarely been used for research, scientists have gone to other countries, Finland, for example, to experiment on fetuses obtained there. After the Supreme Court's decision, the National Institute of Health began to work on guidelines that would limit the kinds of research possible on live, aborted fetuses. These included forbidding research on viable fetuses or any fetuses of a certain size or keeping a fetus alive by artificial means for experimentation.[25] The fear that aborted fetuses would be subject to improper experimentation, as well as distaste at the idea of experimentation, led Congress to accept as a rider to a federally-funded medical research bill the proviso that no funds would be used for any research on a live fetus.[26] The states also acted to regulate fetal research. Even before Edelin's trial, the Massachusetts legislature passed a law prohibiting Massachusetts doctors from giving experimental drugs or vaccines to women planning abortions.[27] New laws in Pennsylvania and Missouri imposed a duty of care for any surviving fetuses on physicians performing abortions. Other states imposed limits on fetal research and wrote various provisions to protect infants who survived abortions, often making them wards of the state.

New Kinds of State Legislation

Laws protecting the fetus were only one kind of abortion-related provision being considered by the states in this period. State legislatures had begun to respond to the Court's decision immediately after it was handed down. Some states acquiesced in the ruling and passed statutes conforming their laws to the new constitutional requirements. Four states—New York, Washington, Alaska, and Hawaii—had already passed liberal laws that required no revision. But in other states, opponents of abortion went back to the legislatures to urge, often unsuccessfully, that measures be passed to circumvent or limit the effect of the ruling. Some of the new state laws were clearly in conflict with the Supreme Court's decision. Utah would permit abortion only to preserve the life or physical health of the mother; North Dakota, only to preserve her life; and Rhode Island's new law stated that

in the furtherance of the public policy of said state, human life and, in fact, a person within the language and meaning of the 14th Amendment to the Constitution of the United States, commences to exist at the instant of conception.[28]

In the first wave of post-*Roe* legislation, three out of seven of the laws enacted were overly restrictive and would later be overturned in the courts. Other legislation seemed to regulate within the limits prescribed by the Supreme Court.

In 1973 nearly two hundred bills (both general- and single-purpose bills) were introduced in state legislatures. Outside of the general regulation of the conditions under which abortions could be performed, two areas were clearly of special concern: the exemption of medical personnel from the necessity of performing abortions if they disapproved on moral or religious grounds and the requirement of parental consent for abortions for unmarried minors.

In the twenty-four months immediately following the Supreme Court's decision, sixty-two laws directly related to abortion were adopted by thirty-two states.[29] The laws fall into seven main categories, although some of the more comprehensive laws contain provisions in each category. With minor exceptions, these categories include most types of legislation adopted through 1979 and outline the basic state legislative response on this topic.

1. *Performance requirements.* These were regulations governing the places where abortions could be performed, by whom, and

when. Five states required that even first trimester abortions be performed in hospitals. Seven states required that abortions after viability be performed only if two physicians agreed that the abortion was necessary to preserve life. New York's law, for example, required that after the twelfth week of pregnancy, abortions be performed only in hospitals; and that after the twentieth week, two physicians be in attendance.[30] Twenty states enacted provisions governing the performance of abortions. Court tests of these laws consistently overturned unduly restrictive regulations of first trimester abortions. Regulations that singled out clinics for special controls were held to violate equal protection of the laws. A state law making it a criminal offense to perform a first trimester abortion except in a hospital or licensed health facility was invalidated by a lower federal court, and the decision affirmed by the United States Supreme Court.[31] *Roe v. Wade* indicated that states could require that abortions be performed only by physicians. The federal courts have also upheld state laws making it illegal for nonphysicians to perform abortions.

The general rule on second trimester abortions has been that the states may pass those regulations that are reasonably related to the protection of the mothers' health. But in the years after 1973, performance requirements multiplied, gradually making access to the operations more difficult and complicated.

2. *Consent requirements.* Consent requirements of different kinds were a feature of many of the new laws. Some states required written consent from the woman before an abortion could be performed. Others included so-called spousal and parental consent requirements. These requirements forbade the performance of an abortion, unless the husband consented, or when the patient was under age and unmarried, unless the parent or guardian consented. Another variation required the woman to be informed of the hazards, physiological and psychological, of abortion and of the methods to be used before an abortion could be performed. Twelve states adopted spousal or father's consent rules, fourteen states enacted parental consent requirements. The "informed consent" strictures were ostensibly designed to keep women who did not want abortions from being coerced into having them, although

an additional motive was the discouragement of some abortions. The spousal and parental consent provisions gave the spouse or parents a veto over the woman's decision. Various combinations of these consent requirements were used. Consent laws were later struck down in eight states; they received a Supreme Court test in 1976, in *Planned Parenthood of Missouri v. Danforth* and, in 1979, in *Bellotti v. Baird*.[32] (These cases are discussed later.)

3. *Reporting requirements.* By 1975 twenty-three states had formulated rules requiring that physicians or hospitals keep records and report all abortions. In some states, this was a purely statistical record, with the name of the mother deleted. Eleven of the twenty-three required that the records be confidential.

4. *Advertising of legal abortions.* In 1975 six states had prohibited advertising of abortion services. This type of law was declared unconstitutional in *Bigelow v. Virginia*[33] in 1975. It was held to put unconstitutional limits on freedom of speech and the press.

5. *Public funding of abortions.* It was not initially clear whether the states were required to fund abortions for the poor under Medicaid programs. Immediately after *Roe v. Wade*, twenty states and the District of Columbia had no provisions *forbidding* the public funding of abortions. However, twenty-nine states (Arizona had no state Medicaid plan) had legislation or administrative regulations that restricted state payments for therapeutic abortions or required some form of special authorization by additional physicians or hospital boards.[34] The public funding picture, however, changed rapidly. A survey by the Alan Guttmacher Institute in 1974 reported that thirty-nine states and the District of Columbia provided Medicaid payments for legal abortions without restrictions. Most of these states had elected to do so; five states, however, had been ordered to fund abortions by federal courts.[35] Appeals from some of these federal court decisions eventually reached the Supreme Court, which was asked for a definitive ruling on whether state funding was required by the Social Security Act, and whether the Constitution's equal protection clause required payment for abortion on the same basis as payment for the medical expenses of

childbirth. After the Court ruled negatively on both of these questions in 1977,[36] many states again reversed direction and refused to fund elective abortions.[37]

6. *Conscience clauses.* In 1975 forty states had laws allowing institutions or individual physicians or both to refuse to perform abortions if their moral or religious principles opposed abortion.[38] Initially, these laws were thought to be constitutional only as they related to private hospitals or individual doctors or nurses. It was even possible that private hospitals receiving funds under the Hill-Burton Act might not be allowed to refuse to supply abortion as a legitimate medical service. A Massachusetts federal District Court held in 1974, for example, that a public hospital could not refuse to perform elective first trimester abortions.[39] This issue was still unclear until resolved by the Supreme Court in *Poelker v. Doe* in 1977; there, it was held that even public hospitals were not constitutionally required to perform nontherapeutic abortions.[40]

7. *Fetal protection.* As mentioned earlier, a variety of different types of regulation related to the fetus itself were passed. States forbade experimentation with aborted fetuses or fetuses *in utero*, required that the physician performing an abortion protect any fetus born alive, and provided that surviving fetuses become wards of the state. Other provisions dealt with the disposal of dead fetuses. Laws such as Rhode Island's and Louisiana's, declaring a fetus to be a person from the moment of conception, were held unconstitutional in lower federal courts.

Back in the Courts: Testing the New Laws

Many of these legislative proposals would now be challenged in the courts. Using the most effective strategy available to them, pro-Choice groups would again go to court to enforce the general guidelines set out in *Roe*, trying to keep first trimester abortions unhindered and to overturn those laws that seemed to move past regulation to prohibition. State legislators often seemed little concerned with the constitutionality of their product and passed the buck with alacrity to the courts. Frank Sussman, a Missouri attorney who had been active in abortion politics in his state and later represented the plaintiffs in *Poelker v. Doe*, commented at the time Missouri's restrictive abortion law was passed that:

Many state legislators really don't give a damn whether or not what they pass is constitutional. All they care about is whether it will be popular with their constituents, whom they perceive, usually incorrectly, to be conservative on the abortion issue. I think that legislators frequently abdicate their legislative responsibility to the judiciary and, unfortunately, there is no way to prevent it. In Missouri, for example, only a handful of legislators voted against the new state abortion law which is so patently unconstitutional.[41]

Missouri's 1974 comprehensive abortion law, combining five of the seven types of restrictions, brought a Supreme Court test of these legislative provisions. It was not surprising that Missouri was one of the earlier states to pass such a law. Catholics in the St. Louis archdiocese were very heavily organized, with Right-to-Life groups in 254 parishes. Under Father Edward J. O'Donnell's leadership, Catholic organizations had used every available strategy to defeat abortion, pushing a strong law through the Missouri legislature, calling on Congress for constitutional amendments and successfully preventing the performance of abortions in the two St. Louis municipal hospitals.[42]

The Missouri Case: *Planned Parenthood of Central Missouri v. Danforth*[43]

In June, 1974, Missouri's 77th General Assembly enacted a comprehensive new abortion statute. This statute had sixteen sections and covered a broad range of matters connected with abortion. It defined *viability* as "that stage of fetal development when the life of the unborn child may be continued indefinitely outside the womb by natural or artificial life-supportive systems." It also made it illegal to perform any abortion before the end of the first twelve weeks *unless* a series of conditions were met. These were:

1. A consenting, licensed, physician must decide that the abortion is necessary.

2. The woman must consent in writing to the abortion.
3. The husband or spouse must consent (unless the abortion is necessary to save the woman's life).
4. The parent or guardian must consent if the woman is unmarried and under age (unless the abortion is necessary to save her life).

The first trimester had been the period the Supreme Court seemed to have contemplated as being largely unregulated, a period in which the woman and her physician were to make a private decision. Now additional conditions would have to be met.

After the first twelve weeks (in the second trimester), abortions must be performed in a hospital and the physician must certify that to the best of his knowledge, the fetus is not viable. In this period, the physician himself would be subjected to a series of regulations.

1. He must take care to ensure that viable fetuses be kept alive and must take care of any fetuses born alive.
2. He is subject to second-degree manslaughter charges, or civil suits if he fails to exercise proper care and a second-degree murder charge if he kills a viable fetus.
3. He may not use saline amniocentesis, an abortion method usually used in later pregnancies, where an injection of saline solution into the amniotic sac is given to kill the fetus or induce labor.
4. He must keep records of all abortions (as must all clinics and hospitals).

Other sections of the statute made infants surviving attempted abortions wards of the state and required that women seeking abortions be informed of these provisions of the law.

The 1974 statute had also introduced a new variant on informed consent, requiring that the physician warn his patient that if a live infant is born as a result of the abortion, it will be a ward of the state and the parents will lose all parental rights. This provision was not reviewed by the Court in *Danforth*, but was later invalidated by the Court of Appeals for the Eighth Circuit. The Court of Appeals held that it invaded rights of privacy and was not reasonably related to the purpose of "informed consent."[44]

In July, 1976, the Supreme Court, Justice Blackmun again writing for the majority, decided an appeal from a federal court decision upholding the Missouri statute. It held that a number of the Missouri law's provisions were in conflict with *Roe v. Wade* and the United States Constitution. It upheld the Missouri legislature's rather circular definition of viability, allowed the state to require the reporting of all abortions and the written consent of the mother, and agreed that premature infants born alive should be given special protection. But it invalidated the parental and spousal consent provisions and the prohibition against use of saline amniocentesis as an abortion technique.

Limiting the Scope of Consent Requirements

The spousal and parental consent requirements of the law were held to conflict with *Roe v. Wade*. The Court ruled that if the state does not have the right to veto a woman's decision to have an abortion, it may not delegate such a power to the child's father or to the woman's parents—it has no right to give a third party the power to veto. The Court rejected Missouri's argument that the state's interest in protecting marriages and families justifies such consent requirements. Justice Blackmun did not believe that marital ties would be strengthened by letting a husband block a woman's request for an abortion or that parental authority would be strengthened by giving parents the right to veto an abortion for a teenage daughter. Mature minors, the Court held, should be permitted to make their own decisions, and even immature minors should be allowed to bypass parental consent when it is clearly shown that an abortion would be in the minor's best interests.

The parental consent provision was found to infringe on the constitutional rights of the minors themselves. "Constitutional rights do not mature and come into being magically when one attains the state-defined age of majority," Justice Blackmun wrote. "Minors as well as adults are protected by the Constitution and possess constitutional rights." This holding was consistent with several earlier cases upholding the constitutional rights of minors. *In re Gault* had held that juveniles being tried in juvenile court proceedings have a right to many of the procedural protections of due process.[45] *Tinker v. Des Moines* protected the freedom of speech of school children,[46] and *Goss v. Lopez* held that school disciplinary proceedings must respect due process.[47] *Breed v. Jones* extended the protection against double jeopardy to juvenile court proceedings.[48]

Parental consent has remained one of the most controversial

areas in the abortion dispute. The numbers of teenage pregnancies and of unmarried adolescents having children rose precipitously during the 1960s and the magnitude of the problem eventually began to intrude on public awareness. In 1976, Planned Parenthood of America published a research report entitled *Eleven Million Teenagers: What Can Be Done About the Epidemic of Adolescent Pregnancies in the Unites States?* Conservatives were convinced that government programs designed to control the "epidemic" of teenage pregnancy, programs of sex education and family planning and the subsidization of contraceptive and abortion services, actually encouraged sexual activity. To make matters worse, allowing teenagers independent access to birth control devices and abortion destroyed fragile family ties. Fears about the stability of the American family were now joined with other concerns about the erosion of morality, parental loss of control over children, and the increase in the number of abortions being performed nationwide. It was not surprising, in view of the seriousness of these concerns, that provisions for requiring written consent from parents or guardians before abortions could be performed on girls under fifteen (and sometimes even older) continued to be written into many legislative proposals in spite of the decision in *Danforth.*

Although *Danforth* forbade a third-party veto of abortions by a spouse or the parents of a minor, it did not answer all of the questions connected with consent. The decision ruled out an absolute parental veto over all teenage abortions. But it did not rule out the possibility of imposing some requirement of parental consultation or approval, and state legislatures continued to look for acceptable methods of imposing such controls.

In 1974, Massachusetts, like Missouri, enacted a comprehensive set of antiabortion laws. Among the statutory provisions was a requirement that unmarried minors have the consent of both parents before an abortion could be performed. If her parents refused consent, a pregnant minor could petition a judge of the Superior Court, and the judge could consent to the abortion "for good cause shown." The law provided that the parents be notified and allowed to present their side of the dispute in court.[49] A test case brought by abortion activist Bill Baird on behalf of himself, his abortion clinic, his medical director, and two anonymous pregnant minors was filed shortly before the law went into effect. It was supported at various times in the six years it was in the courts by the Massachusetts Civil Liberties Union and by Planned Parenthood of Massachusetts. The Supreme Court first heard this case (*Bellotti v. Baird I*) in 1976; it was argued at the same time as the *Danforth* case, and the decision was handed down the same day.[50]

The statute differed from that considered in the Missouri case because it applied to all unmarried women under eighteen and because it allowed appeals from a parental refusal of consent to a judge. Because there were unresolved questions about the intent of the state legislature and the meaning of several provisions, the Supreme Court remanded the case to federal District Court for certification to the Supreme Judicial Court of Massachusetts. After the state Supreme Court handed down a definitive reading of the statute, the case started its long legal journey back to the United States Supreme Court. The Justices reheard the case, reaching a final decision in 1979.[51] The Court ultimately rejected the consent requirement as failing to provide enough protection for the minor's own needs. Even after a finding by a state judge that a minor was mature enough to make her own decision about abortion and had, in fact, decided that an abortion was the best course to take, the judge was still empowered to overrule her decision.

Although the Supreme Court rejected the provision, it was badly split as to why the law was unconstitutional. Four Justices objected to the law because it contained an absolute third-party veto; no minor, no matter how capable or mature, could have an abortion without the consent of both parents or a Superior Court judge. Four other Justices thought that distinctions had to be made between mature and immature minors. Mature minors should be allowed to make their own decisions. Even immature minors were entitled to decisions made in their best interests, a right not adequately protected by the state law. Justice Powell's opinion for one of the four-Justice blocs suggested to Massachusetts that it provide some route that would allow mature minors to bypass the parental consent requirement and go directly to court; if the court agreed that a minor was responsible enough to make her own decision, she should be allowed to make her own choice even if the judge disagreed. If it could be shown that an abortion would be the best solution for a minor, the court should be required to authorize it. Again, as stated above, even immature minors were entitled to a decision based on their own best interests. If the state followed these guidelines, the opinion suggested, the resulting statute would probably be upheld.

Because of the split on the Court, the *Bellotti* litigation was resolved without clarifying rules to be used in defining the separate rights of parents and children. The decision was in effect a compromise that affirmed the importance of parental involvement, but required some formal recognition of a minor's rights. After the decision was handed down, the Massachusetts legislature quickly enacted a statute that embodied Justice Powell's compromise. The state ended up with an expensive system in which judges rubber-stamp the requests of those minors who go to court. One Massachusetts judge summed up the situation: the Supreme Court and the Massachusetts legislature have given "half a loaf to the anti-abortion forces and dumped the other half on us." The practical results of the law were mixed. The number of abortions performed on minors in Massachusetts declined, but there was some evidence that adolescents often went out of state to avoid the consent requirements.[52] There was no evidence that the law decreased teenage sexual activity or improved family communication. After five years of litigation and six published opinions by state and federal courts, it was still unclear how much parental consent and consultation could be required when minors sought abortions, how their best interests should be protected, and how acceptable legislation should be worded.

One method of avoiding the problems presented by consent provisions is to require that physicians notify parents when a minor seeks an abortion. Although there is a technical difference between the two, parental notification provisions address the same concerns as parental consent requirements; practically speaking, when parents are notified that a minor is seeking an abortion, they will often be able to veto the decision. Notification is designed to guarantee, at the very least, that some kind of discussion between parents and child will take place. Two years after *Bellotti*, in *H. L. v. Matheson*, the Court upheld a parental notification law.[53] H. L., an unemancipated fifteen-year-old, living at home claimed that the law abridged her rights and that it would not be in her best interests to tell her parents about the proposed abortion. The issue in this case was narrowly defined, since her lawyer wanted to test the constitutionality of the notification requirement itself, divorced from any particular factual situation. H. L. did not, therefore, claim that she was an emancipated minor or explain the reasons for her stand. The Court upheld the law, but only as it applied to immature and unemancipated minors, refusing to extend the *Danforth* ruling by holding that parental notification was unconstitutional in all instances.

It was now becoming clear that one of the underlying concerns of the Court in parental consent cases was the integrity of the family. The Justices were uneasy about conservative contentions that government-sponsored programs of sex education, family planning, and abortion services tie the adolescent girl to the state and loosen her dependence on her parents. Even though it did not repudiate its holding that there was a constitutional right to choose whether or not to bear a child, the Court did not want to undercut family ties by upholding claims to constitutional rights that allowed minors to bypass family decisions. The *Bellotti* decisions and *H. L. v. Matheson* were not, however, the last word on parental consent. The issue would be confronted again in the *Akron* and *Ashcroft* decisions in 1983.

Testing Statutory Requirements Designed to Ensure Fetal Survival

Pennyslvania, like Missouri and Massachusetts, enacted comprehensive abortion legislation in 1974 as part of the first wave of restrictive state laws. As was true also in Massachusetts, the legislation was passed over the Governor's veto. The Pennsylvania Abortion Control Act of 1974 required informed consent and spousal and parental consent, prohibited abortion after viability except to save the life or health of the mother, required reports and record keeping, prohibited the advertising of abortions and the use of public funds, and authorized the Department of Public Health to make rules governing the performance of abortions. It also attempted to define the viability and prescribe the physician's responsibilities in caring for viable and potentially viable fetuses. *Colautti v. Franklin*, which reached the Court in 1979, was part of a protracted litigation effort commenced shortly after the enactment of this legislation.[54] The original suit, brought by

Planned Parenthood and various organizations and physicians, challenged most of these provisions on constitutional grounds. A United States District Court upheld some provisions and overturned others.

By the time the case reached the Supreme Court, many of the issues it presented had been considered in other cases, and it was remanded for reconsideration in light of *Planned Parenthood of Missouri v. Danforth* and other abortion decisions. On remand all issues were disposed of by stipulation, except for one section regulating the physician's responsibilities for fetal survival. The sole question remaining for decision in 1979 was the constitutionality of Section 5, Subsection (a) of the 1974 act, subjecting a physician to criminal penalties if he failed to take certain steps to preserve the life of a fetus when it was "viable" or when there was "sufficient reason to believe" that it might be viable. The Court was asked to decide whether this section was too vague and overbroad to form the basis for a criminal prosecution.

The Court divided on this issue, six to three. Justice Blackmun discussed the issue of viability for the majority, saying that the Court, in *Roe*, had left the exact limits of viability flexible, recognizing the need for medical decisions based on a broad range of variable factors that might affect the fetus's ability to survive.

The Pennsylvania statute did not, the Court held, allow the physician the discretion required by *Roe*, but rather subjected him to criminal penalties on the basis of a vague and ambiguous standard. The phrase "may be viable" was even less definite a concept than "viable." The physician was thus subjected to liability without regard to fault; under the law, he might act in good faith and still risk prosecution. The Court also held that the statute failed to reconcile the fetal care provisions with the doctor's parallel responsibilities for the protection of the mother's health. In sum, the majority concluded that abortion was a complex medical problem that the Pennsylvania legislation had not handled within the framework of the 1973 decisions.

State Legislation After 1977

More abortion laws were enacted in 1977 than in any previous year since 1973. The tone of the statutes was becoming increasingly restrictive, reflecting the growing power and presence of anti-abortion forces in state politics. The Right-to-Life groups seemed to be better organized and better motivated and to work harder than the pro-Choice forces.[55] For the most part, the devices proposed in 1977 and afterward were not new but represented tougher versions of familiar regulations. None led to increased access to abortion. Conscience legislation allowed physicians and hospitals to refuse to perform abortions. Reporting requirements became stricter, requiring physicians to report all abortions to state agencies. A Minnesota proposal required that the names of doctors, the numbers of abortions performed, and the fees received be made part of the Public Records Act.[56] Following the Supreme Court's decisions allowing the states to refuse to fund abortions for low-income women, funding restrictions were increasingly imposed. By March, 1978, only sixteen states and the District of Columbia were paying for all or most abortions.[57] The NARAL claimed that federal funding was now near zero; in 1978 only 385 medical abortions and 61 abortions for rape or incest victims were funded.[58] Many other kinds of restrictive provisions were in effect. Protection-of-the-fetus laws imposed criminal penalties on physicians who failed to take all possible steps to save the lives of fetuses that survived abortion attempts.[59] Waiting periods, pregnancy tests, and informed consent proposals were passed. State laws required registration of hospitals, clinics, and abortion counsellors and required licensing and inspection. They regulated advertising and forbade referral fees. They cut off funding not only for abortions, but also for family planning and referral organizations.[60]

THE AKRON ORDINANCE CASES[61]

The most extensive attempt by a state or local government to hedge the abortion procedure with restrictions was written into a city ordinance and enacted by the city council of Akron, Ohio, in February, 1978. Drafted with the help of Right-to-Life organizations, the ordinance served as a model for laws in eleven states, including Oklahoma, Illinois, Kansas, Louisiana, and Nebraska.[62]

Local governments have ordinarily limited their concern with abortion to zoning, clinic inspection, and the provision of emergency services. The Akron ordinance, however, went beyond the regulation of facilities and equipment, providing a complex arrangement of seventeen provisions designed to restrict access to abortions and discourage those considering abortions. It required a twenty-four-hour waiting period, notice to the supposed father or the women's parents or guardian, parental consent for minors, and written consent by the woman herself. In addition, the ordinance required that the physician give the woman a lecture on the physical development of the fetus, explain to her that the "unborn child is a human being from the moment of conception," and describe its "appearance, mobility, tactile sensitivity, including pain perception or response, brain and heart functions," and the presence of internal and external organs. Further, the woman must be told that the fetus may be viable if twenty-two weeks have elapsed and that she would have no parental rights to a live child. The ordinance also placed various restrictions on abortion clinics and prohibited the use of saline abortions after the first trimester, requiring the doctor to use the technique most likely to save the life of the fetus if the possibility of viability exists.

None of these provisions were unique: all had been used in one form or another in state statutes. But in conjunction they resulted in an extremely restrictive system.

In 1978, three abortion clinics and a physician brought suit challenging the constitutionality of the ordinance. Decisions in the District Court and the Court of Appeals for the Sixth Circuit invalidated some of the provisions and upheld others. The case finally reached the Supreme Court in 1982 and was decided, with two companion cases, in 1983. *City of Akron v. Akron Center for Reproductive Health, Planned Parenthood, Kansas City, Missouri v. Ashcroft,* and *Simopoulos v. Virginia* provide us with a benchmark, ten years after *Roe v. Wade,* from which to measure the course of decisions defining the limits of state authority to restrict abortions.

The decisions in the three cases demonstrated that the Court was still willing, despite political pressure from the Reagan administration and the addition of a new Justice, to stand by the main principles of *Roe v. Wade.* But the 1983 cases also revealed that, while the Court was willing to reaffirm its decision in *Roe,* there had been some subtle erosion of the dividing line, marked out in the 1976 *Danforth* decision, between acceptable and unacceptable state regulation. They also tell us something about the positions of the individual Justices in 1983. Justice Sandra Day O'Connor, newly appointed, joined the two Justices with the most conservative views on abortion, Justices White and Rehnquist. While the remaining six Justices were still disposed to follow the 1973 precedent, disagreement continued between Justices Brennan, Marshall, and Blackmun in a pro-Choice position, and Justices Burger, Powell, and Stevens who were more tolerant of state regulation. The Court now split six to three; the decision in *Roe v. Wade* had been seven to two.

Abortion opponents had had hopes that the Supreme Court would take this opportunity to overrule *Roe v. Wade* and retreat from the conflict altogether. But Justice Powell's majority opinion invoked the doctrine of *stare decisis* and reaffirmed the basic principles asserted in the earlier case: the right of privacy and the concept of personal liberty in the Fourteenth Amendment create constitutional protections broad enough to encompass a woman's decision whether or not to terminate her pregnancy, and freedom of choice in matters of marriage and family life are essential aspects of liberty. The limits on these rights were also reiterated: the woman's right is not unqualified, and abortion is a medical procedure that can be regulated by the state.

In *Roe v. Wade* Justice Blackmun had tried to balance the conflicting interests about abortion by dividing pregnancy into trimesters and allowing the balance of interests to shift as the pregnancy progressed: the woman's choice was predominant in the first three months; first trimester regulations could not operate to limit a woman's ability to choose an abortion, make it more costly, or influence her choice. Nor could they place unnecessary restrictions on physicians. After the first trimester, the state's legitimate interests in regulation to protect maternal health and the developing fetus became more important—substantial in the second trimester and nearly dominant in the third. The Court retained this basic formula in the 1983 decisions. Some regulation was permissible in the first trimester. Written consent and record-keeping requirements had been upheld in *Danforth*. If the regulations were justified by important state health objectives and had little or no impact on the woman's right to choose, they would be upheld.

The Akron ordinance required signatures on a consent form, a lecture by the physician on abortion procedures and the development of the fetus, and a twenty-four-hour waiting period. While the requirement of written consent and the provision of information about abortion procedures was found to be reasonably related to state concerns about health, the Court did not accept the necessity of a lecture on the development of the fetus or the need in all cases for a waiting period. The lengthy and inflexible recitation about fetal development was likely to influence the woman's decision, and the waiting period was costly and burdensome, would delay early abortions, and might, in some instances, expose the woman to additional risk. The provision requiring parental consent (or that of a legal guardian) for minors was inconsistent with earlier decisions, since it did not provide a definite procedure by which mature minors would be allowed to make their own decisions, thus foreclosing entirely the abortion option for these women if their parents disagreed. Regulations during the second trimester were valid in so far as they actually protected the patient's health and safety. The standard to be used in deciding what regulations were necessary to protect health and safety was to be *accepted medical practice*, rather than the views of either the state legislature or the Supreme Court. The Akron ordinance required *all* second trimester abortions to be performed in regular hospitals rather than clinics; the Court held that such provisions were costly and unrelated to medical necessity and that many abortions could be performed safely and more cheaply in well-equipped clinics. Finally, the court overturned the provision requiring "humane and sanitary" disposal of aborted fetuses. The Court held that the term "humane," in this context, was unconstitutionally vague.

The *Akron* decision indicated that the Court would not repudiate the basic holdings in *Roe v. Wade* and was still willing to overturn excessively restrictive state regulations. But the Akron ordinance was an extreme measure, admittedly designed to discourage the performance of abortions. The provisions of the Missouri law reviewed in the second case, *Planned Parenthood, Kansas City, Missouri v. Ashcroft*, were more clearly within the range of restrictions that the Court was now willing to accept as reasonable. In *Ashcroft*, while the Court followed *Akron* in rejecting hospitalization for all second trimester abortions, it upheld three other restrictions: a requirement that a second physician be present at second trimester abortions to protect infants who were alive, a requirement that all fetal tissue be sent to a pathologist for a report, and a parental consent requirement. This consent requirement met objections that had been raised in earlier consent cases because it provided a procedure that allowed mature minors to make their own abortion decisions.

The third case, *Simopoulos v. Virginia*, the criminal prosecution of a physician for performing a second trimester abortion in his unlicensed clinic, indirectly supported the general proposition that second trimester abortions be allowed in licensed outpatient clinics rather than in hospitals. The actual decision turned on a narrow question of statutory interpretation.

This group of decisions gave observers the first clear indication of Justice O'Connor's position on reproductive rights. She had been questioned aggressively about abortion in her confirmation hearing and had insisted that, while she was personally opposed to abortion, she would maintain proper judicial neutrality about abortion cases until after she had the chance to read the briefs and hear the arguments. Her dissenting opinion in *Akron* criticized *Roe v. Wade* as not providing "neutral principles" on which to decide abortion cases. In her view, inevitable changes in medical technology cause the temporal guidelines (the trimesters) used in that case to blur. Thus, the point of viability is pushed back toward conception as techniques for saving premature infants improve. Yet abortions in the second trimester also become safer, decreasing the need for state regulations premised on the need to protect the woman's health and safety. The framework set forth in *Roe* is thus "on a collision course with itself." O'Connor proposed a new standard that could be used to replace the allegedly unworkable trimester rule. She would have the Court ask only a single question: does the state regulation "burden" the right to choose an abortion? If it does not, the Court should uphold regulations that are rationally related to legitimate state objectives.

It is not clear why Justice O'Connor found this manifestation of the impact of changing technology on constitutional law so unprecedented.[63] The need to adapt legal principles to techno- logical change is not uniquely present in medical cases. The Court is constantly involved with the consequences of changing tech- nology. Basic legal principles are always being molded to fit the new "state" of some science—as the steamboat and railroad replace the riverboat and wagon; as electronics augments human sight, hearing, ability to compute and remember; as campaigning by television replaces the hard cider campaign and the whistlestop. The value of the trimester approach lay in its formula for resolving conflicts between and among the three sets of overlapping and, to some extent, mutually exclusive interests involved in the unique condition of pregnancy. The protection of fetal life necessarily conflicts with a woman's objection to childbearing. The trimester approach was a formula for compromise. In response to Justice O'Connor's objection that the trimester formulation involves the Court too fully in evaluating medical techniques, the majority might have responded that this is exactly what it does not do. Using accepted medical knowledge at any given time as a reference point that can be objectively assessed, it marks out certain boundaries and, within these boundaries, leaves the abortion decision to the woman and her physician. Such a standard keeps the Court from becoming a medical review board and leaves the abortion decision where it belongs, in private and medical hands. Justice O'Connor's "unduly burdensome" standard would not require the state to justify its regulations unless they "drastically limited the availability and safety of the desired service." Such a test supplies neither a neutral principle nor the promise of results free from personal predilections. What "burdens" reproductive choice will be no clearer to warring litigants than what "burdens" interstate commerce has been in the past. If all regulation that does not "drastically limit" abortion is to be accepted, the way is opened to a continuous narrowing of abortion rights through the piling up of technical requirements.

The Ritual Dance Continues

The Supreme Court's 1983 decisions seem to have inhibited the further introduction of legislation on waiting periods, informed consent, and hospitalization for second trimester abortions, but other techniques for restricting abortion remained to be explored. In 1985, when forty-nine legislatures were in session, sixty-five state laws were passed on fertility related topics—the largest number since 1973. In states with strong antiabortion political pressures, legislators still tested for new ways to legislate in the interstices of court decisions. The laws continued to deal with a list of familiar topics: prohibitions on abortion funding, parental notification of minors' abortions, restrictions on abortion coverage in health insurance schemes, counselling, clinic licensing, and the care for viable fetuses. But fertility-related legislation no longer seemed to be dominated by the abortion issue. Many of the new laws were concerned with broader issues of maternal and infant health.[64]

Although many of the newer laws tended to follow well-established patterns, there were some novel topics and innovative approaches. A few bills were introduced to address the emerging problem of violence against abortion clinics.[65] Washington State's Anti-Harassment Act of 1985 imposed strict penalties and provided that repeated offenses would be prosecuted as felonies. State "Baby Doe" statutes mandated care for newborn infants with severe handicaps. A number of states began experimenting with spousal notification laws, that is, legislation requiring the notification of husbands about impending abortions. Illinois required spousal consent for post-viability abortions unless the mother's life was endangered. Fetal pain statutes, introduced after 1985, required doctors to inform women about to undergo abortions that the fetus might be able to feel pain—a response to a Right-to-Life propaganda film shown on television in March, 1985, entitled "The Silent Scream."

Even though the political furor over abortion had not abated, and activists on both sides of the dispute continued to be vocal and emotional, by 1985, the battles were taking place within fairly well-defined boundaries. The conflict had been tamed, limited, and confined by the ritual dance, back and forth, between legislatures and courts.

THORNBURGH AND DIAMOND: RETHINKING *ROE V. WADE?*

Court watchers on both sides of the abortion dispute were surprised when the Court accepted two new abortion cases for review in May, 1985.[66] No one was quite sure what this action meant, coming as it did so soon after the supposedly definitive rulings two years earlier. A number of imaginative theories were advanced.⁶⁷ One view was that four Justices had voted to hear the cases with the expectation that by the time the cases actually reached the Court at least one new Reagan-appointee would be in place, ready to vote against abortion rights—or at least to reexamine the entire trimester approach.

It was possible, on the other hand, that four of the majority Justices had decided to hear these appeals in order to fine-tune the guidelines before the rumored resignation of Justice Powell, who had been seriously ill. If this was indeed the true reason, the new cases might have been selected as vehicles for firming up the law, for clarifying the "bright line" between permissible and impermissible statutes. Other theories were that sentiment on the Court had shifted concerning the range of acceptable state regulation or that the Justices had found the Court of Appeals decisions in the two cases "too harsh and one-sided." A fourth supposition was that the Court had mistakenly agreed to hear these cases, unaware of how closely the Pennsylvania law in *Thornburgh v. American College of Obstetricians* paralleled the unconstitutional Akron ordinance and ignorant of the fact that the state of Illinois was no longer a party in *Diamond v. Charles* (since the offending state law had since been changed), and that the appeal was being pursued by an antiabortion organization, Americans United for Life, rather than by the state.⁶⁸ The Illinois case raised a number of serious technical problems, and it seemed reasonable to predict that the Court might dispose of the case on procedural grounds. Although all these theories were plausible, the most likely possibility was that the cases presented unresolved issues that the Court wished to lay to rest before another period of inaction.

The laws challenged in the *Thornburgh* and *Charles* cases were not new. These cases were part of a final round in litigation that dated back to the first wave of comprehensive state abortion laws. The Pennsylvania statute was the last in a series of antiabortion laws beginning in 1974; the Illinois law was a much revised version of legislation dating back to 1975. Both the Illinois and the Pennsylvania laws contained provisions requiring physicians to use certain medical techniques to save fetuses that might be viable (even when these techniques could put the mother at risk). The Pennsylvania act imposed extremely detailed reporting procedures on physicians, required physicians to take out insurance policies, and specified that certain abortion techniques be used in order to maximize the chances of fetal survival. Maternal health and safety seemed to be of secondary concern. The law also required second physicians at abortions in which a fetus might be viable and had informed consent provisions that were very detailed. Criminal penalties were imposed and viability was defined by law. The Illinois law had an informed consent provision that required doctors to tell women patients that some methods of contraception were "abortifacient." In reviewing this statute, the Court of Appeals had concluded that such a requirement in fact decided that conception was the point at which "life begins," a legislative determination with extensive legal ramifications. The statute also made it a felony to fail to use the same standard of care in protecting a viable fetus resulting from an abortion as would be used where the fetus was intended to be born. All in all, the statutes constituted a massive invasion of what doctors believed to be areas reserved to medical judgment.

In the Akron ordinance case the Court had emphasized "accepted medical practice" and the responsibilities of physicians, but it had not undertaken a definitive discussion of the impact of new kinds of restrictive laws on the practice of medicine or the degree to which the medical judgment of physicians should be left unhampered by legislative mandates. The fact that the parties in these newer cases were doctors and medical organizations rather than pregnant women, abortion clinics, or civil rights groups may reflect a growing presence in the political equation—that of organized medical interests and health and welfare officials, professionals concerned about the invasion of ideologues onto their professional and scientific turf. To add to the suspense about these cases, in July, the Justice Department announced that it would submit a brief supporting the state legislation and urging the Court to overrule *Roe v. Wade,* a move that some columnists believed reflected raw politics more than anything else.[69] The Justice Department's brief urged overruling. If this had been done, the whole dance would have begun again. After all of the hullabaloo, the actual decisions were almost anticlimactic. On April 30, 1986, the Court unanimously dismissed the *Diamond* case, declaring that the state of Illinois was no longer a party and that the petitioner, a pro-Life pediatrician, did not have standing as a private citizen to pursue an appeal in the Supreme Court.[70] Although there were some differences on the Court about the proper underpinning of the decision, all of the Justices agreed that the pediatrician was not properly before the Supreme Court.

On June 11, the Court decided the *Thornburgh* case, affirming the Court Appeals decision to overturn six sections of the Pennsylvania Abortion Control Act of 1982.[71] The Court divided five to four. Justice Blackmun wrote an opinion joined by Brennan, Marshall, Powell, and Stevens. Stevens wrote a separate concurring opinion. The dissenting Justices filed three opinions.

Justice Blackmun found that the Pennsylvania statute required procedures that went beyond reasonable regulation of abortion and that the Court of Appeals had been correct in striking down six provisions. Rather than simply giving women information that would allow an intelligent weighing of risks and alternatives, the informed consent provisions provided information in a manner designed to actively discourage abortions. In addition, the reporting provisions were written in such a way that they encouraged the invasion of privacy and the loss of physician-patient confidentiality. Provisions that might, in some circumstances, provide marginally improved opportunities for fetal survival, did so at the expense of the woman's health and safety by increasing her medical risks. Justice Blackmun saw most of these regulations as substituting state regulation for the physician's judgment and intruding on the private doctor-patient relationship. The Pennsylvania statute seemed to be a very similar, if slightly more moderate, incarnation of the Akron ordinance—a law clearly intended to discourage abortion.

The majority opinion affirmed *Roe v. Wade*, followed the precedents set in the *Akron* and *Ashcroft* cases decided three years before, and again identified the constitutional rights being protected as those of privacy and liberty. The majority was not willing to accept the Pennsylvania legislation as a neutral attempt to regulate abortion within the limits set out in earlier cases. To this group of five Justices, the statutory provisions were obviously hostile to an unimpeded right to choose.

In a lengthy dissenting opinion, Justice White undertook a systematic refutation of the majority position. While precedent should be respected, he wrote, the Court has a responsibility for correcting bad decisions based on faulty reasoning. Abortion rights are different from other reproductive rights, he explained, because there is a new entity involved, the fetus, an entity "that bears in its cells all the genetic information that characterizes a member of the species." Barring a clear constitutional basis for protecting abortion, the people should be allowed to determine the balance to be struck between competing values. White went on to argue that even if one accepted abortion rights as constitutionally protected, the Pennsylvania regulations were well within the state's authority to regulate abortion and to encourage childbearing as a preferable alternative.

After the wild speculation during the summer and fall of 1985 about the possible outcome of the two new abortion cases, the actual decisions seemed fairly routine. In spite of the urgings of Acting Solicitor General Charles Fried, members of the Court, except for Justices White and Rehnquist, showed little enthusiasm for an outright overruling of *Roe v. Wade*. The five-to-four vote did, however, reflect differences of opinion on the Court over the kind and amount of state regulations permissible within the limits set out in the original decision.

A week after the *Thornburgh* decision was handed down, President Reagan proposed changes in the Court's membership that might ultimately lead to more drastic changes in the law governing abortion. It was announced that Chief Justice Burger would retire and Justice Rehnquist would be nominated to take his place. Judge Antonin Scalia of the Court of Appeals for the District of Columbia, a staunch conservative and a Roman Catholic, would be nominated as Associate Justice to succeed Justice Rehnquist. These moves would not in themselves guarantee changes in the lineup of Justices on the underlying constitutional question. Whether additional conservative appointments would follow, and whether new Justices would vote to take new abortion cases and use them as a vehicle for reopening the controversy, was still entirely speculative.

On the National Level:
Federal Action and Inaction

6

Social conservatives whose votes, PACs, and campaign money had helped elect President Reagan expected results once their candidate had been sworn in as president. Antiabortion planks in the Republican platform, profamily rhetoric in Reagan's acceptance speech to the Republican National Convention, and promises made to conservative leaders during the campaign led them to expect more than symbolic gestures from the new administration. But the fact is that there is little that the president can do *directly* to restrict access to abortion or to promote many of the other conservative "social issues." Once in office, a president interested in influencing abortion policy can provide national leadership, exert influence on Congress, and make telling administrative and judicial appointments. Presidents Ford and Carter had been reluctant to become entangled with such a volatile political issue, one that seemed to lie largely outside the ambit of national policy-making capabilities. Congress has perhaps more power to affect abortion policies, although its power is related to major national programs of health insurance and funding for medical care, hospital facilities, medical research, foreign aid, and social service programs offering family-planning services. A Congress so inclined can cut off federal funding for abortion services and remove abortion as an option in various types of federal programs. But to reverse a Supreme Court decision establishing reproductive rights, an amendment to the

Constitution is necessary. In this process Congress, rather than the president, plays a leading role.

Strategies for Reversing *Roe*: Constitutional Amendment

Abortion opponents knew from the beginning that the most direct and efficient way to counter *Roe v. Wade* would be to amend the Constitution. They were to find, however, that major difficulties beset this strategy. In the first place, the amendment process designed by the Framers is exceedingly difficult to use with success unless there is a clear consensus in favor of change—a consensus that failed to develop on the abortion issue. Second, the types of amendments favored by antiabortionists were too radical; they proposed language that seemed likely to make unpredictable, perhaps drastic, changes in constitutional theory. Even members of Congress who were strongly opposed to abortion were reluctant to introduce into the fundamental document words and concepts that might turn out to be loose cannons on the gundecks of constitutional construction. By 1986, although a number of amendments continued to be introduced in each session of Congress, hopes of overturning *Roe v. Wade* by this strategy were increasingly dim.

Usually, amendments are proposed in Congress by joint resolution and passed by a two-thirds vote in each house (signature by the president is not necessary); a resolution so passed is then sent to the states to be ratified. If three-fourths of the state legislatures accept the amendment, it becomes part of the fundamental law. The difficulty of using this complicated process is attested to by the fact that over ten thousand proposals for amendments have been submitted to Congress since 1789.[1] Only thirty-three of these, including the first ten amendments, have received the necessary two-thirds vote. And only twenty-six have been successfully ratified.

Immediately after the 1973 decision, a number of proposals for an antiabortion amendment were introduced in each house. Over fifty proposals for constitutional amendments were introduced during the first session of the 94th Congress, with growing support for an amendment giving constitutional protection to a right to life and some loss of support for the simpler states rights proposal that first had seemed to be favored.[2]

The states rights proposal, jocularly referred to as "local option," provided that "The power to regulate the circumstances under which pregnancy may be terminated is reserved to the States." There was precedent for such an approach; after the repeal of Prohibition, liquor control was handed back to the states to regulate. The Twenty-first Amendment prohibited the transportation of liquor into states that elected to remain dry, allowing the states to impose prohibition locally by state law. One of the objections to applying a federal solution to the regulation of abortion is that it would allow each state to delineate abortion rights as it chose, possibly creating fifty different sets of abortion laws. From the pro-Life point of view this type of amendment was undesirable because it was unlikely to lead to recriminalization in every state. From the pro-Choice point of view it was undesirable because it did not accept the idea of a constitutional right to choose an abortion.

Dozens of congressmen sponsored a wide range of differently worded types of proposals. One popular approach redefined the word *person* in the due process clauses of the Fifth and Fourteenth Amendments to include unborn persons. But the language of both due process clauses provides only that government shall not deprive any person of life *without due process of law;* anti-abortionists wanted to go further and directly guarantee a constitutional right to life. Senator Jesse A. Helms (R., N.C.) introduced Senate Joint Resolution 6 (94th Cong., 1st sess.), an early formulation of this concept. The resolution provided that "every human being shall be deemed, from the moment of fertilization, to be a person and entitled to the right to life." Another version, introduced by Senator James L. Buckley (R.-Cons., N.Y.) extended the category of persons to "all human beings, including their unborn offspring at every state of their biological development irrespective of age, health, function, or condition of dependency."[3]

An amendment written by the National-Right-to-Life Committee was also introduced in this session, sponsored by Senators Buckley and Garn (R., Utah). It tied protection of the fetus to the older language of the Fifth and Fourteenth Amendments, but then added an enormously broad provision protecting the unborn from deprivation of life by "any person." This addition was designed to protect the fetus against injury by private persons as well as from government or government-sponsored programs. The amendment, later called the Garn-Oberstar Amendment, or Human Life Amendment, became the preferred version of many organized right-to-life groups. It read:

Section 1. With respect to the right to life, the word "person," as used in this article and in the fifth and fourteenth articles of the amendment to the Constitution of the United States, applies to all human beings, irrespective of age, health, function, or condition of dependency, including their unborn offspring at every stage of their biological development.

Section 2. No unborn person shall be deprived of life by any person; *Provided however*, that nothing in this article shall prohibit a law permitting only those medical procedures required to prevent the death of the mother.

Section 3. Congress and the several states shall have the power to enforce this article by appropriate legislation in their respective jurisdictions.[4]

All of the Senate resolutions were referred to a Subcommittee of the Senate Judiciary Committee, under the chairmanship of Birch Bayh (D., Ind.). In 1974 and 1975, the committee held sixteen days of public hearings, compiling four thick volumes of testimony and data from over eighty-three witnesses. Representatives of all shades of opinion on abortion appeared before the committee to testify, and the testimony covered abortion as it related to many fields: medicine, demography, public health, law, politics, religion, and philosophy.[5]

Members of the Judiciary Committee found that most of the proposed amendments were likely to present serious legal and constitutional problems. After a September 14, 1975, vote, the Subcommittee refused to report out any of the Senate Joint Resolutions.[6] The only open debate on the issue took place in April, 1976, after a clever piece of procedural manipulation by Senator Helms allowed him to bypass the Senate Judiciary Committee and bring an amendment he was sponsoring directly to the floor of the Senate.

In the debate that followed, in a long speech, Senator Bayh explained some of the misgivings that he and members of the Subcommittee had with the proposals in their various forms.[7] By establishing a right to life, the amendments would still fail to resolve the conflicts that might arise between the rights of the woman and the fetus. But in assigning personhood to unborn humans, the amendments would force drastic changes of direction in existing areas of law, especially in torts, property, tax, and criminal law. The law of tort, for example, might have to be modified to allow an unborn person to sue for injuries by any person, including its mother, from the time of conception onward. A child would, in theory, be able to sue a mother who damaged it in the womb by drinking, taking drugs, or smoking.[8] Doctors would be liable to such persons for malpractice for any treatment of the mother that adversely affected the child *in utero*. In the past, courts had recognized the fetus as an individual apart from its mother only in limited contexts. Until birth it has been treated as part of the mother. Inheritance rights were sometimes recognized, but they were contingent on live birth. Tort law allowed claims for prenatal injuries if the child was subsequently born alive, compensating children and their parents for tortious conduct against the pregnant woman. Feticide was a crime in some states, but the focus of the statutes was the protection of women whose pregnancies were threatened by the violent acts of third parties.[9] Protection of the fetus as a separate individual would turn much private law in an entirely new direction. The recognition of a positive right to life for all persons would also affect public law in many areas, perhaps causing a rethinking of the military draft and the death penalty. Senator Bayh pointed to the fact that some versions of the amendments did not allow exceptions for rape, incest, or disease; did not deal with the issue of contraception; and were likely to create excessive governmental intrusions on privacy. Most amendments that have been adopted, Senator Bayh noted, have established underlying principles of government, rather than trying to resolve moral choices on which there is a great deal of controversy.[10] The Subcommittee had decided that it would not be a responsible course of action to report out such amendments favorably.

One of the central causes of concern, brought out by other testimony before the Senate committee, was that protection of the right to life from the moment of conception and proposals giving the fetus personhood under the Constitution would involve a basic shift in our underlying constitutional philosophy. The Constitution as presently in force does not guarantee a right to life to anyone. It merely forbids government (state or national) from depriving anyone of his life "without due process of law" or from denying to any person "equal protection of the laws." A constitutional right to life could be interpreted as making government responsible in a positive sense for the lives of all its people, born and unborn, citizens and resident aliens. Such a change in the approach to government would be revolutionary. Since it could be read as guaranteeing support for life not only from the cradle to the grave, but from "womb to tomb," from the moment of conception to the moment of death, it could create the ultimate welfare state.[11] No one could be quite sure what new duties a constitutional guarantee of life would impose on government. Would it, perhaps, require government to provide minimum requirements of food, clothing, medical care, housing, and education to all its citizens? Desirable as such a broad protection of life might be when seen abstractly as the proper function of a just government in a just society, it would present many practical difficulties for flesh-and-blood politicians.

Amendments such as that sponsored by the National Right-to-Life Committee sought to ensure the protection of the fetus not only against government but against private individuals. The Garn-Oberstar amendment, as it was later designated, contained a clause protecting the unborn against deprivation of life "by any person."[12] Such a clause would allow the national government to pass laws in circumstances where it cannot now act. Under the Fourteenth Amendment Congress can legislate to remedy state actions that deprive persons of life—but cannot pass laws that act directly on private parties. The protection of life, liberty, and property from the criminal acts of others is the realm of state criminal law. The old state-national division of power would be eroded by an amendment giving Congress a general power to enact criminal laws to protect unborn persons. Here again, a great extension of national law and enormous complications in the existing federal system might occur if the amendment were adopted.

Evidently some of these considerations struck the Senators on the Bayh subcommittee as conclusive. After a September 14, 1975, vote, the Subcommittee refused to report out any of the Senate

Joint Resolutions. Because of the failure of the Senate to take action, Right-to-Life forces put pressure on the House to act; hearings were held throughout the spring of 1976 on House-sponsored amendments, but no action was taken before adjournment.[13] The last of the House hearings was held in April.

THE HATCH AMENDMENT, 1983

After 1976, large numbers of amendments continued to be introduced in each session of Congress and there has been continuous experimentation with different phraseology, but no further action was taken on any of these proposals until 1983. Hearings were held in early 1983 on an amendment suggested by Senator Orrin Hatch of Utah. Senator Hatch's amendment (S.J. Res. 3, 98th Cong, lst sess.), first proposed in 1981, was terse and simple, unlike the complicated, unpredictable personhood and right-to-life amendments.[14] It read:

A right to abortion is not secured by this Constitution.
The Congress and the several States shall have concurrent power to restrict and prohibit abortion: Provided, That a provision of law of a State which is more restrictive than a conflicting provision of a law of Congress shall govern.

On the suggestion of Senator Eagleton (D., Mo.) the second sentence of the amendment was dropped, and the final vote was taken on a version containing only the first ten words. Written in this manner, the amendment seemed to have several strong points. It would wipe out the legal abortion right, erase the decision in *Roe v. Wade,* and return the law to the *status quo ante* when abortion was a matter for each state to decide. According to its supporters, it had the advantage of avoiding radical solutions with unknown ramifications. This type of amendment was not, however, acceptable to hard-liners. It would permit antiabortion legislation and allow the most restrictive law, federal or state, to control, but there was no guarantee that Congress or all of the states would enact prohibitions against abortion. The Hatch amendment was reported out of committee, but after ten hours of debate it was defeated forty-nine to fifty, eighteen votes short of the two-thirds vote needed. It was the first time that either chamber of the Congress had had the opportunity to vote directly on such an amendment.[15]

Strategies for Reversing *Roe*: A New Constitutional Convention

Congress alone cannot prevent resort to the amending process when there is an insistent demand for alteration of the Constitution. Article Five allows two-thirds of the state legislatures to initiate constitutional change when Congress refuses to act.

The Congress . . . on the application of the legislatures of 2/3 of the several states, shall call a convention for proposing amendments.

The convention alternative has never been used, although over the years more than 400 petitions have been received by Congress requesting that it "call" a constitutional convention. Most of the petitions propose that the convention be called to address specific problems. Only a few have received substantial support from the states.[16] At the present time, one call for a convention is close to success; only two more states need submit requests to reach the total of thirty-four necessary to propose an amendment requiring the federal government to balance its budget. The drive to use the same method to propose an antiabortion amendment has had some success, but by 1984, petitions from only nineteen states had been received.[17] But since the convention method of proposing amendments has never been used, there are a great many unresolved technical questions relating to such an action. It is not clear, for example, that petitions for the convention, differing widely in wording, would all be valid, and there are other unresolved procedural problems that would make the actual convening of a convention problematical. The proposed Constitutional Convention Implementation Act, now pending, responds to many of these concerns.[18] But there are also doubts about the wisdom of resorting to an untested process, and in the past Congress itself has been persuaded to propose new amendments in order to avoid the uncertainties of the convention alternative. The specter of a runaway convention that would take the bit in its teeth and attempt to rewrite the whole constitutional document creates apprehension among observers of all political persuasions.[19] Conservatives are afraid of a convention dominated by "wild-eyed radicals," liberals by the prospect of deliberations controlled by "right-wing crazies." The proposed implementation legislation authorizes Congress to limit a convention to a single topic, although there is some doubt that the Constitution itself empowers Congress to impose such restrictions on the amending process. All in all, the convention route to constitutional amendment, attractive as it appears on paper, presents a greater number of snags, pitfalls, and buried obstacles than the more traditional method of proposing amendments.

Amending by Subterfuge: The Human Life Bill

Frustrated by the difficulties inherent in the amending process, pro-Life strategists sought another means of negating the Supreme Court's abortion decision. In 1981, Senator Jesse Helms introduced a Human Life Bill as a piece of ordinary legislation that would require only passage by simple majorities in both houses of Congress and signature by the president, rather than the complicated procedure required by the formal amending process. A similar bill was introduced in the House of Representatives by Congressman Henry Hyde (R., Ill.). The Human Life Bill had two provisions. The first section contained a declaration by Congress that it had determined, as a finding of fact, that human life begins at conception and that fetuses are "persons" protected by the Fourteenth Amendment. The second section, invoking Congress's constitutional power to regulate the appellate jurisdictions of the federal courts, banned federal District Courts and United States Courts of Appeal from hearing cases that challenged any of the new state abortion statutes.[20] Congressmen and legal scholars immediately expressed doubt about the constitutionality of both provisions. The new tactic was the brainchild of Stephen H. Galebach, an attorney with a private Washington law firm. Galebach had outlined his scheme in a 1981 article in the *Human Life Review*, presenting a sophisticated defense of the unusual approach.[21] He argued that since the Supreme Court has refused to decide when life begins, the question is open and it is appropriate for Congress to make such a determination as a legislative finding of fact. Congress often lays out the factual background supporting legislation as a series of "findings of fact." The model relied on by Galebach was the Voting Rights Act of 1965, where Congress had based its rejection of literacy tests for voting on findings that such tests are often used in a discriminatory manner to prevent minorities from exercising their voting rights. In a similar fashion, he contended, Congress can make a finding of fact that life begins at conception and then legislate to protect such life under Section 5 of the Fourteenth Amendment—a section that allows Congress to "enforce this amendment by appropriate legislation."

Although this scheme seemed both plausible and ingenious, many scholars thought it subverted the accepted constitutional order, arguing that the proper avenue for such a drastic change is the formal amending process provided by the Constitution. Thomas I. Emerson, Professor of Law at Yale, took issue with Mr. Galebach, stating that Section 5 of the Fourteenth Amendment was designed to allow Congress to implement and enforce the Amendment, but does not give Congress the option of rejecting or changing the Supreme Court's interpretation of the Constitution. The grant of enforcement powers, he maintained, was a one-way ratchet; it was designed to provide remedies for rights that have been determined by the courts to fall under the protection of the Amendment and does not allow the changing or diminishing of those rights by legislative fiat.[22]

The second device adopted in the bill was the restriction of the appellate jurisdiction of the federal courts. This provision was one of the twenty-seven "Court-stripping" proposals introduced in the 97th Congress—legislative efforts to circumvent Supreme Court decisions on abortion, school prayer, and busing.[23] Conservatives newly elected to office in 1980 were in a hurry to implement their campaign promises. Their attitude, summed up by one newspaper-man, was "Why go to the trouble of winning the support of two-thirds of the Congress and three-fourths of the states when a parliamentary maneuver can accomplish the same result."[24] The *Washington Post* called this maneuver a "rerun of the great 'kill the court' campaigns of the 50's and 60's."[25] Court-stripping bills were politically attractive, but there was always the possibility that the Supreme Court would declare jurisdictional statutes of this kind unconstitutional.

As it turned out, there was not much legislative support for a Human Life Bill or for the idea of protecting antiabortion legislation from litigation by repealing federal court jurisdiction over abortion cases. Although the Separation of Powers Subcommittee of the Senate Judiciary Committee, under the chairmanship of Senator East (R., N.C.), held several days of hearings on the question of "when life begins," the Senate took no further action on this legislation.[26]

Strategies for Reversing *Roe*: The Federal Legislative Route

In 1975 the director of the U.S. Coalition for Life, Randy Engel, put out a "Pro-Life Guide to Practical Politics," which recommended tacking antiabortion amendments onto all federal legislation on health and related areas. This approach would have a number of advantages, she asserted. It would allow Right-to-Life forces to get experience in national politics, especially with legislative committees and public hearings; it would keep Congress on its toes and force legislators to record their votes on abortion-related issues; it would educate the public and give an opportunity for antiabortionists to write their congressmen. In the long run, this strategy would build support for an antiabortion amendment and whet the political skills of those expected to maneuver it through Congress.[27]

Engel had given her troops superb political advice. Since the Constitution gives Congress no direct constitutional authority to pass laws controlling abortion, or any other kind of surgical operation for that matter, any attempt to legislate on the subject must be made by indirection. What federal authority exists is related to specific national responsibilities, such as abortions in the military services or in federal institutions or in connection with the spending of federal tax money for various medical and welfare programs. Riders attached to federal health programs and appropriations bills can prohibit the spending of any funds for abortion (and usually for birth control or sterilization programs as well.)[28] A *rider* is a provision that probably could not pass on its own merits, but that often can be attached as an amendment to an important piece of legislation and be given a free ride when the main bill is passed. Once an amendment has been attached, supporters of the main bill may not want to jeopardize its chances of passing by trying to detach the rider. Riders are admirably suited for minority blackmail; often the majority will let an amendment go through because it is afraid that minority partisans will obstruct the passage of the central bill if the rider is defeated—perhaps by a filibuster in the Senate or by one of the many procedural rules that can easily be used to block or delay legislation in either house.

A conscious strategy was actively pursued along these lines by antiabortion congressmen and senators. Although many riders were deleted in committee or conference committee or voted down on the floor of the House or Senate, a few were passed, and the tactic has remained an effective method for forcing political bargaining.

Although 1974, the first year following the Supreme Court's decision, did not produce any major abortion legislation, many funding bills—on subjects such as Medicaid, the antipoverty program, military procurement, the debt ceiling, and community services (OEO)—and parts of the Social Security Act were subjected to harrassing amendments. Several of these riders were passed.

1. *Fetal research.* The fear that aborted fetuses would be subject to improper experimentation as well as a public reaction to the very idea of such experimentation led Congress, in 1973, to accept as a rider to a federally funded medical research bill the proviso that no funds would be used for any research on a live fetus.[29] The National Research Service Awards and Protection of Human Subjects Act of 1974 put a moratorium on fetal research until a commission could work out a long-term policy on the matter. This act also added a "conscience clause" exempting individuals from any HEW service or research activity that might be contrary to their moral or religious convictions.[30]

2. *Health care.* The Church amendment, added by Senator Frank Church (D., Idaho) to a routine extension of health care services, the Health Programs Extension Act of 1973, added a conscience clause for hospitals receiving federal funds. No physician or hospital could be required to perform sterilizations or abortions if doing so violated his religious or moral convictions, even if the

hospital was financed by federal funds and was the only community health facility in the area.[31]

3. *Foreign aid.* Senator Jesse Helms (R., N.C.) specialized in riders to foreign aid bills, succeeding in amending the Foreign Assistance Acts of 1973 and 1974 to ban the use of any foreign aid money to support "abortion as a method of family planning."[32]

4. *Legal services.* The Legal Services Corporation Act, a measure providing various legal services to the poor, was amended to keep any lawyer from helping an indigent client secure an abortion.[33]

5. *Medicaid.* Amendments to appropriations bills for Medicaid were introduced in every session of Congress after 1973 in an attempt to forbid the use of such funds for abortion. Representative Roncallo's (R., N.Y.) 1974 attempt was typical of these moves; he tried to attach a rider to the Fiscal Year 1975 appropriations bill for the Department of Labor and HEW, which would have barred the use of medicaid funds for abortions for indigent women and for abortion research of abortifacient drugs and devices. This bill produced the first full-scale debate on an antiabortion rider; after an emotional two-hour debate in the House, the provision was defeated, 247 to 123.[34]

The Medicaid Battle

Although the Roncallo amendment prohibiting the use of Medicaid funds for abortion failed in 1974, it was introduced again in the following years and would ultimately be successful. Medicaid was the main source of funds for abortions for welfare recipients. By 1977 it accounted for nearly a third of the 1 million or so operations performed annually, and the fact that the government not only permitted abortion but was actually financing over three hundred thousand a year, at a cost of $50 million, scandalized those who opposed abortion. "Taxpayers should not have to pay for something they regard as a crime," argued Senator Jake Garn. Jesse Helms, North Carolina's senior senator, thought that the funding of abortions compels the American taxpayer to finance a form of killing. Under pressure from antiabortion forces, both

President Ford and candidate Carter took stands against abortion funding during the 1976 presidential primary campaign.

Antiabortion riders, like the Roncallo amendment, were introduced in 1973 and 1974 in the House and in 1974 and 1975 in the Senate. In the spring of 1976, the rider was introduced again, this time by Congressman Henry J. Hyde (R., Ill.), who attached it to the big $56.7 billion Health, Education and Welfare Department appropriations bill that Democratic leaders were trying to push through Congress before the fall adjournment. Hyde's rider would have stopped the use of any federal funds "to pay for abortions or to promote or encourage abortions." In an election year, many congressmen were afraid to vote against such a measure, and the bill passed the House 207 to 167 in June. The Senate refused the amendment, and the bill went to conference committee, where it was hoped that the House and Senate differences could be resolved. The conference could not agree, and the measure was sent back to the House and Senate. The House took several more votes on the rider, passing it each time with a larger majority, the last vote, in August, 223 to 150. The pressure to pass the HEW bill was enormous, because without it many federal programs for education, health, and welfare would go unfunded. Finally, in September the Senate gave in, accepting a modified wording of Congressman Hyde's amendment. In its final form, the amendment read:

None of the funds contained in this Act shall be used to perform abortions except where the life of the mother would be endangered if the fetus were carried to term.

Opponents hoped that this wording was ambiguous enough to be interpreted broadly and that under it administrators could fund some abortions; or possibly, that courts would declare the amendment unconstitutional as denying equal protection to poor women. President Ford's veto of the HEW bill as too expensive seemed to end the controversy, but Congress passed the bill over his veto.

In October, 1976, Judge John F. Dooling, Jr., of the Brooklyn federal District Court, issued a temporary restraining order to keep HEW from implementing the new limitations while the Court heard arguments on a number of constitutional challenges. This restraining order was eventually lifted after the Supreme Court's Medicaid decisions, but three years later, the District Court still had not come to a final decision on other constitutional issues that had been raised.[35]

By the early summer of 1977, while the United States Supreme Court was still deliberating on the constitutionality of state laws refusing funds for abortions, Congress decided to try again to end Medicaid payments. A $61.3 billion appropriations bill for the Department of Labor and HEW was again amended to ban Medicaid-financed abortions, except when the mother's life was at stake—the Hyde Amendment again. In spite of a two-week lobbying campaign by the National Womens Political Caucus, the Hyde Amendment clearly had the votes to pass.[36] A last-minute amendment to the bill made it even tougher, removing the exception to abortions when the mother's life was endangered. Surprisingly, proabortion groups supported this amendment, hoping that it would show the extremism and callousness of their opponents and strengthen the case against the constitutionality of the bill if it reached the courts. The amended bill passed 201 to 155. Majority Leader Jim Wright said in an interview that the bill as passed by the House was "an abomination" and predicted it would not become law in this form.[37] The Senate later restored the exception allowing abortions to save the mother's life and also in cases of rape, incest, and medical necessity. But while the Senate deliberated, the Supreme Court issued a major ruling affecting the right to Medicaid-funded abortions.

The Medicaid Decisions[38]

On Monday, June 20, 1977, the Supreme Court handed down its long awaited decision on Medicaid abortions. The issue at stake was the degree to which Medicaid payments must be made available to cover elective abortions (often called abortions on demand). The court did not rule on the congressional funding of Medicaid, the provisions occupying Congress at the time of the decision. The 1976 Appropriations Act (for Fiscal Year 1977) for the HEW program, with its limitations on spending for abortions, had been challenged in court after passage in 1976 but had not yet reached the Supreme Court. The two cases decided by the Court in June, 1977, were concerned with *state* laws that refused to allow Medicaid payments for "elective" as opposed to "therapeutic" abortions —those required for health reasons. Before these cases were decided, forty-five states and the District of Columbia allowed Medicaid coverage for all legal abortions, therapeutic or not. In two states, North Carolina and Kentucky, funding was allowed for early abortions, but not for later ones. Three other states—Indiana, Ohio, and Louisiana—refused to pay out any Medicaid money for elective abortions.[39] Nine states had tried to restrict such abortions but had been ordered to end their restrictions by federal courts. Two of these states, Pennsylvania and Connecticut, had appealed from the court orders and were now in the Supreme Court.

The laws passed by the Pennsylvania and Connecticut legislatures both provided Medicaid reimbursement for abortions only if the abortion was "medically necessary" to preserve the woman's life or health, including her mental health. The two cases, however, raised slightly different legal issues. In the Pennsylvania case, the Supreme Court was asked to determine whether the Social Security Act (Title XIX, Medicaid) required the states to pay for nonmedical abortions. Medicaid is a cooperative program between the states and the federal government, where each governmental unit assumes part of the cost of providing medical care to welfare recipients. Some states also provide care for persons defined as *medically indigent*—too poor to handle their own medical care needs. Under the Medicaid program, the states set up their own programs for reimbursement of medical expenses within the guidelines set out by the act. The question in *Beal v. Doe*, the first case, was a question of statutory interpretation, of the meaning of the Medicaid provisions and the intent of Congress in passing the legislation. Had Congress meant to require payment for all abortions, or had it left the matter up to the judgment of the states? If pregnancy requires medical care, does the Social Security Act permit states to pay for some forms of care (for instance, childbirth) and not others (abortions)? The Pennsylvania case was concerned with the meaning of the federal law.

The Connecticut case, *Maher v. Roe*, raised a constitutional question. In that case, it was argued that if a state pays medical expenses for pregnancy and childbirth, it must also pay for abortions; to pay the medical expenses of women giving birth, but allowing no funds for those women who choose to terminate their pregnancies, is discriminatory and denies the women who choose to have abortions equal protection of the laws. The basic question here was whether a woman has in fact been denied her right to choose whether or not to bear a child if the state will pay medical expenses connected with childbirth, but will not pay for an elective abortion. Poor women who are dependent on Medicaid, it was argued, will not have a free choice.

The Supreme Court, in a six to three decision, ruled that neither the Social Security Act nor the Constitution required the states to finance nontherapeutic abortions, but the states may choose to do so. States that oppose abortion must pay when the abortions are medically indicated, but need not pay for elective abortions.

Pro-Choice forces were appalled by the decision, agreeing with the three dissenting Justices that the Court had backed away from its 1973 holdings.

Until this point, federal courts had held the line against a variety of ingenious state attempts to avoid the implementation of the principles enunciated in *Roe v. Wade*. Now that the barriers were down, states could refuse to fund elective abortions. Justice Brennan wrote, in dissent, "None can take seriously the Court's assurance that its conclusion signals no retreat." Justice Blackmun, who had written the majority opinion in *Roe v. Wade* and *Planned Parenthood of Missouri v. Danforth*, was sure that states would "now accomplish indirectly" what the Court had said they could not do directly.[40] Congress and the states will not, in view of the political pressures, authorize funds for nontherapeutic abortions, Justice Blackmun wrote in dissent. "Why should any politician incur the demonstrated wrath and noise of abortion opponents when mere silence and nonactivity accomplish the results the opponents want?" It is unrealistic to tell a poor woman she has the right to an abortion when she does not have the funds to pay for one. Justice Blackmun was reminded of Marie Antoinette's advice to the starving poor at the time of the French Revolution; if they had no bread, "let them eat cake." Justice Brennan quoted Anatole France's cynical remarks about equality under the law: "The law in its majestic equality, forbids the rich as well as the poor to sleep under bridges, to beg in the streets, and to steal bread."

Justice Marshall, also dissenting, wrote that the practical effect of the decision will be to coerce women "to bear children whom society will scorn for every day of their lives."[41]

The Supreme Court's majority position was that *Roe v. Wade* had held only that a woman has a right to make a choice whether or not to bear children and that the states may not deny this right to choose by making abortion a criminal offense. There is a vast difference, six Justices believed, between freeing abortion from state prohibitions and positively encouraging it by governmental funding. Of the 1.1 million abortions performed in the United States in 1976, three hundred thousand were paid for under Medicaid. Many of these abortions were not medically necessary. This funding was not, they held, required by either the law or the Constitution.

A third case[42] decided on June 20 dealt with an unsolved problem, the responsibility for abortions by publicly funded hospitals. It had never been clearly decided whether such hospitals had the right to refuse to perform abortions. Most lower court cases had agreed that private hospitals had such a right, especially if the group supporting the hospital (e.g., the Roman Catholic church) was morally opposed to abortion.[43] Amendments to federal statutes funding hospitals and providing health care had provided that no loss of funds to hospitals occurs when abortions are refused for moral or religious reasons. Now the Supreme Court held that public hospitals had the right to refuse to perform nonmedical abortions. Just as the government is not required to pay for elective abortions, so also public medical institutions are not required to provide this particular service if the community opposes it.

These three decisions meant that the expansion of abortion services would be checked, at least for a time. Some states would now undoubtedly refuse to fund further nonmedical abortions. Public hospitals would no longer be under pressure to provide elective abortions. Since in 1975-76 only about 18 percent of all public hospitals in the country actually provided such services, and ten states had no hospitals performing nontherapeutic abortions, the decision would curtail services that were already limited.

In May, 1977, Planned Parenthood Institute released its third annual survey of doctors, hospitals, and clinics. The study indicated that contrary to what many people believed, legal abortions have never been readily available to some classes of women (young, poor, or rural women). Eighty percent of all public hospitals and 70 percent of non-Catholic general hospitals have never performed abortions.[44] Those women most likely to receive such services live in the big cities, in one or two metropolitan areas in most states. Many women have always had to leave their own states and travel to a different area to find abortion services; in 1975, 83,000 went to another state in search of an abortion. The study also found that a third of those obtaining abortions in 1975 were teenagers and about a third nonwhite.

The rulings in *Beal v. Doe* and *Maher v. Roe* meant that states were now free to eliminate all spending for nontherapeutic abortions if they wished to do so. But the Supreme Court still had not decided how far spending could be cut off for medically necessary abortions under Medicaid, or whether Congress could adopt a policy of funding all medical services except abortion.

After 1977 the states began gradually to withdraw from abortion funding. In March 1978, only sixteen states and the District of Columbia were paying for all or most abortions.[45] By the end of 1978, only eight states provided full coverage, nine states covered "medically necessary abortions," twenty-two states had adopted the then current HEW formula (severe and long-lasting health damage when life was threatened or when rape or incest had occurred), and twelve funded only if the woman's life was threatened.[46]

Each year Congress also came under heavier pressure to cut back federal funding for abortions. The Hyde Amendment, first passed in 1976, forbade all funding except when the life of the mother was endangered. In the summer of 1977, the House again tried to attach the Hyde Amendment to the Labor-HEW budget bill,[47] but the Senate held out for a compromise that would allow "medically necessary" abortions. The final compromise, reached after a five-month battle between House and Senate, permitted Medicaid abortions in three situations: when the mother's life would be endangered, when rape or incest had taken place, or when severe or long-lasting health damage would result from the pregnancy.[48] The last provisions required that the determination of possible health damage be made by two physicians. The two-physician proviso was evidently the key change that allowed the House and

Senate to compromise. The wording of the provision in the federal
funding bill was important not only because it determined which
abortions could receive federal funds, but also because many of the
states tended to key their state funding provisions to the federal
definition.[49] The fight over abortion funding would be repeated
in each subsequent year, with the language becoming narrower and
narrower after each battle. By 1979 Congress's gradual retreat
had resulted in the most restrictive language ever adopted. In
continuing resolutions providing emergency funds for a number of
federal departments, Congress dropped coverage when there was
severe and long-lasting health damage to the mother, allowing
payments only when her life was directly threatened or when
rape or incest had occurred.[50]

By this time, some sentiment was beginning to appear for changing
the House rules to restrict the practice of attaching riders to
appropriations bills, since it allowed antiabortion congressmen to
delay the discussion of other important issues and to hold the
orderly appropriation of money for the federal departments
hostage to the abortion issue.[51] In 1978 Congressman Herbert
E. Harris (D., Va.) began a campaign to prohibit all policymaking
riders. His proposal was not acted upon; Congress was not yet
ready for this change.[52] After 1977, in addition to yearly battles
over abortion funding in the Department of Labor-HEW appropriations bill, the House and Senate had to fight off antiabortion
amendments to other appropriation bills and to health and community services legislation.[53]

The most vigorous battle was over the 1979 Pregnancy Disability Act, an amendment to the Civil Rights Act designed to
prohibit discrimination, because of pregnancy, in the granting of
disability pay and benefits. Pregnancy was frequently excluded
from the coverage of employers' disability plans and such exclusions
had been upheld by the Supreme Court.[54] The act, which passed in
October, 1978, originally included protection and benefits for women
who need abortions, but Catholic lobbyists sought exemptions that
would allow employers to refuse to provide insurance coverage,
paid leave, or disability pay for abortions or complications following abortions. A compromise in conference committee eventually
allowed employers to refuse coverage for abortions, except when
the life of the woman was endangered.[55] The act went into effect

in April, 1979, but the enforcement of its abortion coverage provisions was delayed until a court challenge, brought by the Catholic church, could be decided. The church, in its brief, argued that the act violated its First Amendment rights as well as those of employers holding moral objections to abortion. This suit was dismissed by the District Court for the District of Columbia in January 1980.

The restrictive Hyde Amendments were very effective. By 1979 few abortions were being paid for by federal funds. Secretary Joseph Califano told a House subcommittee in March, 1979, that only 2,421 abortions had been paid for in 1978. Before various versions of the Hyde Amendment had gone into effect, the federal government had funded about 250,000 such abortions a year.[56] Califano told the House Committee that 1,857 of the 2,421 abortions involved the life of the mother; 385, physical health damage; and 61, cases of rape or incest. Some states continued to use their own funds to pay for abortions for low-income women even though federal matching money was not available.

Congress had become sensitized to the pressures on the abortion issue. In the House, which had more and stronger pro-Life sentiment than the Senate, those members from districts with strongly organized Right-to-Life forces tended to favor that position. The Senate, with fewer Catholics and longer terms, was more evenly divided.[57]

The Hyde Amendments in Court: The *McRae* Case

Additional constitutional questions about Medicaid funding remained unanswered until the *McRae* decision in June, 1980.[58] A big class action suit brought by Cora McRae and other low-income women unable to obtain abortions, a number of physicians, Planned Parenthood of New York City, and the Women's Division of the Board of Global Ministries of the United Methodist Church, it challenged the constitutionality of the Hyde Amendment under the First and Fifth amendments, as contrary to the Court's earlier ruling in *Roe v. Wade*. The suit began as a request for a temporary injunction against the enforcement of the 1976 Hyde Amendment restrictions on funding.[59] After an appeal to the Supreme Court, the case was remanded for consideration in light of the rulings in the *Maher* and *Beal* decisions. In a thirteen-month trial before Judge John F. Dooling, Jr., in the District Court for the Eastern District, New York, the plaintiffs were represented by attorneys from the Center for Constitutional Rights, Planned Parenthood, and the American Civil Liberties Union, many of whom had been involved in earlier abortion litigation.[60] The defendant was Joseph A. Califano, Secretary of Health, Education and Welfare. There were a number of *amicus curiae* briefs, including one filed by fifteen other national religious groups backing the plaintiffs.[61] The plaintiffs and their attorneys made First Amendment religious claims a central part of their case. Pro-Life groups, they argued, were attempting to write an essentially religious view of the fetus into law without relating this provision to any clear secular purpose, as required by the Constitution. Such a course constitutes an establishment of religion, since it imposes the religious views of certain groups upon others. The policy also impairs the religious freedom of those who take the view that their religious responsibilities require them, under some circumstances, to abort children for whom they cannot care properly.[62] As evidence that anti-abortion sentiment was primarily religious in nature, testimony was introduced about the extensive involvement of the Catholic hierarchy, its use of money, personnel, and organizational resources to defeat abortion funding.[63] Although the Constitution gives religious organizations the right to lobby, the argument went, they should not be allowed to push through legislation justified mainly by religious dogma.[64] The trial record ultimately contained four hundred exhibits and a transcript of over five thousand pages, much of it directed at the religious involvement of the Catholic church.

Judge Dooling's decision, announced in January, 1980, with a 340-page opinion, rejected the establishment argument, but held that the Hyde Amendment violated liberty interests guaranteed to pregnant women by the First and Fifth amendments. An appeal to the Supreme Court was taken from his decision.

The Supreme Court announced its five to four decision in June. A five-judge majority, speaking through Justice Stewart, rejected all of the constitutional claims. The religious issue was settled with dispatch. There is clearly no establishment of religion, Justice Stewart wrote, merely because public policy happens to agree with a sect's religious views. As to the other claim, the litigants in this case had not established the standing necessary to raise the claim of interference with their free exercise of religion.[65]

The constitutional problem that gave the majority the most difficulty was that of the relationship of the right to choose an abortion, established in *Roe v. Wade*, to the fact that without public funding, most poor women are unable to make this choice. Stated simply, the question was: does government have any obligation to equalize access to constitutional rights when poverty creates the conditions that prevent their exercise? If the Court were to answer this question conscientiously, it would have to assess the "relevance of economic inequality to issues of personal liberty."[66] This was a particularly difficult matter for the Court, because an affirmative answer would set a precedent for other areas; obviously, the poor are at a disadvantage in their ability to exercise many of their constitutional rights including the right to vote and rights to freedom of speech, freedom of the press, and freedom to enjoy the blessings of liberty in many areas. In fact, the abortion-funding cases opened up again to debate questions of the nature of the constitutional guarantees in our governmental system; are these guarantees primarily negative, are they constitutional *limitations* only, or are there more positive duties that the government owes to its citizens.[67] Indeed, in some areas, the Court has already held that the government has positive obligations to equalize access to constitutional rights. States must supply lawyers to the indigent in criminal cases as part of the right to a fair trial. There are also positive obligations to provide trial transcripts free of charge, to allow appeals on a basis of equality, and to make the civil courts available to indigents who want to divorce. There may be a right to a public education—which surely involves a positive governmental obligation to act.[68] Although the Court has never held that there are constitutional entitlements to public assistance, minimum levels of housing, education, or health care, some cases foreshadow trends in those directions.[69]

The majority of the Court was not ready to accept any such doctrine in the abortion-funding cases. Justice Stewart rested his decision squarely on *Maher v. Roe*. In *Maher* the Court had held that a basic difference exists between a law that interferes with a constitutional right and one that merely provides encouragement for an alternative course of behavior. If state legislatures decide to encourage childbirth by paying for it under Medicaid, and to discourage elective abortions by not funding them, this decision does not interfere with the right to choose an abortion.[70] The majority thus denied the proposition that the Court has any responsibility for removing conditions that make the exercise of constitutional rights impossible and thus effectively deny them.

The abortion-funding cases thus raised questions about the nature of abortion rights. Are they essentially individual, alienable, and negative, like rights to freedom of religion or the guarantee against unreasonable searches and seizures, calling for government to refrain from action but implying no governmental responsibility for positive protection? Or do they require government to take steps to assure equal access? Laurence Tribe has pointed out that some constitutional rights are individual, alienable, and negative, but others require affirmative governmental protection because of their systemic importance.[71] Systemic rights require more than a negative guarantee because of their importance to the proper working of the political system: voting rights belong in this latter category, as does the right to counsel. A society that aspires to equality, democracy, and justice cannot afford to leave such rights to individual initiative, fail to protect them from alienation, or allow public or private entities to discourage their exercise. The Court's decisions in the abortion-funding cases characterized abortion rights as negative and held that the Court had fulfilled its reponsibility when it vetoed governmental prohibitions against their exercise. The dissenters believed that failure to guarantee access to abortion for those financially unable to avail themselves of their "right to choose" legally reinforced subordination of women to a childbearing role—limiting liberty and denying equality.

The Supreme Court is very sensitive to changes in the direction of the political wind. By 1980, after all the politicking on the issue, abortion had become as much a political as a legal matter, and the Court may have been reluctant to thrust itself into a confrontation with Congress on such a politically explosive subject. To preserve judicial authority, it may have seemed desirable to reprove state legislatures when they attempted an end run around a major decision. But Congress is a coequal department of government, and the Court has never tried to force Congress to fund programs of which it disapproves or that it finds politically inexpedient. The Court might overturn a statute clearly designed to abridge the right to choose an abortion, but it was unwilling to demand that Congress use tax money to underwrite such controversial services. All in all, the political climate in 1980 was better suited to self-restraint than to judicial activism.

The constitutional questions raised by religious involvement in antiabortion political activity, so summarily disposed of in the *McRae* case, soon resurfaced in another form. In 1980, a pro-Choice organization, Abortion Rights Mobilization (ARM), brought suit in the federal District Court in New York City against the U.S. Catholic Conference, the National Conference of Catholic Bishops, and the Internal Revenue Service (IRS), charging that the church had forfeited its tax-exempt status by entering the electoral arena to oppose and support specific candidates. As part of the suit, ARM asked the Catholic organizations to produce documents related to their involvement in political campaigns to overturn *Roe v. Wade.* Although the District Court judge later dismissed the religious bodies as parties, leaving only the IRS as defendant, he also ruled that the church must respond to discovery subpoenas and supply information concerning its political activities. Church officials delayed and stonewalled, and, in 1986, the bishops were cited for contempt and fined $50,000 a day for each day the documents were not produced. U.S. District Judge Robert Carter ruled that the church conferences had willfully misled the court about their willingness to comply with its orders and had made a travesty of the judicial process. Judge Carter's action in 1986 was only the most recent move in litigation that had already lasted five and a half years. ARM and twenty other pro-Choice groups were hoping to get a court ruling fixing limits on the involvement of churches in open political campaigning and the direct endorsement of candidates. The ARM attorney contended that the Catholic Church was proceeding according to its 1975 political master plan for pro-Life activities, and that the IRS was doing nothing to enforce restrictions in the federal tax code.[72]

Although Judge Carter later delayed the fines, pending appeal, the case promised to be a major test case on religion and politics.

Federal Legislation after 1980

After 1976, except for a seven-month period in 1980, federal payments for abortions were sharply restricted, and, since June,

1981, Medicaid abortions have been funded only if the woman's life would be endangered were she to carry the pregnancy to term.[73] Even before the Hyde Amendments, only a small proportion of the costs of abortion were paid under Medicaid. After Hyde, subsidized abortions dropped from 285,000 in 1977 to 194,000 in 1978. By 1985, only fourteen states and the District of Columbia continued to pay for abortions with their own funds.[74] In so far as the impact of these restrictions could be assessed, the funding cut-off did not keep women from having abortions, although they did have other side effects. When there was difficulty finding money for the fees, pregnant women often postponed abortions for two or three weeks. A postponement of two or three weeks might mean that the abortion was performed in the second trimester, rather than in the first. Funds for abortions, or for travel to places where abortions could be had, were diverted from household money.[75]

In Congress, in spite of President Reagan's victory at the polls, the New Right did not have the votes to enact a conservative social agenda, but had to be content with the old strategy of attaching riders to specific funding programs.[76] The Pregnancy Disability Act of 1978, amending the Civil Rights Act to forbid discrimination in employment and employee benefits for pregnant women, was itself amended to exempt employers from any requirement to include elective abortions in medical disability plans.[77] Government-funded health insurance plans for federal workers were barred from abortion funding.[78] The Civil Rights Restoration Act of 1985, a piece of legislation designed to overturn the Supreme Court's *Grove City* decision (a decision that limited the cut-off of federal funding to institutions practicing gender discrimination), was stalled in the Senate, probably permanently, because of attempts to add antiabortion amendments.[79]

At the end of 1985, with no clear-cut legislative victories on the issue, conservative leaders made a major effort to cut off all federal spending that might even indirectly promote abortion. Because a number of 1986 funding bills had not cleared Congress, a long-term continuing appropriations resolution combined a number of these bills in a catch-all spending bill. Nine antiabortion measures were proposed as amendments to the omnibus resolution.[80] Senator Orrin Hatch of Utah and Representative Jack Kemp (R., N.Y.) proposed amendments to Title X of the Public Health Service Act, which funds family-planning services, to forbid abortion counselling and referrals, and they added other amendments that would have crippled the family-planning program. Amendments were proposed to the District of Columbia appropriations bill that would have barred the use of any funds, even those raised privately or by the District, to pay for any abortions in Washington, D.C. Senator Jesse Helms tried unsuccessfully to bar the use of federal funds for abortions for federal prison inmates. The Senate later rejected his proposed amendment on the grounds that it was probably unconstitutional.

Foreign and international family-planning programs were easy political targets. Throughout 1985, conservative groups had lobbied for proposals that would limit U.S. funding of population programs abroad to those teaching "natural family planning," a modernized version of the rhythm method.[81] The Agency for International Development (AID), a federal agency involved with channelling family-planning money to the Third World, responded to conservative pressures by allocating a substantial amount of money for such a program. A conference committee on foreign aid appropriations later changed the policy, specifying that only agencies that offer access to a broad range of family-planning methods be given federal funding.[82] The administration also cut off funds to the U.N. Fund for Population Activities (UNFPA) and International Planned Parenthood Federation under the Kemp Amendment, a continuing resolution that bars United States contributions to international agencies that participate in programs using coerced abortion or sterilization.[83] International Planned Parenthood had been accused of using government funds to finance programs in China that forced women to have abortions.

Guerrilla warfare, using the amendment strategy, was still sometimes successful where other legislative moves failed, and it continued to serve the purposes outlined by Randy Engel in 1975. It kept the abortion issue alive, created publicity, and convinced supporters back home that their elected representatives were forcefully pursuing tough antiabortion policies. The director of Planned Parenthood's Washington, D.C., office, involved in lobbying efforts to save family-planning programs, called the amendment tactic a "shotgun approach to try to batter and badger Congress with the abortion issue."[84]

However, there were signs of a gradual shift of emphasis from single-issue abortion actions to a broader campaign to promote conservative family policies as alternatives to abortion.[85] In 1981, Senator Jeremiah Denton (R., Ala.) was successful in pushing his Adolescent Family Life Bill through Congress—a pilot program designed to provide alternatives to abortion by encouraging chastity, abstention, adoption, prenatal medical care, and some support programs for mothers and infants. Denton's bill set up demonstration projects designed to encourage teenagers to postpone sexual activity or to put their babies up for adoption if they did become mothers. The Children's Health Assurance Plan (CHAP) received support from both pro-Choice and antiabortion congressmen. It provided federal matching funds to states that set up medical coverage for poor women who were pregnant for the first time and for women and young children in families where the principal wage earner was unemployed. The WIC Program, providing food to women and infants, was continued, although the Reagan administration was charged with trying to cut its funds and downplay its effectiveness.[86] Conservatives were also successful in adding amendments to the Child Abuse Prevention Act that brought handicapped infants under the protection of the act. The Child Abuse Amendments were a partial response to highly publicized incidents where it was alleged that treatment had been withheld from Baby Does, children born with serious defects.[87] Some observers saw in these recent developments an indication of a gradual shift from legislation focused only on abortion prevention to programs offering alternatives to abortion—programs tailored to conservative ideas. The conservative approach to family policy differs from the older liberal approach; it rejects government support of sex education, contraception, abortion counselling, and payments to unmarried mothers as offensive and counterproductive. It was unlikely, however, that new funding projects, even those designated profamily, proadoption, and antisex, would thrive and flourish in a period of drastic budget cuts.

Strategies in Congress designed to modify and confine the decision in *Roe v. Wade* have been most successful in preventing federal funding of abortions under any of the existing government health or welfare programs. They have not been successful in undermining the decision itself. By 1986, the best hope of reaching that goal seemed to be by changing the political complexion of the judicial branch.

New Strategies: Revising *Roe* by Changing the Supreme Court

President Reagan's first opportunity to nominate a member of the Court came with the retirement of Justice Potter Stewart, an Eisenhower-appointee, in 1981. Court watchers predicted that President Reagan would look for a conservative Republican with high credentials as a lawyer, probably a judge, who would be a strict constructionist, who would oppose further "judicial activism" by the Court, and who would have the "right views" on such touchy matters as the exclusionary rule, federal-state relations, affirmative action, and abortion. The Republican platform adopted in the summer of 1980 pledged the Republican party to adopt a Human Life Amendment to restrict abortions. A plank in the platform also promised to seek "the appointment of judges who respect traditional family values and the sanctity of innocent human life." After the 1980 election, President Reagan's New Right supporters, as expected, were determined to make abortion a litmus test for any new Supreme Court appointment. Although seven of the sitting Justices had been appointed by Republican presidents, political conservatives were increasingly dissatisfied with the Burger Court because of its failure to repudiate what were considered unfortunate decisions by the "activist" Warren Court. Antiabortionists went further, demanding that the President appoint a Justice who was orthodox on the single issue of abortion and who would vote for revision or relaxation of the constitutional rule laid down in *Roe v. Wade*. This political promise would be a hard one for President to keep. There was no guarantee that the nomination of a hard-line Right-to-Life candidate with an established anti-abortion record would slide through the Senate without opposition.

The president does not have a completely free hand in choosing justices, since he must secure the approval of his nominees by a majority vote in the Senate. When Congress and the presidency are dominated by the same party, the president can usually count on the Senate's support of his choices. But when the opposition party dominates the Senate, when the margin of control is slim, or when the president looks beyond questions of professional qualification and judicial temperament to questions of ideology, he is likely to run into trouble. Cabinet appointments are supposed to be political. No one begrudges the president his claim to have his own men, henchmen who share his policy preferences and point of view, in key administrative positions. But even though its decisions do affect policy, the public expectation is that the Supreme Court will be above the grosser levels of political conflict and that justices will be selected who are able to be fair, detached, neutral, and just in their judgments. Courts are seen by the public as places where justice is done to the best ability of the fallible human beings staffing them. Appointees already committed to ideological positions are out of harmony with this ideal of judicial impartiality and can be expected to run into outraged opposition from political opponents. In theory it is possible to reverse an objectionable decision by changing the composition of the Supreme Court by appointing new justices with appropriate views, but in practice the president will succeed only if he plays his political cards skillfully.

The choice of Sandra Day O'Connor, a state court judge who had also served in the Arizona state legislature and the state Attorney General's office to fill the Supreme Court vacancy, was a very shrewd political move by President Reagan. Judge O'Connor had stated that she opposed abortion personally, and, even though she had a somewhat ambiguous record on abortion as a state senator and did not have firm antiabortion credentials, her nomination satisfied most pro-Life senators. She was a conservative Republican and would undoubtedly be a conservative Justice. As the first nomination of a woman to a position on the Supreme Court, the O'Connor appointment was greeted enthusiastically by liberal women who might otherwise have opposed a conservative judge. Because O'Connor's record on abortion had not been completely unblemished (she had cast votes, several on rather technical motions, that could be interpreted as favoring abortion), Pro-life leaders were hostile to her nomination. The Religious Roundtable, a group that brings together major Christian leaders in a series of seminars, formed an anti-O'Connor alliance with the objective of blocking her nomination. Opposition was coordinated by Paul Viguerie's direct-mail organization.[88] During the hearings on her nomination before the Senate Committee on the Judiciary, Judge O'Connor was quizzed mercilessly by Senators Hatch (R., Utah), Denton (R., Ala.), and East (R., N.C.) on her views on abortion and the proper role of the Supreme Court, but she managed to avoid any statements that would compromise her neutrality in future cases. She handled herself with aplomb, emphasizing her personal views, but refusing to discuss legal issues that could be raised in cases coming before her as a Justice.[89] To the dismay of the opposition, every one of the Senators who had received pro-Life support in 1980 voted to confirm. Paul Brown of the American Life Lobby voiced the frustration of the antiabortionists by commenting, "I'm not at all adverse to making up a hit list for 1982 made up entirely of Republicans."[90]

The role of Senate hearings is ostensibly to inform the Senate; if they are to play their constitutional role of advising and consenting to presidential selections, senators must be informed about the policy preferences and the past track records of nominees. In the past, especially when a strong party majority has rubber-stamped the appointees of a president of their own party, the Senate's role has sometimes been perfunctory. When there are no pressures for ideological purity, or when the appointment is low in symbolic value, the Senate may consent to a nomination with a minimum of examination. Nominees who are qualified professionally, meet expectations of geographical representation, and are mainline in their views can count on confirmation with a minimum of opposition. Justice William Rehnquist, discussing the Senate hearings on President Eisenhower's nomination of Justice Charles Whittaker, complained that the Senate had shirked its responsibility in examining the nominee; the hearings had "succeeded in adducing only the following facts: (a) proceeds from skunk trapping in rural Kansas assisted him in obtaining his early education; (b) he was both fair and able in his decisions as a judge of the lower federal courts; (c) he was the first Missourian ever appointed to the Supreme Court; (d) since he had been born in Kansas but now resided in Missouri, his nomination honored two states."[91] But Whittaker's appointment did not involve, as Rehnquist's own controversial nomination did, conflict between the President and Senate on basic political philosophy.

Although controversy over the policy-making proclivities of courts has encouraged the Senate to review the political views of judicial candidates with great care, the examination of prospective justices for political orthodoxy may put a candidate in a no-win situation. She cannot be confirmed if she displeases the Senate, but she must also appear to fill the hiring specifications of the appointing president. The nominee's only defense against attack by a senator who is opposed to her candidacy on policy grounds and is determined to use the hearings to ensure ideological purity or to get a commitment to vote correctly on future issues is often the invocation of the need for neutrality. Questioning during the hearing is partly designed to satisfy constituents, but it can also be used to sensitize the appointee to the importance of specific points of view. It may result in an unspoken commitment by the nominee to consider both sides of an issue with care and may predispose the candidate to refute any suggestions of bias by voting in favor of the controversial viewpoint in later cases. O'Connor's catechism in the hearings and the attacks on her nomination by abortion opponents may have served the purpose of heightening her sensitivity to the abortion issue. Her dissenting opinion in the *Akron* case in 1983 and her reexamination in that case of "viability" as a bright line, marking out the limits of a right to choose an abortion, may reflect the careful conditioning she was given during the nomination process.

Justice O'Connor's appointment kept alive the hope that a reconstructed Supreme Court would overrule or at least modify *Roe v. Wade*. But as President Reagan's second term moved toward its halfway mark, and the prospects for continued Republican control of the Senate after 1986 began to look less than certain, the only prediction that could be made with assurance was that candidates with monolithic conservative ideologies or strong opinions on single issues would be subjected to hostile questioning by Senate Democrats, and their confirmation would depend on the size and cohesiveness of the Republican majority.

Thirteen years after the original abortion decision, after skirmishing in the electoral system, battles at every level of the federal system, in all branches of government, the war was still going on, but the battlelines were now fairly well marked out. The campaigners had now settled down for a long siege. It looked less and less likely that the conflict over abortion could be resolved definitively by victories at the polls, by constitutional amendment, or by a massive change in the composition and outlook of the Supreme Court. Minor compromises had been thrashed out, new strategies tested, related issues had emerged and been considered at all levels of the political process for over a decade. The conflict had not abated but the structure of the dispute was now quite different from what it had been in 1973.

Afterword

From the foregoing description of the events that followed the decision in *Roe v. Wade,* it seems evident that some decisions of the Supreme Court have such extended consequences that they rival elections in bringing about changes in society. Obviously, we need better analytical tools for dealing with the impact of Court decisions. One approach to this subject that might be useful would be to work out a typology of decisions. In this typology, decisions that have a broad across-the-board impact, like *Brown v. Board of Education* or *Roe v. Wade,* would be identified as "restructuring decisions," similar to the "realigning elections" used in the analysis by Angus Campbell and his associates in *The American Voter.* Below this megadecision level, there could be descending categories of decisions that have a much more limited potential for impact—either because they deal with routine, technical, or procedural matters that are unlikely to generate much change in the way legal business is transacted; because they are primarily structural in their importance; because they target a specific abuse; or because they settle disputes of very little interest to the general public.

Certain pivotal decisions, however, reach more broadly beyond the Court reports, are important political events in their own right, and set off a chain reaction.[1] *Roe v. Wade* clearly belongs in the

megadecision category. Even a random list of some of the consequences, whether directly caused by the decision or not, would
surely include those discussed in the following section. Notice that
they affect a wide range of respondents—or, to use an analysis
employed by Johnson and Canon, interpreters, implementers, and
consumers.[2] They also cause indirect changes across a broad
spectrum of activities: political, governmental, medical, social,
religious, moral, organizational.

The consequences of the abortion decision for the medical profession and medical research were enormous. With safe, legal
abortions, deaths and surgical complications from abortion among
women of childbearing age were reduced almost to zero. Increased
numbers of abortions were performed every year until 1981, when
the curve seemed to be levelling off. Medical procedures were also
affected: safer surgical procedures for pregnancy termination were
developed and low-cost outpatient gynecological services
(including clinics and services in doctors' offices) became
available.[3] A boost was given to research on contraception, and a
number of new methods and devices were developed. Some of
these, perhaps, may eventually moot the controversy over
abortion by allowing women to control conception at home, with
drugs.[4] Concern for prenatal life spurred the development of new
techniques for saving premature infants and expanded research into
fetal development and neonatology.[5]

Politics and elections were transformed by the political
organizing of Right-to-Life and pro-Choice forces. Abortion and
the rights of the fetus became a rallying point for conservative
voters. Single-issue election campaigning on abortion became
common as abortion and right-to-life concerns were introduced
into political campaigns for local, state, and federal offices.[6] Pro-
and antiabortion political action committees emerged on the
electoral scene. There was a vast increase in law-making activity in
state legislatures on abortion and fertility and related topics, and
litigation to test the constitutionality of the new laws and the limits
of the Supreme Court's decision began to move through the courts.
Even Congress became a forum for debate over abortion, family
planning, and teenage pregnancy as federal programs funding
medical services and family planning were attacked. Bills directed
at maternal health, child care and abuse, pregnancy prevention,

and various family issues, some quite new in design, were introduced.

Hostile responses to the decision took many forms. Dozens of proposals for constitutional amendments related to abortion and the right to life were introduced each session. Court-stripping bills reappeared, and plans to influence the judicial process by recruiting judges opposed to abortion were initiated. Abortion turned up as a policy issue in presidential position papers; it became a plank in the platforms of each political party and was included as a topic in the State of the Union Address. Religious participation in political campaigns and the statements of religious leaders on political matters became commonplace. Marches and picketing occurred, as did the bombing of abortion clinics. The ERA was defeated, in part, at least, due to the furor over abortion. Some courts began to make decisions granting fetuses rights separate from and in conflict with those of their mothers in such areas as medical treatment and prenatal care.[7]

There were other social ramifications related to the decision. Although it is often difficult to pinpoint the causes of social changes directly, enhanced ability to control reproduction may have had some effect on decreasing rates of marriage and increasing rates of divorce.

Even this random selection of the events that followed the Court's decision indicates that it was more than a court decree, the compliance or non-compliance with which could be measured, but an important political event, much like an election.

In addition to events like these that followed in the train of the decision, whether "caused" by it or not, *the decision restructured the dispute itself* in a number of important ways before turning it back into the political process. It laid down a new major premise: after 1973, barring overruling or a constitutional amendment, early abortions were legal and free access to them was constitutionally protected. This was a result very different from the kind of abortion law reform that had come from state legislatures. The reform legislation that was initially proposed was based on the American Law Institute's Model State Abortion Statute; it kept abortion in the hospital setting, monitored by review boards of physicians. Even where abortion was permitted, it was costly, access was limited, and it was controlled by the medical profession.

In this context, there was no incentive to develop new medical techniques or inexpensive outpatient services; there was, rather, an incentive to restrict the number of abortions being performed. *Roe* created a market demand for cheap, safe, locally available services and new techniques and equipment, tailored to some extent to the needs of consumers.

Immediately after the decision the political alignment of forces was unstable and fluid, but it soon became apparent that the cast of political actors would be different in the post-*Roe* period. Well-organized opposition emerged to attack the decision. Loose coalitions of reformers, physicians, womens' organizations, church, and social groups on the pro-Choice side began to consolidate into national organizations and then to build grassroots networks. The theater of action was no longer the state legislature, but spread across the whole political scene. The *New Republic* was to comment later that the decision was "the worst thing that ever happened to American liberalism. Almost overnight it politicized millions of people and helped create a mass movement of social-issue conservatives that has grown into one of the most potent forces in our democracy."[8] The decision provided a symbol and a rallying point for a new kind of politics, "fetal politics," and eventually helped put a conservative Republican into the White House. Initially elated by the victory, then demoralized by the mobilizing of antiabortion forces, the women's movement did not begin to recover until after 1980. Its leaders belatedly recognized the necessity of organization to harness the energies and political ambitions of women as a separate political force.[9] The "gender gap" was barely visible in the 1980 election, but became large enough to be politically significant in 1984. But despite all these changes, the action, unless the decision could be overturned, was now confined by the guidelines laid down by the Supreme Court and would have to take place within the framework set out by its decision.

Although extreme antiabortionists were irreconcilable, public opinion in the middle range was not out of line with the Court's abortion compromise. There was little change in the polls between 1975 and 1986. Most Americans favor abortions in some situations, for example, when the life or health of the mother are in danger. Support falls off sharply for abortions for personal reasons.[10] A

Louis Harris poll done for *Ms.* magazine in 1984 showed about 65 percent of men and 60 percent of women were opposed to a constitutional amendment prohibiting abortion.[11] Underneath this limited consensus were controversial issues that were not resolved, most of them related to the family. And as the conflict moved back and forth from legislatures to courts, to the polls, to the legislatures, and back to the courts again, new issues began to emerge. Should parental consent be required for distribution of contraceptives to teenagers or for resort to abortion? How should the adolescent pregnancy explosion be handled? What protections should be required to save premature infants, including those that survived abortions? It became apparent that abortion was a symbolic issue and that it symbolized public concern about a whole range of social issues dealing with the transformation of the family and social pressures affecting traditional family patterns. The Supreme Court had not recognized these underlying family issues but had tried to solve the dispute in terms of a balancing of interests stated in the familiar constitutional language of liberty and privacy. It had not really examined the irreconcilable nature of the conflict between the pregnant woman and the fetus and had not realized that the moral issues in this conflict would be impossible to avoid.[12] Nor had it predicted that its legalization of abortion would be seen as an attack on the traditional family, loosening already fragile strands of control between parents and children.[13]

While the Court itself did not anticipate the full dimensions of the underlying issues, its decision provoked thorough discussion. Books and articles galore were published between 1973 and 1986, exploring the moral, political, and social ramifications of the abortion controversy from every possible point of view.[14] Criticism of substance combined with criticism of the decision as an abuse of the judicial function; the dispute was a political thicket that the Court never should have entered. This type of criticism centered on three propositions: that the decision was unprincipled, was grounded in the private policy views of the Justices rather than in the Constitution or established principles of constitutional law, and that political decisions of this kind displace democratic, legislative decision making.

Thirteen years of legislative activity on abortion have refuted the charge that Congress and the state legislatures were shut out of the process of democratic decision making. As they have reacted to court decisions, legislatures at all levels have had a significant impact in molding the contours and limits of abortion rights. They decided that abortions would not, for the most part, be publicly funded, forcing the Supreme Court to back away from this issue. Legislation required that every precaution be taken to protect the lives of any viable fetuses. Legislators struggled to work out a compromise between conflicting rights on another level: the rights of children old enough to reproduce and the traditional parental rights to control and monitor the activities of minors. Legislation marked out the boundaries of the decision, and political and legislative activity provided avenues for expressing opposition to it. The Court's decision made significant changes, but it was not out of line with majoritarian opinion on at least one of its central holdings, that women had a limited right to assert control of their reproductive functions.

Nor was the decision unprincipled. Part of the difficulty with seeing the majority opinion in *Roe v. Wade* as a legitimate holding within accepted constitutional principles is that the Court misidentified the underlying issue, and the doctrinal solution did not address the central problem. It is not that liberty and privacy doctrines were irrelevant; liberty and privacy can be reasonably read to include a holding that individuals have rights to make reproductive choices free from state coercion. Even if one insists that constitutional decision making be attuned to the intent of the Framers, it is hard to argue that proponents of limited government, as were most of the members of the Constitutional Convention, would have rejected the idea that government should be prohibited from interfering with individual decisions whether or not to conceive and bear children. There is also a strong tradition of family privacy rooted in common law principles. But the real constitutional principle at issue in *Roe v. Wade* was equality, gender equality, the proposition that only with the right to accept or reject responsibilities for procreation could women choose to play roles as free, autonomous, participating citizens in a democratic system on an equal basis with men. For a number of reasons, the development of constitutional doctrine in the equal protection area has failed to reconcile the idea of equality with the reality of biological differences.[15] Reasoning based on privacy and liberty may have seemed inadequate because it was not accompanied by a discussion of equality.[16]

The Supreme Court's principal contribution to policy making about abortion was its removal of constraints on abortion, formulated in an earlier era and frozen into law, that were impeding the process of gradual change. In its initial decision, the Court took the kind of action that has, historically, been its forte; it gave a sharp negative to restrictive state laws and freed political forces to find a new balance on the abortion issue. It opened up the subject to a new cycle of argument and discussion and forced state legislatures to rewrite their older abortion laws. Increased political activity raised public awareness, and the education of the public, government officials, lawyers, and judges that accompanied such airings of opinion went forward.

Like other landmark decisions of the past twenty years, the initial thrust of *Roe v. Wade* was the negating of old social adjustments, allowing the law and the Constitution to change. The decision could have gone the other way and reinforced the traditional patterns, leaving the business of change to the legislatures. By so doing it might have avoided the tumultuous aftermath, leaving old laws in place and letting change come more slowly. The abortion issue was, however, one particularly unsuited to rational decision by democratic, deliberative bodies because of its highly charged emotional content, its entanglement with moral and religious issues, the ferocity of pressure-group activity on the subject, and the obsessive single-mindedness of its partisans.[17] The Supreme Court's decision gave structure and limits to the dispute and displaced some of the emotion into heated arguments over constitutional law.

As of this writing, the outcome of the controversy is still uncertain; it is still possible that the Supreme Court, with newly appointed conservative Justices, could reverse the decision or that a constitutional amendment would return the problem to the states. It is also possible that new ways of controlling conception will make abortion unnecessary. What is certain is that it would be very difficult to reimpose government prohibitions on voluntary reproductive control.

Chronology 1980–1986

1980

Ja 7 Federal Judge M. Joseph Blumenfeld rules that Connecticut must pay for all abortions that a doctor declares "medically necessary," overturning a state regulation.

Ja 15 Federal Judge John F. Dooling of New York rules that the Hyde Amendment of 1978, which permitted federal Medicaid payments for abortions only in cases in which a woman's life was endangered or in cases of rape and incest, is unconstitutional.

Ja 23 A crowd of between 28,000 to 45,000 rallies in Washington, D.C., to mark the anniversary of the Supreme Court's 1973 abortion decision.

Fe 5 Republican presidential-hopeful Ronald Reagan assails fellow candidate George Bush for his stance on abortion; Bush responds that he personally opposes abortion and supports federal funding only in cases of rape, incest, or when the life of the mother is threatened.

Fe 12 Solicitor General Wade McCree asks the Supreme Court to move quickly on Dooling's ruling to avoid disruption of the Medicare system.

Fe 16 Justice Thurgood Marshall issues a stay on Dooling's ruling.

Fe 19 The Supreme Court votes six to three to lift Marshall's stay on the New York ruling and announces it will review the case, *Harris v. McRae*, during the current term, along with three Illinois cases on the same issue.

Fe 25   The Supreme Court agrees to review the constitutionality of a Utah law that requires physicians to notify parents before performing abortions on teenage girls (*H. L. v. Matheson*).

Ap 21   The Supreme Court hears arguments in four cases testing the validity of the Hyde Amendment: *Harris v. McRae, Williams v. Zbaraz, Miller v. Zbaraz,* and *U.S. v. Zbaraz.*

Je 24   Democrats adopt a draft of the 1980 platform that contains stronger opposition to a proposed antiabortion constitutional amendment than a plank favored by President Carter.

Je 30   The Supreme Court votes five to four that neither the federal government nor the states are constitutionally required to fund abortions for poor women, upholding the Hyde Amendment that limits Medicaid funding of abortions.

Jl 9   Republicans adopt a draft of the 1980 platform strongly favoring a constitutional amendment banning abortion.

Jl 15   Republicans adopt the draft platform.

Ag 6   The American Bar Association condemns a plank in the Republican platform calling for "the appointment of judges at all levels of the judiciary who respect traditional family values and the sanctity of human life."

Ag 13   President Carter disavows a plank in the newly ratified party platform endorsing federal funding of abortions, stating that he is personally opposed to it.

Se 16   Despite unusually strong opposition from the Roman Catholic church, two proabortion candidates in Massachusetts win Democratic nominations for the U.S. House of Representatives.

Se 17   The Supreme Court denies petitions to rehear the cases of Medicaid funding limits decided June 30.

Se 30   Ronald Reagan clarifies his stance on judicial appointments, saying he will select Supreme Court justices on the basis of their "whole broad philosophy" and not just on their position on abortion.

No 6   President-elect Reagan reaffirms his support for the antiabortion policies of the Republican platform.

1981

Ja 12   The Supreme Court refuses Arizona's request to grant a stay of a lower court order that it continue to honor a contract with the state's Planned Parenthood organizations to provide family-planning services.

Ja 22   Fifty thousand abortion foes march from the White House to the Capitol to demand a constitutional amendment to protect the life of the unborn; representatives meet with congressional leaders, President Reagan, and administration officials.

Fe 18   The Massachusetts Supreme Court orders the state to pay for all "medically necessary" abortions for women on welfare even if their lives are not in danger; it overturns 1979 state law limiting public financing of abortions to life-threatening cases.

Mr 3   President Reagan suggests that an antiabortion constitutional amendment can be avoided if Congress determines that the fetus is a human being.

Mr 15   Georgia eliminates state payments for abortions, effective March 15, except in cases in which the mother's life is endangered or for victims of rape or incest.

Mr 23   The Supreme Court votes six to three that a state may require a doctor to notify the parents of a teenage girl before performing an abortion on her or face criminal penalties, at least when the girl is still living at home and is dependent on her parents (*H.L. v. Matheson*).

Ap 23   Five doctors testify that human life begins at conception at Senate Judiciary Committee's Subcommittee hearings on a bill to outlaw abortions.

Ap 27   The Supreme Court upholds without comment the constitutionality of an Indiana law that requires that all abortions after the first three months of pregnancy be performed in a hospital (*Gary-Northwest Indiana Women's Services v. Orr*).

Ap 28   In response to a proposed bill, the National Academy of Sciences passes a resolution asserting that there is no way to absolutely define when human life begins in clear-cut scientific terms.

My 21   The Senate, voting fifty-two to forty-three, approves an amendment already approved by the House that places stringent restrictions on federal funding of abortions.

Je 1   The House and Senate ratify the most stringent restrictions ever placed on Medicaid abortions after rejecting a House-passed measure that would have forbidden medical insurance payments for abortions for federal employees.

Je 3   Senator Jake Garn and Representatives Henry J. Hyde and Robert A. Young resign in protest from an advisory board of the National Pro-Life Political Action Committee after it designates nine Congressmen as targets for defeat in 1982.

Je 9   Both sides claim victory as the Senate Judiciary Committee's subcommittee on Separation of Powers passes a "Human Life Bill" that says a fetus is a human being. But the vote delays action on the bill, and opponents say that this places it on the back burner.

Je 12   Theologians express strongly conflicting views on abortion during a three-hour hearing before the Senate Judiciary Committee's Subcommittee on Separation of Powers. Ex-Solicitors General Archibald Cox and Robert H. Bork testify that a proposed anti-abortion bill is unconstitutional.

Je 17   Liberals in a House-Senate Conference Committee temporarily block C. Everett Koop's nomination as Surgeon General because of his antiabortion stance.

Jl 7   Antiabortion groups attack the nomination of Sandra Day O'Connor to the Supreme Court because she once opposed an Arizona Senate antiabortion bill.

Jl 29   Massachusetts Appeals Court overrules a lower court's order that a 14-year-old must consult her parents before having an abortion.

Se 21   The Senate confirms Sandra Day O'Connor's nomination to the Supreme Court despite qualms about her past record on abortion.

No 6   The National Conference of Catholic Bishops endorses a constitutional amendment that would empower Congress and individual states to adopt laws regulating and banning abortion.

No 16   The Senate, voting sixty-eight to twenty-four, confirms Dr. C. Everett Koop, a prominent abortion foe, as United States Surgeon General and Public Health Service Director.

De 16   The Senate Judiciary Committee's Constitution subcommittee approves four to zero the proposed "human life federalism" constitutional amendment that would give "concurrent power" to Congress and the states to ban or regulate abortion.

1982

Ja 19   President Reagan refuses to answer a question about whether he would personally approve abortion if a member of his family was a rape victim, but says he "would be hesitant" to allow use of government funds under such circumstances.

Ja 21   An AP-NBC News Poll shows that 75 percent of Americans opposed a proposed constitutional amendment to ban abortions.

Ja 22   An estimated 25,000 people march on Washington, D.C., to mark the nineth anniversary of the Supreme Court's decision to legalize abortion; Following the march, antiabortion leaders meet with President Reagan.

Ja 23   Arson damages abortion clinic in Granite City, Illinois, run by Dr. Hector Zevallos.

Mr 10   The Senate Judiciary Committee, voting ten to seven, approves a proposed constitutional amendment sponsored by Senator Orrin

Hatch that would enable Congress and individual states to adopt laws banning abortion.

My 24 Supreme Court justices agree to rule on the constitutionality of the array of obstacles that state and local governments have placed in the path of access to legal abortions.

My 29 In St. Petersburg, Florida, abortion clinics are firebombed. The "Army of God" group later claims responsibility.

Je 11 Pennsylvania Governor Dick Thornburgh signs a bill that prohibits abortions except when a physician determines that a mother's well-being is at stake.

Jl 29 The Justice Department, in a twenty-two-page brief filed with the approval of Attorney General William French Smith and administration aides, formally urges the Supreme Court to "give heavy deference" to state and local laws restricting abortion rights and strongly implies that the Court's 1973 decision legalizing abortion is wrong.

Ag 13 Dr. Hector Zevallos, operator of an abortion clinic called Hope Clinic for Women of Granite City, Illinois, and his wife Rosalie Jean are kidnapped; an "Army of God" group is suspected.

Ag 16 Liberals begin a filibuster in the Senate over an anti-abortion measure introduced by Senator Jesse Helms.

Ag 18 The FBI joins in the search for Zevallos.

Ag 20 Zevallos and his wife are released.

Ag 25 Planned Parenthood files a federal court challenge to a new Indiana law requiring that parents of underage girls requesting abortions be notified at least twenty-four hours before the procedure.

Se 15 The Senate, after failing in two attempts to stop a liberal filibuster, votes forty-seven to forty-six to kill Senator Helms's proposal to impose severe restrictions on womens' right to have an abortion. Senator Hatch withdraws his proposed constitutional amendment.

No 22 The FBI arrests Matthew Maxon Moore and Wayne Allen Moore and seeks Don Benny Anderson, members of self-styled "Army of God," for kidnapping abortion clinic operator Dr. Hector Zevallos and his wife.

No 24 The FBI arrests Don Benny Anderson in the Zevallos kidnapping.

No 30 The Supreme Court hears arguments on the constitutionality of the Akron Ordinance and related cases.

De 4 Justice Harry Blackmun, in a television interview, says he resents the names he has been called as the author of the Court's 1973 decision.

De 22 California Superior Court Judge Eli Chernow rules that a state law banning abortions after the twentieth week of pregnancy violates the Supreme Court's 1973 decision.

1983

Ja 14 A letter from Faye Wattleton, president of Planned Parenthood Federation of America, criticizes the Health and Human Service Department's proposal to require family-planning clinics receiving federal assistance to use separate facilities, staffs, supplies, and equipment for abortion services.

Ja 19 The League of Women Voters endorses for the first time the right of women to obtain a legal abortion.

Ja 21 Tenth anniversary of the Supreme Court ruling legitimizing abortion. About 26,000 people march on the Capitol to demand legislation overturning the ruling; a coalition of groups supporting the right to have an abortion pledges to carry on the cause.

Ja 22 President Reagan, in his weekly radio address, says he will continue to support legislation to end the practice of abortion-on-demand.

Ja 25 The attorney for Don Benny Anderson, who is on trial in Alton, Illinois, for the abduction of Dr. Hector Zevallos, who performed abortions, makes his client's opposition to abortion a central part of his defense; prosecutors say that Anderson and two others threatened to kill Zevallos and his wife if President Reagan did not announce an end to legal abortion.

Ja 27 Anderson is found guilty and later sentenced to thirty years in prison. His accomplices were also sentenced to long prison terms.

Ja 31 President Reagan vows to renew efforts for a ban on abortion in a speech to a convention of Christian broadcast preachers in Washington, D.C.

Fe 13 The Florida Board of Medical Examiners unanimously revokes the license of Dr. Edgar Gonzalez, a physician accused of performing an illegal third trimester abortion that nearly killed a 12-year-old girl.

Fe 14 Federal District Judge Henry F. Werker's temporary injunction in New York blocks the implementation of a Reagan administration rule that would require federally funded clinics to notify parents after giving prescription birth control devices to teenagers.

Fe 18 Federal District Judge Thomas A. Flannery issues a similar injunction in Washington, D.C.

Fe 23 Roman Catholic Archbishop Edmund Szoka of Detroit demands the resignation of a nun, Sister Agnes Mary Mansour, who is the State Department of Social Services director; Sister Mansour has refused to oppose state payments for abortions.

Fe 25 Margaret M. Heckler, Reagan's nominee for Secretary of Health and Human Services, testifies to her long-standing opposition to abortion during her confirmation hearings before the Senate Finance Committee.

Mr 7 Sister Mansour defies Archbishop Szoka's order.

Mr 8 President Reagan urges federal legislation to restrict abortions in an address to the National Association of Evangelicals, Orlando, Florida. Mansour tells a legislative confirmation hearing that, while she is opposed to abortion, her conscience permits her to carry out the law under which the state pays for abortions for poor women.

Mr 9 Mansour confirmed; Sisters of Mercy, her order, says she can keep her post.

Mr 25 The Vatican orders Mansour to denounce Michigan's policy of paying for abortions for poor women or quit as director of the state's welfare agency.

Ap 19 Senate Judiciary Committee, voting nine to nine, sends a constitutional amendment to the floor that would reverse the 1973 Supreme Court decision legalizing abortion.

My 11 Mansour announces she has given up religious vows rather than face expulsion from her order.

Je 6 An antiabortion rider on a $12 billion appropriations bill prompts House liberals to join conservatives in defeating the bill.

Je 15 The Supreme Court (*Akron v. Akron Center for Reproductive Health*) forcefully reaffirms the constitutional right to obtain an abortion and strikes down an array of local curbs on access to abortions; the Court, voting six to three, declares unconstitutional an Akron, Ohio, ordinance that places obstacles in the path of access to abortion.

Je 20 The Supreme Court refuses to hear an appeal by a Minnesota city from a ruling that it could not prohibit staff physicians from performing abortions at city's public hospital (*Virginia v. Nyberg*).

Je 28 The Senate rejects a proposed ten-word constitutional amendment asserting that the right to an abortion is not secured by the Constitution; the vote is fifty to fifty-nine, eighteen short of a two-thirds required majority.

Jl 10 Democratic presidential candidates Gary Hart, Walter Mondale, Alan Cranston, Ernest Hollings, and John Glenn assert their support for abortion rights at the National Women's Political Caucus convention in San Antonio, Texas.

Ag 2 Wichita officials, in response to complaints by anti-abortionists, ban the practive of disposing of human fetuses at city-owned incinerator.

Ag 22 Barbara Honegger, a critic of Reagan's women's rights policies (including abortion), resigns her position as a special assistant in the Justice Department's Civil Rights Division to protest Reagan's policies.

Ag 30 The U.S. Court of Appeals for the Seventh Circuit, Chicago, Illinois, bars the enforcement of an Indiana law requiring doctors to notify parents before performing abortions on minors.

Se 22 The House of Representatives approves an appropriations bill after adding an amendment banning the use of any federal funds for abortions under any circumstances.

Se 28 The El Paso, Texas, jury that found Dr. Raymond Showery guilty of murdering a fetus in 1979 abortion sentences him to fifteen years in prison.

Oc 3 Twenty demonstrators for the Pro-Life Action League march in front of the Supreme Court building to mark the opening of the term.

Oc 20 A long-delayed $104.4 billion appropriations bill clears Congress for the Departments of Labor, Health and Human Services, and Education; it contained a controversial provision barring the use of the funds to pay for abortions unless the life of the mother was endangered.

No 14 An amendment to a stop-gap spending bill in Congress forbids insurance coverage of abortions for federal workers unless the woman's life was endangered.

No 17 Joseph Cardinal Bernardin says during the National Conference of Catholic Bishops that he will renew an antiabortion campaign.

1984

Ja 23 An estimated 30,000 to 50,000 people mark the eleventh anniversary of the Supreme Court's 1973 abortion decision at a protest rally in Washington, D.C.

Ja 25 President Reagan urges banning abortion during his State of the Union speech in Washington, D.C.

Ja 30 President Reagan, speaking to the National Religious Broadcasters' convention in Washington, D.C., renews his call for a constitutional ban on abortion.

Fe 11 Democratic candidates Reuben Askew (for) and Jesse Jackson (against) debate a proposed constitutional amendment restricting abortions during a debate among the eight major Democratic candidates in Des Moines, Iowa.

Fe 17 Pipe bombs explode near an abortion clinic in Norfolk, Virginia.

Mr 6 President Reagan, addressing the National Association of Evangelicals, says the fetus suffers "excruciating pain" during an abortion and calls for a constitutional amendment banning elective abortion.

Je 24   Archbishop John J. O'Connor of New York says he does not believe that a Catholic "in good conscience" can vote for a political candidate who approves of abortion or favors leaving the decision to women.

Jl 7   A bomb explodes outside an Annapolis, Maryland, office of Planned Parenthood—the second such bombing in a week.

Jl 8   A Planned Parenthood survey shows that the number of abortions declined by 3,400 in 1982, the first such decline since *Roe v. Wade* in 1973.

Jl 13   The White House gives final approval to a policy statement that would deny government family-planning money to international organizations supporting abortion; the measure will affect Planned Parenthood.

Jl 17   Democrats include a plank calling for "Reproductive Freedom" and the right to choice in their party platform.

Jl 25   President Reagan, campaigning among Catholics in New Jersey, attacks the Democratic Mondale-Ferraro ticket's support of abortion.

Ag 3   New York Governor Mario Cuomo accuses Archbishop John J. O'Connor of New York of telling Catholics not to vote for politicians disagreeing with O'Connor's views on abortion.

Ag 9   Walter Mondale, campaigning in Madison, Alabama, tells antiabortion demonstrators that he cannot support a constitutional amendment banning abortion. Bishop James W. Malone of Ohio, president of the United States Catholic Conference, says it is "not logically tenable" for candidates to make a distinction between their private views and those they advocate in public.

Ag 21   The Republican party platform endorses "a human life amendment" to the Constitution and opposes the use of public funds for abortions.

Se 9   Senator Edward Kennedy says that the Roman Catholic hierarchy is wrong to insist that politicians of any faith advocate a government ban on abortion.

Se 10   Geraldine Ferraro responds to criticism by Archbishop John J. O'Connor on the abortion issue by saying that she would resign if she felt it impossible to reconcile her religious views with her constitutional obligations.

Se 11   Vice President George Bush is pressed on inconsistencies in his record of opposing abortion in cases of rape and incest.

Se 13   Walter Mondale reiterates his stand on abortion and denies the accusation that his party is antireligious.

Se 25   The Senate votes to widen permitted uses of Medicaid funds for abortion.

Oc 7   Reagan and Mondale include the abortion issue during a debate in Louisville, Kentucky.

Oc 10   Security is tightened in the Supreme Court building after Justice Blackmun receives a death threat and an antiabortion protestor (Oc 9) interrupts oral arguments in the Court's central chamber.

Oc 11   Final action by the Senate approves a $470 billion spending bill, but not until the Senate drops a controversial proposal to allow Medicaid funding of abortions in cases of rape and incest, in addition to instances in which the mother's life was endangered.

Oc 12   Chief Justice Warren E. Burger lifts a stay on a ruling by a Maryland state court that the mother of a handicapped woman could obtain an abortion for her blind, deaf, and severely retarded daughter, the apparent victim of a rape.

No 6   Colorado voters ban state funding of abortions; Washington State voters narrowly defeat a similar measure.

De 4   FBI figures on terrorism do not include abortion clinic bombings because they are not attributable to organized groups.

De 18   Twenty-four nuns who signed a public statement on October 7 differing from the Roman Catholic church's position on abortion are told that they face expulsion from their orders unless they renounce their position.

De 25   A bomb explodes at a Pensacola, Florida, abortion clinic, causing extensive damage.

De 30   Federal agents in Pensacola, Florida, arrest Matthew J. Goldsby, age twenty-one, on charges of bombing three abortion clinics on Christmas and a similar bombing in June. Other suspects are arrested on January 2, 1985.

1985

Ja 3   President Reagan and Moral Majority leader Jerry Falwell condemn recent bombings of abortion clinics.

Ja 14   House Republicans issue a policy agenda for 1985 that omits the goal of an antiabortion amendment to the Constitution that the 1984 Republican platform had included.

Ja 19   Abortion rights groups say that they are satisfied with the way federal investigators are handling abortion clinic bombing cases. Federal agents arrest three men for bombings at abortion clinics in Maryland, Virginia, and Washington, D.C.

Ja 21   President Reagan includes a brief remark about "the unborn" during his second inaugural address in the Capitol Rotunda.

Ja 22   President Reagan supports antiabortion demonstrators in a speech marking the anniversary of the 1973 Supreme Court's abortion decision.

Fe 6   President Reagan says abortion must be stopped and asks a joint session of Congress for legislation to protect the unborn during the State of the Union address.

Fe 17   The controversial film, *The Silent Scream*, is shown on Jerry Falwell's television program. The film contended that fetuses feel pain during abortion attempts.

Fe 28   One shot is fired into Justice Harry F. Blackmun's apartment in Arlington, Virginia; Blackmun had received an anonymous death threat. Similar threats are received by Justice William F. Powell and Senator Alphonse D'Amato.

Mr 12   The Alan Guttmacher Institute reported that the United States, as compared to other industrialized countries, has twice the rate of teenage pregnancy.

Mr 15   Attorney General Edwin Meese III says that the Justice Department will fill federal judgeships with appointees who believe in the "sanctity of life."

Ap 15   The Supreme Court agrees to hear arguments on whether Pennsylvania's Abortion Control Act violates the Constitution; the law was substantially invalidated in 1984 by a United States Court of Appeals.

Ap 24   Matthew Goldsby and three others charged with bombing abortion facilities in Pensacola, Florida, in 1984 are convicted.

Ap 26   The Alan Guttmacher Institute reported that, in 1981, one out of every four pregnancies in the United States ended in abortion.

My 6   The NARAL begins a "Silent No More" campaign, urging women to speak out about their abortion experiences.

My 20   The Supreme Court agrees to hear a joint appeal by the State of Illinois and an antiabortion group, Americans United for Life, of a federal District Court ruling that elements of the 1975 Illinois Abortion Law were unconstitutional.

My 24   The Universal Press Syndicate decides not to distribute six "Doonesbury" comic strips satirizing the antiabortion film "The Silent Scream."

My 28   Panelists at the annual meeting of the American Association for the Advancement of Science assert that medical advances in keeping fetuses alive are eroding the Supreme Court's 1973 abortion decision as it related to the "viability" of the fetus.

Jl 11   A federal District Court in New Jersey voids a law requiring abortions after the sixteenth week to be performed in hospitals.

Jl 15   Acting Solicitor General Charles Fried files an *amicus curiae* brief in the Supreme Court, asking the Court to overturn *Roe v. Wade.*

Jl 27   Convicted clinic bomber Thomas Eugene Spinks is sentenced to fifteen years in prison by the United States District Court, Baltimore, Maryland. Co-conspirators were sentenced earlier to shorter terms.

Ag 31   The NARAL and other pro-Choice groups file an *amicus curiae* brief in the Supreme Court in new abortion cases. Eighty-one members of Congress file a brief opposing the government's position.

Se 9   The Reagan administration withdraws funding for the United Nations Fund for Population Activities (UNFPA) to protest involvement in China's allegedly coercive abortion policy.

Se 18   The Supreme Court denies the government's request to participate in oral argument in the new abortion cases.

No 5   Antiabortion referenda on the ballot in three New England towns are turned down by the voters. (Bristol, Conn.; Dover, N.H., Derry, N.H.).

No 6   The Supreme Court hears oral argument in two new abortion cases.

De 6   Bomb and arson attacks against abortion clinics occur in five states. The Pennsylvania Supreme Court upholds restrictions on Medicaid funding of abortions.

De 18   The New York Court of Appeals rejects Roman Catholic attempts to block abortion clinics in several New York localities.

1986

Ja 19   President Reagan proclaims January 19 as National Sanctity of Life Day.

Ja 22   President Reagan addresses the annual March for Life.

Fe 4   President Reagan's State of the Union Address includes a statement supporting a right to life for the unborn.

Mr 9   The NOW stages a pro-Choice March for Women's Lives in Washington, D.C. An estimated 85,000 to 125,000 attend.

Mr 16   The NOW stages a March for Women's Lives in Los Angeles; about 30,000 attend.

Ap 30   The Supreme Court dismisses *Diamond v. Charles,* the Illinois abortion case, holding that the appellant had no standing to defend the law in court.

Je 11   The Supreme Court decides *Thornburgh v. American College of Obstetricians and Gynecologists* by a vote of five to four, overturning six sections of Pennsylvania's Abortion Control Act.

Notes

Introduction

1. Clement E. Vose, *Constitutional Change: Amendment Politics and Supreme Court Litigation since 1900* (Lexington, Mass.: D. C. Heath, 1972); Jack Greenberg, *Judicial Process and Social Change: Constitutional Litigation* (St. Paul, Minn.: West Publishing Co., 1977); Richard Kluger, *Simple Justice* (New York: Knopf, 1976).

2. Lee Epstein, *Conservatives in Court* (Knoxville: University of Tennessee Press, 1985).

3. Donald L. Horowitz, *The Courts and Social Policy* (Washington, D.C.: Brookings, 1977); Abram Chayes, "The Role of the Judge in Public Law Litigation," *Harvard Law Review* 89 (May 1976): 1281-1316.

4. Michael Meltsner, *Cruel and Unusual: The Supreme Court and Capital Punishment* (N.Y.: Random House, 1973). See also Greenberg, *Judicial Process and Social Change* (St. Paul, Minn.: West Publishing Co., 1977).

5. Bellotti v. Baird, 428 U.S. 132 (1976); see Robert H. Mnookin, *In the Interest of Children: Advocacy, Law Reform and Public Policy* (New York: W. H. Freeman and Co., 1985).

6. Epstein, *Conservatives in Court.*

7. Ruth B. Cowan, "Women's Rights through Litigation: An Examination of the American Civil Liberties Union Women's Rights Project, 1971-1976," *Columbia Human Rights Law Review* 8 (Spring-Summer 1976): 373-412.

8. Vose, *Constitutional Change,* p. 290. The case was Love v. Griffin, 266 U.S. 32 (1924).

9. See Lawrence Lader, *Abortion* (Boston: Beacon Press, 1967); and idem., *Abortion II: Making the Revolution* (Boston: Beacon Press, 1973), for accounts of the early organizational efforts. See also Bernard N. Nathanson, *Aborting America* (Garden City, N.Y.: Doubleday, 1979). Diane Schulder and Florynce Kennedy, *Abortion Rap* (New York: McGraw-Hill, 1971), illustrate the cooperative, client-involved nature of early abortion suits.

10. See Heather Sigworth, "Abortion Laws in the Federal Courts: The Supreme Court as Platonic Guardian," *Indiana Law Forum* 5 (Fall 1971): 130-42.

11. Roger M. Williams, "The Power of Fetal Politics," *Saturday Review,* June 9, 1979, pp. 12-15. Mulhauser is quoted in this article.

12. Theodore J. Lowi, *The Politics of Disorder* (New York: Norton, 1971) discusses the congealing of social movements.

13. Roy Lucas, "Federal Constitutional Limitations on the Enforcement and Administration of State Abortion Statutes, *North Carolina Law Review* 46 (June 1968): 730-78.

14. Mnookin, p. 160, points out that test case litigation "provides an opportunity for moral discourse on difficult issues on which there is little consensus."

15. Sylvia Law, "Rethinking Sex and the Constitution," *University of Pennsylvania Law Review* 132 (June 1984): 981.

16. Mnookin, p. 246. "Litigation is in no sense neutral—it may amplify the voices of certain actors and groups and mute those of others."

17. Michael A. Rebell and Arthur R. Block, *Educational Policy-Making and the Courts* (Chicago: University of Chicago Press, 1982), p. 216.

Chapter 1

1. James George, Jr., "The Evolving Law of Abortion," in *Abortion, Society and the Law,* ed. David F. Walbert and J. Douglas Butler (Cleveland and London: Case Western Reserve University, 1973), pp. 3-32.

2. William Hawkins, *A Treatise on the Pleas of the Crown,* 4th ed. (London: Richardson and Lintot, 1762), bk. 1, ch. 31, sec. 16. This book was first published in 1716.

3. Roe v. Wade, 410 U.S. 113, 135-36 (1973).

4. James C. Mohr, *Abortion in America: The Origins and Evolution of National Policy* (New York: Oxford University Press, 1978). Mohr's fascinating new study of the origins of abortion policy appeared in 1978. Before this study, there were many unanswered questions about the

flood of legislation in the 1860-80 period. See also Linda Gordon, *Woman's Body, Woman's Right* (New York: Penguin, 1977).

5. Mohr, *Abortion in America*, p. 18.

6. Another reason for the law's lack of interest in abortion must have been the fact that infanticide was widespread and was of greater concern. Historian William L. Langer documented its widespread use in Europe in the eighteenth and nineteenth centuries, William L. Langer, "Europe's Initial Population Explosion," *American Historical Review* 69 (October 1963): 8-10. See also Gordon, *Woman's Body*, pp. 50-51.

7. Mohr, *Abortion in America*, p. 25.

8. Cyril C. Means, Jr., "The Law of New York Concerning Abortion and the State of the Foetus, 1664-1968: A Case of Cessation of Consti-tutionality," *New York Law Forum* 14 (Fall 1968): 419-26. For a short account of the common law writings on this subject and an attempt to explain some of the inconsistencies therein, see "Testimony of Professor Cyril C. Means, Jr." U.S., Congress, House, Committee on the Judiciary, Subcommittee on Civil and Constitutional Rights, *Hearings on Proposed Constitutional Amendments*, 94th Cong., 2d sess., February-March, 1976, pt. 1.

9. Mohr, *Abortion in America*, ch. 2.

10. Ibid., ch. 5.

11. Hugh L. Hodge, "Foeticide, or Criminal Abortion, A Lecture Introductory to the Course of Obstetrics," in *Abortion in Nineteenth Century America*, Sex, Marriage and Society series (New York: Arno Press, 1974), pp. 35-36.

12. Mohr, *Abortion in America*, ch. 4.

13. *Abortion in Nineteenth Century America*, other pamphlets in this collection. See also Gordon, *Woman's Body*, pp. 49-60 and ch. 8.

14. All of the material on the passage of state abortion laws is from Mohr, *Abortion in America*.

15. George, "The Evolving Law of Abortion," pp. 3-33.

16. Ibid., p. 8.

17. Gordon, *Woman's Body*, pp. 60-71.

18. Mohr, *Abortion in America*, pp. 240-45.

19. Lucinda Cisler, "Unfinished Business: Birth Control and Women's Liberation," in *Sisterhood is Powerful*, ed. Robin Morgan (New York: Vintage Books, 1970), pp. 245-89.

20. Zad Leavy and Jerome M. Kummer, "Criminal Abortion: Human Hardship and Unyielding Laws," *Southern California Law Review* 35 (Winter 1962): 126. Daniel Callahan surveyed the figures on illegal abortion in his book *Abortion: Law, Choice and Morality* (New York: Macmillan, 1970), pp. 132-36, and pointed out some of their shortcomings.

21. Harold Rosen, "A Case Study in Social Hypocrisy," in *Abortion in America*, ed. Harold Rosen (Boston: Beacon Press, 1967), p. 299. This is a new edition of an earlier book, published in 1954 under the title of *Therapeutic Abortion*, and contains articles by doctors and psychiatrists on the subject.

22. Rosen, "Case Study," pp. xviii, 319-21.

23. Betty Sarvis and Hyman Rodman, *The Abortion Controversy* (New York: Columbia University Press, 1973). This book reviews the early literature on the subject, drawing on an M.A. thesis by Barbara Plant, "A Survey of the U.S. Abortion Literature, 1890-1970" (University of Windsor, Windsor, Ontario).

24. Glanville Williams, *The Sanctity of Life and the Criminal Law* (New York: Knopf, 1957).

25. Sarvis and Rodman, *The Abortion Controversy*, pp. 7-9.

26. Fred P. Graham, "Review of Abortion," *New York Times*, 10 September 1967.

27. Barbara Deckard, *The Women's Movement* (New York: Harper and Row, 1975), ch. 9.

28. Judith Blake, "Abortion and Public Opinion: The 1960-1970 Decade," *Science* 171 (February 12, 1971): 540-49. The article analyzes five polls taken by Gallup and other organizations in this period.

29. Robert H. Walker, *Reform in America* (Lexington, Ky.: University Press of Kentucky, 1985), pp. 11-12.

30. Lawrence Lader, *Abortion II: Making the Revolution* (Boston: Beacon Press, 1973), p. 68.

31. Keith Monroe, "How California's Abortion Law Isn't Working," *New York Times Magazine*, December 29, 1968, p. 11.

32. Ibid., p. 17.

33. *New York Times*, 12 March 1967.

34. Monroe, "How California's Abortion Law Isn't Working," p. 17.

35. Roy Lucas, "Federal Constitutional Limitations on the Enforcement and Administration of State Abortion Statutes," *North Carolina Law Review* 46 (June 1968): 735, n. 26.

36. *Congressional Quarterly Fact Sheet*, July 24, 1970, p. 1914.

37. Lader, *Abortion II*, has an excellent, detailed account of this bitter struggle, chs. 10-11.

38. Ibid., described the early organizational efforts. See also Bernard N. Nathanson, *Aborting America* (Garden City, N.Y.: Doubleday, 1979).

39. Arlene Carmen and Howard Moody, *Abortion Counseling and Social Change* (Valley Forge, Pa.: Judson Press, 1973), gave the story of the Clergy Consultation Service on Abortion.

40. Lader, *Abortion II*, pp. 34-36.

41. Deckard, *The Women's Movement*, pp. 332-36, discussed the radical women's groups.

42. *New York Times*, 9 September 1967.

43. Diane Schulder and Florynce Kennedy, *Abortion Rap* (New York: McGraw-Hill, 1971), pp. 3-4.

44. Cisler, "Unfinished Business," p. 246.

45. Ibid., p. 276.

46. Nancy Stearns et al., "Abortion Brief," in *Radical Lawyers*, ed. Jonathan Black (New York: Avon Books, 1971), pp. 264-68.

47. Sagar C. Jain and Steven W. Sinding, *North Carolina Abortion Law: 1967*, Carolina Population Center Monograph No. 2 (Chapel Hill, N.C.: University of North Carolina, 1968), p. 32.

48. Ibid, p. 42.

49. Sagar C. Jain and Laurel F. Gooch, *Georgia Abortion Act, 1968: A Study in Legislative Process* (Chapel Hill, N.C.: University of North Carolina, School of Public Health, 1972).

50. Lader, *Abortion II*, pp. 85-86.

51. Graham, "Review of Abortion," p. 11.

52. Herbert L. Packer, *The Limits of the Criminal Sanction* (Stanford: Stanford University Press, 1968), p. 344.

53. Cisler, "Unfinished Business," p. 275; Monroe, "How California's Abortion Law Isn't Working," p. 10.

Chapter 2

1. Increasing attention has been paid, in recent years, to litigation campaigns. See Jack Greenberg, *Judicial Process and Social Change: Constitutional Litigation* (St. Paul: West Publishing Co., 1977); and idem., "Litigation for Social Change: Methods, Limits and Role in Democracy," *Record of the Association of the Bar of New York* 29 (1974): 320. On the importance of the courts in the making of social policy, see also Donald L. Horowitz, *The Courts and Social Policy* (Washington, D.C.: Brookings, 1977); and Abram Chayes, "The Role of the Judge in Public Law Litigation," *Harvard Law Review* 89 (May 1976): 1281. Clement E. Vose, *Constitutional Change: Amendment Politics and Supreme Court Litigation since 1900* (Lexington, Mass.: D. C. Heath, 1972), described a number of litigation campaigns.

2. Greenberg, *Judicial Process and Social Change*, pp. 57-89.

3. Pearson v. Murray, 169 Md. 478, 182 A. 590 (1936); Missouri *ex rel.* Gaines v. Canada, 305 U.S. 337 (1938); Sipuel v. University of Oklahoma, 332 U.S. 631 (1948); Sweatt v. Painter, 339 U.S. 629 (1950);

McLaurin v. Oklahoma State Regents, 339 U.S. 637 (1950).

4. 163 U.S. 537 (1896).

5. 83 U.S. 130 (1873).

6. Ruth B. Cowan, "Women's Rights through Litigation: An Examination of the American Civil Liberties Union Women's Rights Project, 1971-1976," *Columbia Human Rights Law Review* 8 (Spring-Summer 1976): 373-412.

7. Laurence H. Tribe, *American Constitutional Law* (Mineola, N.Y.: Foundation Press, 1978), pp. 53-56.

8. Baker v. Carr 369 U.S. 186 (1962).

9. See Louis L. Jaffe, "The Citizen as Litigant in Public Actions: The Non-Hohfeldian or Ideological Plaintiff," *University of Pennsylvania Law Review* 116 (1968): 1033-47.

10. Tribe, *American Constitutional Law*, pp. 102-14.

11. For a summary of the rules governing declaratory judgments and some of their history, see Perez v. Ledesma, 401 U.S. 83 (1971); separate opinion, Brennan, J.

12. Good Samaritan Hospital v. Attorney General, No. 140504 (Super. Ct. Ariz., July 30, 1962). This was the Sherri Finkbine case. See also "Note: Declaratory Relief in Criminal Law," *Harvard Law Review* 80 (May 1967): 1490-1507.

13. See Blackmun, J., plurality opinion, in Singleton v. Wulff, 428 U.S. 106 (1976).

14. Roy Lucas, "Federal Constitutional Limitations on the Enforcement and Administration of State Abortion Statutes," *North Carolina Law Review* 46 (June 1968): 753.

15. Buck v. Bell, 274 U.S. 200 (1927); Skinner v. Oklahoma, 316 U.S. 535 (1942).

16. Norman E. Hines, "A Decade of Progress in Birth Control," *Annals of the American Academy* 212 (1940): 88-95.

17. The birth control cases had some of the same difficulties meeting the technical requirements of lawsuits that were to beset the initial attempts to get tests of abortion laws. Thus in Tileston v. Ullman, 318 U.S. 44 (1943), the Supreme Court held that a doctor trying to test a law forbidding him to advise his patients on the use of contraceptives did not have standing to bring the suit. In Poe v. Ullman, 367 U.S. 497 (1961), the Court held that no real case or controversy existed, because no grounds existed for believing that the state intended to prosecute anyone under the statute.

18. Douglas, J., dissenting, in Public Utilities Commission v. Pollak, 343 U.S. 451, 467 (1951).

19. Poe v. Ullman, at 543.

20. Griswold v. Connecticut, 381 U.S. 479 (1965).

21. See C. Thomas Dienes, *Law, Politics and Birth Control* (Urbana, Il.: University of Illinois Press, 1972), pp. 162-66.

22. Thomas I. Emerson, "Nine Justices in Search of a Doctrine," *Michigan Law Review* 64 (December 1965): 219. Emerson, a professor at the Yale Law School, was one of the attorneys in this case.

23. Emerson, "Nine Justices," p. 228.

24. Griswold v. Connecticut, at 486.

25. See cases such as Mapp v. Ohio, 367 U.S. 643 (1961); and Stanford v. Texas, 379 U.S. 479 (1965).

26. Dienes, *Law, Politics and Birth Control*, pp. 163-64.

27. Lucas, "Federal Constitutional Limitations," pp. 752-76.

28. Ibid., p. 756.

29. People v. Belous 71 Cal. 2d 954, 458 P.2d 194 (1969).

30. Lawrence Lader, *Abortion II: Making the Revolution* (Boston: Beacon Press, 1973), pp. 1-17.

31. United States v. Vuitch, 402 U.S. 62 (1971).

32. Tom C. Clark, "Religion, Morality and Abortion: A Constitutional Appraisal," *Loyola (Los Angeles) Law Review* 2 (April 1969): 1-11.

33. This assertion is made by Robert A. Destro, "Abortion and the Constitution: The Need for a Life Protective Amendment," *University of California Law Review* 63 (September 1975): 1268. The reference is to Cyril C. Means, Jr, "The Phoenix of Abortional Freedom: Is a Penumbral or Ninth Amendment Right about to Arise from the Nineteenth-Century Legislative Ashes of a Fourteenth-Century Common Law Liberty?" *New York Law Forum* 17, no. 2 (1971): 335-410.

34. Janice Goodman, Rhonda Copelon Schoenbrod, and Nancy Stearns, "Doe and Roe: Where Do We Go From Here?" *Women's Rights Law Reporter* 1 (Spring, 1973): 24-26. See also Diane Schulder and Florynce Kennedy, *Abortion Rap* (New York: McGraw-Hill, 1971), pp. 6-88, 91-102.

35. *Congressional Quarterly Fact Sheet*, 24 July 1970, p. 1913. See also Heather Sigworth, "Abortion Laws in the Federal Courts: The Supreme Court as Platonic Guardian," *Indiana Legal Forum* 5 (Fall 1971): 130-42. The cases are collected as of spring, 1972, in Pat Vergata et al., "Abortion Cases in the United States," *Women's Rights Law Reporter* 1 (Spring, 1972): 50-55.

36. Jo Freeman, *The Politics of Women's Liberation* (New York: McKay, 1975), pp. 242-43.

37. Schulder and Kennedy, *Abortion Rap*. This book, written by two lawyers, is an account of the New York case and includes depositions given in the case by women and a selection of the legal documents that were filed. The case is Abramowicz v. Lefkowitz, 305 F. Supp. 1030 (S.D.N.Y. 1969).

38. Schulder and Kennedy, *Abortion Rap*, p. 95.

39. Ibid., p. 96.

40. Ibid., appendix.

41. Citing Algeyer v. Louisiana, 165 U.S. 578 (1897).

42. Citing Thorpe v. Housing Authority, 393 U.S. 268, 271 (1969), where pregnancy and illegitimate children were accepted as factors that could be weighed in the decision to exclude persons from public housing. Schulder and Kennedy, *Abortion Rap*, appendix.

43. Schulder and Kennedy, *Abortion Rap*, appendix. Emily Jane Goodman was the attorney for the *amici curiae* in Abramowicz v. Lefkowitz.

44. Goodman, Schoenbrod, and Stearns, "Doe and Roe," p. 22.

45. Y.W.C.A. of Princeton, N.J. v Kugler, 345 F. Supp. 1048 (D.N.J. 1972).

46. Women of Rhode Island v. Israel, Civil No. 4605 and No. 4586 (D. R.I. Feb. 7, 1973).

47. Women of Massachusetts v. Quinn, Civil No. 71-2420-W (D. Mass. Feb. 21, 1973).

48. Wheeler v. State of Florida, Case No. 41,708 (S. Ct. Fla. May 18, 1972).

49. Abele v. Markle, 452 F.2d 1121 (2d Cir. 1971). On remand, 342 F. Supp. 800 (D. Conn. 1972).

50. 31 N.Y. 2d 194; 335 N.Y.S. 2d 286, 390 N.E. 2d 887 (1972).

51. Goodman, Schoenbrod, and Stearns, "Doe and Roe," pp. 22-23.

52. 342 F. Supp. 1048 (D. N.J. 1972).

53. 310 F. Supp. 293 (E.D. Wisc. 1970).

54. 342 F. Supp. 800 (D. Conn. 1972).

55. Sigworth, "Abortion Laws," p. 132.

56. Ibid.; and Vergata et al., "Abortion Cases," pp. 50-55.

57. 402 U.S. 62, 78 (1971).

Chapter 3

1. Roe v. Wade, 410 U.S. 113, 222 (1973).

2. Archibald Cox, *The Role of the Supreme Court in American Government* (New York: Oxford University Press, 1976), p. 108.

3. Ibid., p. 3.

4. Donald L. Horowitz, *The Courts and Social Policy* (Washington, D.C.: Brookings, 1977). ch. 2.

5. Cox, *The Role of the Supreme Court*, p. 77. Some of these developments are discussed in Horowitz, *The Courts and Social Policy*; in Abram Chayes, "The Role of the Judge in Public Law Litigation, *Harvard Law Review* 89 (May 1976): 1281-1316; and in Arthur S. Miller, "Supreme

Court: Time for Reform," *Washington Post*, 11 January 1976.

6. Chayes, *The Role of the Judge*, p. 1302; Horowitz, *The Courts and Social Policy*, pp. 45-46.

7. Millikin v. Bradley, 418 U.S. 717 (1974).

8. James v. Wallace, 382 F. Supp. 1177 (M.D. Ala. 1974), and order issued January 13, 1976. See *C.J. Bulletin*, March 1976.

9. See Chayes, *The Role of the Judge*, p. 1296; Horowitz, *The Courts and Social Policy*, pp. 1-21.

10. Miranda v. Arizona, 384 U.S. 436 (1966).

11. John Hart Ely, "The Wages of Crying Wolf: A Comment on *Roe v. Wade*," *Yale Law Journal* 82 (April 1973): 920-49.

12. Janice Goodman, Rhonda Copelon, and Nancy Stearns, "Doe and Roe: Where Do We Go From Here?" *Women's Rights Law Reporter* 1 (Spring 1973): 27.

13. Cox, *The Role of the Supreme Court*, p. 113.

14. 410 U.S. 113, 209-13 (1973).

15. *Time*, February 5, 1973, p. 51.

16. Bob Woodward and Scott Armstrong, *The Brethren* (New York: Simon and Schuster, 1979), pp. 170-75.

17. Ibid., pp. 171-75.

18. Ibid., pp. 186-89; *Time*, February 5, 1973, p. 51.

19. Woodward and Armstrong, *The Brethren*, pp. 230-34.

20. Walter F. Murphy, *Elements of Judicial Strategy* (Chicago: University of Chicago Press, 1964), ch. 3.

21. Woodward and Armstrong, *The Brethren*, p. 233.

22. For a discussion of these problems, see Richard A. Epstein, "Substantive Due Process by Any Other Name: The Abortion Cases," *Supreme Court Review* (1974): 159-65. Epstein did not think that Roe and Doe had standing but that other appellants did.

Women's rights attorneys believe the Court would not have decided the case if the women's claims had not been made. Copelon and Stearns, "Doe and Roe," p. 23.

23. U.S., Congress, Senate, Committee on the Judiciary, Subcommittee on Constitutional Amendments, 94th Cong. 1st sess., 1975. Testimony of Sarah Weddington, April 11, 1975, p. 304.

24. Poe v. Ullman, 367 U.S. 497 (1961), Harlan, J., dissenting; also Gerald Gunther, "The Subtle Vices of the 'Passive Virtues'—A Comment on Principle and Expediency in Judicial Review," *Columbia Law Review* 64 (January 1964): 1.

25. Abele v. Markle, 351 F. Supp. 224 (D. Conn. 1972).

26. *Van Nostrand's Scientific Encyclopedia*, 5th ed. (New York: Van Nostrand Reinhold Co., 1976), p. 1859.

27. Robert F. Drinan, "The Inviolability of the Right to be Born," in

Abortion and the Law, ed. David T. Smith (Cleveland: Case Western Reserve University, 1967), pp. 107-23.

28. Lucinda Cisler, "Unfinished Business: Birth Control and Women's Liberation," in *Sisterhood is Powerful*, ed. Robin Morgan (New York: Vintage Books, 1970), pp. 273-74.

29. Eisenstadt v. Baird, 405 U.S. 440, 470 (1972).

30. Although it is impossible to find out whether these particular considerations influenced the Court's opinion, internal evidence suggests that a decision was made to avoid certain problems. Strategic considerations do play a part in Supreme Court decisionmaking. See Murphy, *Elements of Judicial Strategy*.

31. Roe v. Wade, at 131.

32. Ibid., at 134-36.

33. Ibid., at 140.

34. Ibid., at 165-66. My italics.

35. Doe v. Bolton, 410 U.S. 179, 196-97 (1973).

36. Roe v. Wade, at 162.

37. Epperson v. Arkansas, 393 U.S. 97, 106-7 (1968).

38. The religious entanglement issue is argued in detail in U.S., Commission on Civil Rights, *Report. Constitutional Aspects of the Right to Limit Childbearing*, April 1975.

39. *Washington Post*, 5 May 1976.

40. Roe v. Wade, at 116.

41. Eisenstadt v. Baird, at 453.

42. Alan F. Westin, *Privacy and Freedom* (New York: Atheneum, 1967), p. 330. See especially ch. 13, "Privacy and the Law."

43. Ibid., p. 337.

44. 277 U.S. 438 (1928).

45. 367 U.S. 497, 509 (1961).

46. Saia v. New York, 334 U.S. 558, 563 (1948).

47. Public Utilities Commission v. Pollak, 343 U.S. 451 (1951).

48. Rochin v. California, 342 U.S. 165, 172 (1952).

49. Frank v. Maryland, 359 U.S. 360, 375 (1959).

50. Gibson v. Florida State Investigating Committee, 372 U.S. 539 (1963).

51. 316 U.S. 535, 541 (1942).

52. See Stanley v. Georgia, 394 U.S. 557 (1969); and Katz v. United States, 389 U.S. 347 (1967); Eisenstadt v. Baird, 405 U.S. 438 (1972).

53. Anthony Burgess, *The Wanting Seed* (New York: Ballantine Books, 1970), is a wonderful science fiction treatment of government attempts at population control. For a discussion of some of the legal issues in the real world, see Jan Charles Gray, "Compulsory Sterilization in a Free Society: Choices and Dilemmas," *University of Cincinnati Law Review*, 41, no. 3

(1972): 529. On U.S. population policy, see Thomas B. Littlewood, *The Politics of Population Control* (Notre Dame, Ind.: Notre Dame University Press, 1977).

54. John Saar, "Birth Control Critics Hit 'Final Solution' Approach," *Washington Post*, 8 November 1976.

55. James C. Mohr, *Abortion in America: The Origins and Evolution of National Policy* (New York: Oxford University Press, 1978), pp. 138-39.

56. Sagar C. Jain and Laurel F. Gooch, *Georgia Abortion Act, 1968: A Study in Legislative Process*, School of Public Health Monograph (Chapel Hill, N.C.: University of North Carolina, 1972).

57. U.S., Congress, Senate, Committee on the Judiciary, Subcommittee on Constitutional Amendments, 94th Cong., 1st sess., 1975. Testimony of Sarah Weddington, April 11, 1975, p. 514.

58. Rosen v. Louisiana State Board of Medical Examiners, 318 F. Supp. 1217 (E.D. La. 1970).

59. Babbitz v. McCann, 310 F. Supp. 293 (E.D. Wis., 1970), *appeal dismissed*, 400 U.S. 1 (1970).

60. 314 F. Supp. 1217 (N.D. Texas, 1970).

61. Abele v. Markle, 351 F. Supp. 224, 231 (D. Conn. 1972).

62. Goodman, Copelon, and Stearns, "Doe and Roe," p. 25.

63. See, e.g., Paul R. Ehrlich, *The Population Bomb* (New York: Ballantine Books, 1968); "Law and the Status of Women: An International Symposium," *Columbia Human Rights Law Review* 8 (Spring-Summer 1976).

64. Lawrence Lader, *Abortion II: Making the Revolution* (Boston: Beacon Press, 1973), gave a detailed account of the attempt to repeal New York's liberal abortion law.

65. Reed v. Reed, 404 U.S. 71 (1971).

66. Frontiero v. Richardson, 411 U.S. 677 (1973). The *Frontiero* case was argued January 17, 1973.

67. Goodman, Copelon, and Stearns, "Doe and Roe," p. 29.

68. Lader, *Abortion II*, p. i.

Chapter 4

1. Barbara Mutnick and Susan La Mont, "The Meaning of the Supreme Court Decision," *WONAAC Newsletter* (Women's National Abortion Action Coalition), February-March 1973, p. 3. This newsletter was published in New York.

2. Barbara Roberts, "Speech Delivered at WONAAC Rally, N.Y.C.," *WONAAC Newsletter*, February-March 1973, p. 6.

3. Roberta Brandes Gratz, "Never Again," *Ms.*, April 1973, pp. 44-45.

4. Marjorie Heyer, "Catholic Bishops Urged Defiance of Any Law Requiring Abortion," *Washington Post*, 14 February 1973.

5. "Abortion: Next Round," *Commonweal*, March 23, 1973, pp. 51-52.

6. Ibid.

7. Heyer, "Catholic Bishops."

8. *Time*, February 5, 1973, p. 51.

9. Marion K. Sanders, "Enemies of Abortion," *Harpers*, March 1974, p. 26.

10. *Congressional Quarterly Weekly Report*, November 10, 1973, pp. 2963-66.

11. Jeffrey A. Tannenbaum, "A New Cause," *Wall Street Journal*, 2 August 1973.

12. James Armstrong, "The Politics of Abortion," *Christian Century* March 10, 1976, pp. 215-16. See also "Bishops begin Anti-Abortion Drive," *Washington Post*, 21 November 1975.

13. Albert J. Menendez, *Religion at the Polls* (Philadelphia: Westminster Press, 1977) p. 176.

14. Ibid.

15. Paul J. Weber, "Bishops in Politics: The Big Plunge," *America*, March 20, 1976, pp. 220-23. Jim Castelli, "Anti-Abortion, the Bishops and the Crusaders," *America*, May 22, 1976, pp. 442-43.

16. Weber, "Bishops in Politics," p. 220.

17. Ibid.

18. Most of these groups preferred this term, which emphasized the woman's right to choose. They did not consider abortion a good solution to problems, but thought it was often necessary. The antiabortion groups preferred the term *pro-Life*.

19. P. David Finks, "Catholic Bishops in the Abortion Debate," *Washington Post*, 15 March 1976.

20. Kevin P. Phillips, "Abortion Issue Not Going Away," *News and Observer (Raleigh)*, 28 July 1976.

21. Roberta B. Gratz, "Never Again," *Ms.* April, 1973, p. 44.

22. Kevin P. Phillips, "Abortion Debate Gaining Momentum," *News and Observer (Raleigh)*, 1 March 1976.

23. Janis Johnson, "Abortion: An Issue That Won't Go Away," *Washington Post*, 18 January 1976.

24. Rowland Evans and Robert Novak, "Carter Whispers on Abortion," *Washington Post*, 17 January 1976.

25. Martin Schram, *Running for President: A Journal of the Carter Campaign* (New York: Pocket Books, 1976), pp. 13-14.

26. Jules Witcover, "Carter Finds his Words are Watched," *Washington Post*, 27 January 1976.

27. *News and Observer (Raleigh)*, 4 February 1976.

28. Ibid.

29. *Washington Post*, 5 February 1976.

30. Ibid.

31. *Newsweek*, February 9, 1976, p. 23.

32. David S. Broder, "Hill Fears Abortion Issue," *Washington Post*, 6 May 1974.

33. *Washington Post*, 11 February 1976.

34. Elizabeth Bowman and Bob Rankin, "Candidates on the Issues: Abortion," *Congressional Quarterly Weekly Report*, February 28, 1976, pp. 463-66.

35. *Washington Post*, 26 February 1976.

36. *Planned Parenthood—World Population Washington Memo*, June 18, 1976.

37. *Washington Post*, 29 May 1976.

38. Menendez, *Religion at the Polls*, p. 176.

39. Ibid., p. 187.

40. *News and Observer (Raleigh)*, 1 September 1976.

41. *Washington Post*, 2 September 1972.

42. Roland Evans and Robert Novak, "Carter's Shifting Abortion Strategy," *Washington Post*, 3 September 1976.

43. On Catholic voting patterns generally, see Norman H. Nie, Sidney Verba, and John R. Petrocik, *The Changing American Voter* (Cambridge, Mass.: Harvard University Press, 1976) and Andrew M. Greeley, *The American Catholic: A Social Portrait* (New York: Basic Books, 1977). See also Menendez, *Religion at the Polls*.

44. "Can Carter Win the Catholic Vote?" *U.S. News and World Report*, September 20, 1976, p. 15.

45. Edward Walsh, "Ford Abortion Stand Encourages Bishops: Amendment Endorsed," *Washington Post*, 11 September 1976.

46. Philip Shabecoff, "Archbishop Asserts Church Is Neutral in White House Race," *New York Times*, 17 September 1976.

47. David S. Broder, "Carter: Effort to Court Catholics Gains," *Washington Post*, 9 September 1976.

48. *U.S. News and World Report* September 20, 1967, p. 17.

49. For discussions of differences of opinion among Catholics, see "Politics and Abortion," *Commonweal*, February 27, 1967, p. 131; Robert N. Lynch, "'Abortion' and 1976 Politics," *America*, March 6, 1976, pp. 177-78.

50. Murray S. Stedman, Jr., *Religion and Politics in America* (New York: Harcourt, Brace and World, 1964), pp. 109-10.

51. Menendez, *Religion at the Polls*, p. 113.

52. Ibid., p. 98.

53. George Thayer, *The Farther Shores of Politics*, 2nd ed. (New York: Simon and Schuster, 1968), ch. 9.

54. "Religious Leaders Seek End to 'Vote Christian' Campaigns," *News and Observer (Raleigh)*, 22 October 1976. Among these groups were the Christian Freedom Foundation, the Crusade for Christ, and the Christian Embassy of Washington, D.C., and the Third Century Publishers of Arlington, Virginia.

55. Clayton Fritchey, "Abortion: 'A National Religious Battle?'" *Washington Post* 7 February 1976.

56. *U.S. News and World Report*, November 15, 1976, p. 20; Harris Poll, *News and Observer (Raleigh)*, 4 November 1976.

57. *New York Times*, 10 September 1976.

58. Frank Trippett, "The Menace of Fanatic Factions," *Time*, October 23, 1978, pp. 73-74. See also David S. Broder, "Let 100 Single Issue Groups Bloom," *Washington Post*, 7 January 1979; and Alan Crawford, *Thunder on the Right*, (New York: Pantheon Books, 1980), ch. 1.

59. Marjorie Randon Hershey and Darrell M. West, "Single-Issue Politics: Pro-Life Groups and the 1980 Senate Campaign," in *Interest Group Politics*, Allan J. Cigler and Burdett A. Loomis, eds. Washington, D.C.: Congressional Quarterly Press, 1983, p. 31-59.

60. Clinton Rossiter, *Parties and Politics in America* (Ithaca, N.Y.: Cornell University Press, 1960), p. 21. On "flea market politics," see Everett Carll Ladd, Jr., *Where Have All the Voters Gone?* (New York: Norton, 1978), pp. 69-71.

61. *National NOW Times*, December 1978-January 1979, p. 5. However, pro-Choice supporters lost three votes in the Senate and had a net loss of from five to twelve votes in the Senate and had a net loss of from five to twelve votes in the House, p. 7.

62. Ibid., p. 5.

63. Robert G. Kaiser, "New Hampshire Ex-Democrat Turned Right into Senate," *Washington Post*, 3 March 1979.

64. "After the Election: Some Clues for '80," *U.S. News and World Report*, November 27, 1978, p. 28.

65. Bill Peterson, "Foes of Abortion Aim at Hill Deadly Dozen," *Washington Post*, 11 February 1979.

66. "The Year of the Loner," *Time*, November 20, 1978, p. 35.

67. *National NOW Times*, December 1978-January 1979, p. 6.

68. Jeremy Rifkin and Ted Howard, "Second Reformation Ahead?" *News and Observer (Raleigh)*, 7 October 1979.

69. Miles Benson, "Bible Right to Take Liberals to Task, "*News and Observer (Raleigh)*, 21 October 1979.

70. Rob Christiansen, "Fundamentalists Target Education," *News and Observer (Raleigh)*, 5 November 1979.

71. Cole C. Campbell and Daniel C. Hoover, "TV Evangelist Calls His Flock to Politics," *News and Observer (Raleigh)*, 3 November 1979.

72. Rifkin and Howard, "Second Reformation," p. 1.

73. Benson, "Bible Right," p. 2.

74. Myra MacPherson, "The New Right Brigade," *Washington Post*, 10 August 1980. See also Crawford, *Thunder on the Right*.

75. Marjorie Hyer, "Catholics Urged Not to Base Votes on a Single Issue," *Washington Post*, 4 November 1979.

Chapter 5

1. Albert P. Blaustein and Clarence C. Ferguson, Jr., *Desegregation and the Law*, rev. ed. (New York: Vintage Books, 1962) ch. 15, "Avoidance, Evasion and Delay," discusses evasive tactics taken after the *Brown* decision.

2. Laurence M. Friedman, "The Conflict over Constitutional Legitimacy," in *The Abortion Dispute and the American System*, ed. Gilbert Y. Steiner (Washington, D.C.: Brookings Institute, 1983). p. 24.

3. *New York Times*, 16 February 1973.

4. Planned Parenthood Federation, *Family Planning/Population Reporter* 2 (October 1973): 121-23. This periodical is published by the Center for Family Planning Program Development of the Planned Parenthood Federation and keeps a running account of state legislation on family planning, abortion, sterilization, and similar laws.

5. Byrn v. New York City Health and Hospitals Corp. 410 U.S. 949 (1973). Appeal dismissed for want of a substantial federal question.

6. *Family Planning/Population Reporter* 2 (April 1973): 25-26.

7. Ibid., p. 26.

8. *Facts on File*, April 16, 1973, p. 314-B3

9. John P. Mackenzie, "Boston Trial Seeks Abortion Curb," *Washington Post*, 22 January 1975. See also William A. Nolen, *The Baby in the Bottle* (New York: Coward, McCann & Geoghegan, 1978), for an account of the trial.

10. Robert Reinhold, "Boston Doctor Is Indicted in Death of Aborted Fetus," *News and Observer (Raleigh)*, 13 April 1974.

11. Richard A. Knox, "Doctors Are Reinstated in Boston Abortion Case," *Washington Post*, 20 April 1974; "Doctors Scapegoated by Anti-Abortionists, Group Claims," *Washington Post*, 15 April 1974.

12. Commonwealth of Massachusetts v. Kenneth Edelin, No. 81823 (Mass. Super. Ct. 1974). The indictment and charge to the jury are

reprinted in U.S. Congress, Senate, Committee on the Judiciary, *Hearings before the Subcommittee on Constitutional Amendments*, 93rd Cong., 2d sess. (1974), pp. 305-16.

13. John P. MacKenzie, "Boston Doctor Convicted in Abortion Case," *Washington Post*, 16 February 1975. See also Nolen, *The Baby in the Bottle*.

14. *News and Observer (Raleigh)*, 17 February 1975.

15. Kenneth C. Edelin, "Speech to Chapel Hill, N.C. NARAL," October 27, 1979.

16. *Washington Post*, 17 February 1975.

17. Laura Shapiro, "Abortion: Back to Square One," *Mother Jones* (September-October 1977): 13-14. See also *Family Planning/Population Reporter* 7 (February 1978): 7.

18. *Washington Post*, 7 May 1978.

19. *Family Planning/Population Reporter* 6 (December 1977): 77; *News and Observer (Raleigh)*, 7 October 1979.

20. *Washington Post*, 31 August 1978.

21. Roe v. Wade, 410 U.S. 113, 160 (1973).

22. Victor Cohn, "Study Finds More Prematurely Born Survive," *Washington Post*, 16 March 1975. See also R. E. Behrman and T. S. Rosen, "Report on the Viability and Non-Viability of the Fetus," Report and Recommendations: Research on the Fetus, Department of Health, Education and Welfare, 1975.

23. For discussion of this issue, see Benjamin B. Sendor, "Medical Responsibility for Fetal Survival under Roe and Doe," *Harvard Civil Rights-Civil Liberties Law Review* 10 (Spring 1975): 444-71.

24. *Family Planning/Population Reporter* 6 (February 1977): 1.

25. Victor Cohn, "Scientists and Fetus Research," *Washington Post*, 1 July 1973; National Science Foundation Authorization Act of 1974, Act of August 16, 1973, Public Law No. 93-96, 87 Stat.

26. Richard L. Lyons, "President Rebuffed on Health," *Washington Post*, 1 July 1973; National Science Foundation Authorization Act of 1974, Act of August 16, 1973, Public Law No. 93-96, 87 Stat. 25.

27. Richard S. Knox, "New Mass. Fetus Law Held to Curb Research," *Washington Post* 29 June 1974.

28. *Family Planning/Population Reporter* 2 (June 1973): 47-49.

29. "Analysis: A Review of State Abortion Laws Enacted Since January 1973." *Family Planning/Population Reporter* 4 (December 1975): 108-13. The information that follows is from this source.

30. *Washington Post*, 16 June 1974.

31. Sendak v. Arnold, 429 U.S. 968 (1976).

32. 443 U.S. 622 (1979).

33. 421 U.S. 809 (1975).

34. "Many State Medicaid Agencies Limit Payment for Abortion, Sterilization," *Family Planning/Population Reporter* 2 (August 1973): 82-83.

35. *Family Planning/Population Reporter* 3 (December 1974): 113.

36. Jeanne Bell Nicholson and Debra W. Stewart, "The Court, Abortion Policy and State Response: A Preliminary Analysis," *Publius* 8 (Winter 1978): 159-78; also idem., "Abortion Policy in 1978," *Publius* 9 (Winter 1979): 161-67.

37. Patricia Donovan, "State Funding of Abortion: Restrictions Prevail, Liberal Policies Face Challenges," *Family Planning/Population Reporter* 7 (April 1978): 20-21.

38. Marc D. Stern, "Abortion Conscience Clauses," *Columbia Journal of Law and Social Problems* 11 (Summer 1975): 571-627.

39. Doe et al. v. Hale Hospital et al., Civil No. 73-1587-C (D. Mass. 1974).

40. 432 U.S. 519 (1977).

41. *Family Planning/Population Reporter* 4 (April 1975): 30-33.

42. *Planned Parenthood-World Population Washington Memo* April 8, 1976. Hereafter cited as *Washington Memo.*

43. 428 U.S. 52 (1976).

44. *Washington Post*, 6 March 1979.

45. 387 U.S. 1 (1967).

46. 393 U.S. 503 (1969).

47. 419 U.S. 565 (1975).

48. 421 U.S. 519 (1975).

49. This section relies heavily on Robert H. Mnookin, *In the Interest of Children: Advocacy, Law Reform and Public Policy* (New York: W. H. Freeman and Co., 1985).

50. 428 U.S. 132 (1976).

51. 443 U.S. 622 (1979).

52. Mnookin, *In the Interest of Children*, pp. 234-42. The Massachusetts judge is quoted at p. 261.

53. H. L. v. Matheson, 450 U.S. 398 (1981).

54. 439 U.S. 379 (1979).

55. Patricia Donovan, "What Can Be Done in the Wake of the Supreme Court Decisions on Publicly Funded Abortions," *Family Planning/Population Reporter* 6 (October 1977): 66.

56. *Family Planning/Population Reporter* 9 (February 1979): 5.

57. Donovan, "State Funding of Abortion," pp. 20-21.

58. *NARAL Newsletter* 11 (April 1979): 2.

59. Ibid., 11 (May-June 1979): 14.

60. Ibid.

61. City of Akron v. Akron Center for Reproductive Health, Inc., 462

U.S. 416, 1983; Planned Parenthood, Kansas City, Mo. v. Ashcroft, 462 U.S. 476, 1983; Simopoulos v. Virginia, 462 U.S. 506, 1983.

62. *Washington Memo*, May 5, 1978, p. 4.

63. See "Late Abortion and Technical Advances in Fetal Viability, "*Family Planning Perspectives* 17 (July/August 1985): 160-4; Nancy K. Rhoden, "Should Medical Technology Dictate a Woman's Right to Choose?" *Technology Review* 89 (April 1, 1986): 21-22.

64. Terry Sollom and Patricia Donovan, "State Laws and the Provision of Family Planning and Abortion Services in 1985." *Family Planning Perspectives* 17 (December 1985): 262-66. See also earlier articles on fertility-related legislation. Patricia Donovan, "Fertility-Related State Laws Enacted in 1981," *Family Planning Perspectives* 14 (March/April 1982): 63-67; *Summary of State Legislation, 1984, Washington Memo*, January 14, 1985, pp. 5-6.

65. Judy Barton, "Abortion Clinics under Siege," *The Progressive* 43 (March 1979): 27-29; Patricia Donovan, "The Holy War," *Family Planning Perspectives* 17 (January/February 1985): 5-9.

66. The cases are American College of Obstetricians v. Thornburgh, 737 F.2d 283 (1984); Charles v. Daley and Diamond, 749 F.2d 452 (1984).

67. Ruth Marcus and Al Kamen, "Is the Court Rethinking Abortion?" *Washington Post*, 26 May 1985.

68. *National Law Journal*, "Was the Court Bamboozled," June 10, 1985.

69. Leslie H. Gelb, "Justice Department Seeking to Reverse Ruling on Abortion," *News and Observer, (Raleigh)* 16 July 1985, p. 1 A; Ellen Goodman, "Waving the Anti-Abortion Banner," *Washington Post*, 23 July 1985, p. A 15.

70. Diamond v. Charles, 54 USLW 1171 (May 6, 1986).

71. Thornburgh v. American College of Obstetricians and Gynecologists, 54 USLW 4618 (June 11, 1986).

Chapter 6

1. U.S., Congress, Senate, Committee on the Judiciary, Report, "Amendments to the Constitution: A Brief Legislative History." October, 1985, p. 95.

2. These early amendments are described in *Washington Memo*, January 20, 1975, and March 20, 1975. Karen J. Lewis, "Abortion: Judicial and Legislative Control, Major Issues Brief #1B 70419, Library of Congress Research Service, Major Issues System, 5-11-81, lists the proposed amendments.

3. Senate Joint Resolution 10, 94th Cong., 1st sess.

4. Senate Joint Resolution 11, 94th Cong., lst sess.

5. See U.S. Congress, Senate, Committee on the Judiciary, *Hearings before the Subcommittee on Constitutional Amendments* 93rd Cong., 2d sess. and 94th Cong., 1st sess., 1974-76. 4 parts.

6. *Washington Memo*, September 19, 1975, and October 6, 1975.

7. See debate on Senate Joint Resolution 178, (earlier introduced in January 1975 as S.J.R. 6), *Congressional Record* (temp. ed.) April 28, 1976, S 6116-42.

8. "Testimony of Harriet F. Pilpel, General Counsel to Planned Parenthood Federation of America." This testimony, before the Bayh subcommittee, was reprinted in the *Congressional Record*, (temp. ed.) April 28, 1976, S6131-33. See also Ron Beal, "Can I Sue Mommy? An Analysis of a Woman's Tort Liability for Prenatal Injuries to Her Child Born Alive." *San Diego Law Review* 21(March 1984): 325-70.

9. Dawn E. Johnsen, "The Creation of Fetal Rights: Conflicts with Women's Constitutional Rights to Liberty, Privacy and Equal Protection," *Yale Law Journal*, 95 (January 1986): 601-3. See also Laurence H. Tribe, "The Abortion Funding Conundrum: Inalienable Rights, Affirmative Duties and the Dilemma of Independence," *Harvard Law Review* 99 (November 1985): 330-43.

10. *Congressional Record* (temp. ed.) April 28, 1976, S6121-23.

11. Pilpel testimony, cited above. See also U.S. Commission on Civil Rights, *Report, Constitutional Aspects of the Right to Limit Childbearing*, April 1975.

12. See the discussion of this type of amendment in Lynn D. Wardle and Mary A. Wood, *A Lawyer Looks at Abortion* (Provo, Utah: Brigham Young University Press, 1982), pp. 201-4.

13. U.S. Congress, House, Committee on the Judiciary, Subcommittee on Civil and Constitutional Rights, *Hearings on Proposed Constitutional Amendments*, 94th Cong., 2d sess., February-March 1976. The last of the House hearings were held in April.

14. See Wardle and Wood, pp. 201-4.

15. The Hatch/Eagleton Amendment is discussed in "Court, Senate Rebuff Anti-Abortion Efforts," *Congressional Quarterly Almanac* (hereafter *CQ Almanac*) 1983, pp. 306-11.

16. On the convention method, see American Bar Association, Special Constitutional Convention Study Committee, *Amendment of the Constitution by the Convention Method under Article V*, Chicago, Ill., 1984.

17. American Enterprise Institute for Public Policy Research, Legislative Analysis No. 46, 98th Congress, September 1984. *Proposed Procedures for a Limited Constitutional Convention, 1984*, p. 4.

18. U.S., Congress, Senate, Senate Report 98-594 on S. 119, S. 2812, H.R. 3373, 98th Congress.

19. *CQ Almanac,* 1984, p. 262; George F. Will, "The Folly of a Constitutional Convention," *Washington Post,* 21 May 1981, A 27. On the various proposals to clarify procedures in calling a convention, see Senate Report 98-594 in note 18 above. See also Walter Dellinger, "Con Con Con," *New Republic,* April 7 1986, pp. 10-11.

20. *CQ Almanac,* 1981, 425-7.

21. The Galebach article is reprinted in *Abortion: Moral and Legal Perspectives,* Jay L. Garfield and Patricia Hennessey, eds. (Amherst: University of Massachusetts Press, 1984).

22. Thomas I. Emerson, "The Power of Congress to Change Constitutional Decisions of the Supreme Court: The Human Life Bill, *Northwestern Law Review* 77 (April 1982): 133-42.

23. Jim Mann, "Bills Pose Serious Challenge to Court's Role," *News and Observer (Raleigh),* 7 June 1981, p. 6I.

24. Richard Reeves, "Protecting Courts Protects the Nation," *News and Observer (Raleigh),* 6 June 1981, p. 5.

25. *Washington Post,* 28 May 1981, p. A 18. See e.g., C. Herman Pritchett, *Congress versus the Supreme Court, 1957-60* (Minneapolis: University of Minnesota Press, 1961).

26. U.S. Senate, Committee on the Judiciary, Subcommittee on Separation of Powers, *Hearings on S. 158, H.R. 900, The Human Life Bill,* 97th Cong., 1st sess., 1982. (Hearings were held during April, May, and June 1981).

27. *Washington Memo,* October 17, 1975, p. 2.

28. Mary Russell, "Taking 'Joy Rides' on the Floor," *Washington Post,* 16 June 1977.

29. Richard L. Lyons, "President Rebuffed on Health," *Washington Post,* 1 July 1973; National Science Authorization Act of 1974, Act of August 16, 1973. Pub. L. No. 93-96, 87 Stat. 25.

30. *Washington Memo,* January 15, 1975, p. 3; National Research Service Awards and Protection of Human Subjects Act of 1974, Act of July 12, 1974, Pub. L. No. 93-348, 88 Stat. 342.

31. Health Programs Extension Act of 1973, Act of June 18, 1973, Pub. L. No. 93-45, 87 Stat. 91.

32. Foreign Assistance Acts of 1973, 1974 (Amendments to, December 17, 1973), Pub. L. No. 93-189, 87 Stat. 714.

33. Legal Services Corporation Act, Act of July 25, 1974, Pub. L. No. 93-355, 88 Stat. 378.

34. U.S., Congress, Senate, *Debate on the Department of Labor/HEW Appropriations Bill,* 93 Cong., 2d sess., June 27, 1974, *Congressional Record* 120: 21687-95.

35. See discussion of Harris v. McRae in chapter 5.

36. *Washington Post,* 18 June 1977.

37. Ibid., 20 June 1977.

38. Beal v. Doe, 432 U.S. 438 (1977); Maher v. Roe, 432 U.S. 464 (1977).

39. *Family Planning/Population Reporter* 5 (February 1976): 11.

40. 432 U.S. 438, at 462.

41. Ibid., at 456.

42. Poelker v. Doe, 432 U.S. 519 (1977).

43. *Family Planning/Population Reporter* 4 (February 1975): 8-9.

44. "Institute Says Abortion Still Hard to Get," *News and Observer (Raleigh)*, 5 May 1977.

45. Patricia Donovan, "State Funding of Abortion: Restrictions Prevail, Liberal Policies Face Challenges," *Family Planning/Population Reporter* 7 (April 1978): 20-21.

46. Jeanne Bell Nicholson and Debra W. Stewart, "Abortion Policy in 1978," *Publius* 9 (Winter 1979): 161-67.

47. *Washington Post*, 30 June 1977.

48. Ibid., 8 December 1977.

49. The measure as finally passed was in the form of a continuing resolution providing operating funds for the Labor/HEW departments and the government of the District of Columbia through 1978. Because antiabortion amendments were added to a number of different appropriations bills, House and Senate stalemates frequently resulted on appropriations legislation. Continuing resolutions were used to provide emergency funding when no agreement could be reached on the principal bill.

50. *Congressional Quarterly Weekly Report*, 13 October 1979, p. 2260. Hereafter cited as *CQ Weekly Report*. See also *News and Observer (Raleigh)*, 17 November 1979.

51. On riders, see *Congressional Quarterly Guide to Congress*, pp. 41, 119, 321, 349, 350.

52. *Washington Post*, 8 March 1979.

53. See *CQ Weekly Report* and *Congressional Quarterly Almanac, 1977-79*, for details of these measures.

54. General Electric Co. v. Gilbert, 429 U.S. 125 (1976).

55. *National NOW Times*, August 1979, p. 9.

56. *Washington Post*, 8 March 1979.

57. "Abortion: How the Members Voted in 1977," *CQ Weekly Report*, February 4, 1978, pp. 258-59.

58. Harris v. McRae, 100 S.Ct 2671. See also the companion case, Williams v. Zbaraz, 100 S.Ct. 2694 (1980).

59. For a history of the case, see Harris v. McRae, at 2681.

60. The District Court decision is summarized in McRae v. H.E.W., 48 U.S.L.W. 2492 (E.D.N.Y. 1980).

61. "Ecumenical War over Abortion," *Time*, 29 January 1979, pp. 62-63.

62. "Symposium on McRae v. Califano," *Christianity and Crisis*, March 5, 1979, pp. 34-43.

63. Linda Ambrose, "The McRae Case: A Record of the Hyde Amendment's Impact on Religious Freedom and Health Care," *Family Planning/Population Reporter* 7 (April 1978): 26-28.

64. "Ecumenical War over Abortion," p. 62.

65. Harris v. McRae at 2689-90.

66. Laurence H. Tribe, *American Constitutional Law* (Minneola, N.Y.: Foundation Press, 1978), p. 931n.

67. Arthur S. Miller, "Toward a Concept of Constitutional Duty," in *Social Change and Fundamental Law* (Westport, Conn.: Greenwood Press, 1979), pp. 129-78.

68. Cf. San Antonio Independent School District v. Rodriguez, 411 U.S. 1 (1973). The Court suggested that there may be a right to a minimum level of education (at 36-37). See also National League of Cities v. Usery, 426 U.S. 833 (1976) and law review comment thereon.

69. See Tribe, *American Constitutional Law*, p. 1135.

70. Harris v. McRae at 2688.

71. Tribe, "The Abortion Funding Conundrum," pp. 330-32.

72. *Washington Post*, 10 May 1986, p. A 7; 15 May 1986, p. A 35; *Time*, 19 May 1986, p. 19.

73. Stanley K. Henshaw and Lynn S. Wallesch, "The Medical Cutoff and Abortion Services for the Poor," *Family Planning Perspectives*, 16, (July/August 1984): 170-80.

74. Patricia Donovan, "The People Vote in Abortion Funding: Colorado and Washington," *Family Planning Perspectives*, 17 (July/August 1985): 155-57.

75. Henshaw and Wallesch, p. 171.

76. "Religious Right: Trying to Link Poll Power and Lobby Muscle," *CQ Weekly Report*, September 22, 1984, pp. 2315-19; "Court, Senate Rebuff Anti-Abortion Efforts, *1983 CQ Almanac*, pp. 306-11.

77. "Federal Abortion Funding Restrictions," *1983 CQ Alamanac*, p. 310. Pregnancy Disability Amendments to Title VII of the 1964 Civil Rights Act, 1977, 1979 (PL 95-215, PL 96-76).

78. See also Margaret Shapiro, "House Votes Ban on Federal Health Coverage for Abortions," *Washington Post*, 28 June 1984, p. A 4.

79. Margaret Shapiro, "Civil Rights Measure Snagged in Congress by Abortion Issue," *Washington Post*, 30 July 1985, p. A 4.

80. Nadine Cohodas, "Array of Anti-Abortion Amendments Planned (Appropriations). *CQ Weekly Report*, November 2, 1985, pp. 2201-2.

81. Lionel Barber, "Natural Family Planning Group Funded," *Washington Post*, 13 August 1985, p. A 15.

82. *CQ Weekly Report*, December 14, 1985, p. 2625. A compromise

dropping these proposals was later approved by the Senate Labor and Human Resources Committee.

83. *CQ Weekly Report,* Sept 1, 1984. Contributions cut off to IPPF. See also *Washington Memo,* January 11, 1985, p. 1.

84. Cohodas, "Array of Anti-Abortion Amendments," p. 2201.

85. Cohodas, "Federal Abortion Alternatives Cut," p. 2949.

86. Idem. See also Guy Munger, "Politics of Hunger: Food Aid to Poor, *News and Observer (Raleigh)* 23 February 1986, p. D 1.

87. Child Abuse Prevention Act, PL 98-457, 98 Stat. 1749, 1984. See also Michael Vitiello, "The Baby Jane Doe Litigation and Section 504: An Exercise in Raw Executive Power," *Connecticut Law Review* 17 (Fall 1984): 95-164. Abigail Lawles Kuzman, "The Legislative Response to Infant Doe," *Indiana Law Journal* 59 (April 1983-4): 377-416.

88. Marjorie Randon Hershey and Darrell M. West, "Single-Issue Politics: Pro-life Groups and the 1980 Senate Campaign," In *Interest Group Politics,* Allan J. Cigler and Burdett A. Loomis, eds., (Washington, D.C.: Congressional Quarterly Press, 1983), pp. 53-56.

89. U.S. Senate, Committee on the Judiciary, "Hearings on the Nomination of Sandra Day O'Connor to be Associate Justice of the United States Supreme Court," 97th Cong., 1st sess., 1981.

90. William S. Sabo, "The New Right and the Fragmentation of American Conservatism," *Journal of the North Carolina Political Science Association* 3 (1983): 35.

91. Grover Rees III, "Scope of Questioning of Supreme Court Nominees at Senate Advice and Consent Hearings," in "Hearings on the Nomination of Sandra Day O'Connor," pp. 174-85. See also G. Calvin MacKenzie, "A Test of Fitness for Presidential Appointment?" in *The Abortion Dispute and the American System,* Steiner, ed. (Washington, D.C.: Brookings, 1982), pp. 47-62.

Afterword

1. Walter F. Murphy and C. H. Pritchett, *Courts, Politics and Judges: An Introduction to the Judicial Process* (New York: Random House, 1985), p. 319.

2. Charles A. Johnson and Bradley C. Canon, *Judicial Policies: Implementation and Impact* (Washington, D.C.: Congressional Quarterly Press, 1984).

3. Willard Cates, Jr. v. 215. *Science* (26 March 1982): 1586-90.

4. Tony Kaye, "Are You for RU-486?" *New Republic,* January 27, 1986, pp. 13-5; Ellen Goodman, "Changing the Whole Abortion Debate," *Washington Post,* 1 March 1986, p. A 23.

5. "Late Abortion and Technical Advances in Fetal Viability," *Family*

Planning Perspectives 17 (July/August 1985): 160-4.

6. Marjorie Randon Hershey and Darrell M. West. "Single-Issue Politics: Pro-Life Groups and the 1980 Senate Campaign," in *Interest Group Politics,* Allan J. Cigler and Burdett A. Loomis, eds. (Washington, D.C.: Congressional Quarterly Press, 1983), pp. 31-59.

7. Dawn E. Johnsen, "The Creation of Fetal Rights: Conflicts with Women's Constitutional Rights to Liberty, Privacy and Equal Protection," *Yale Law Journal* 95 (January 1986): 599-625.

8. *New Republic,* February 25, 1985, p. 4.

9. Dom Bonafede, "A Woman's Place," *National Journal,* December 11, 1982, 2108-11.

10. "American Adults Approval of Legal Abortion Has Remained Virtually Unchanged since 1972," *Family Planning Perspectives* 17 (July/August 1985): 181. See John E. Jackson and Maris A. Vinovskis, "Public Opinion, Elections, and the 'Single Issue,'" in *The Abortion Dispute and the American System,* Gilbert Y. Steiner, ed. (Washington, D.C.: Brookings, 1983), pp. 64-81.

11. "How Women Live, Vote, Think," (Louis Harris National Survey) *Ms.* July 1984, pp. 51-66.

12. Laurence Tribe, "The Abortion Funding Conundrum: Inalienable Rights, Affirmative Duties, and the Dilemma of Dependence," *Harvard Law Review* 99 (November 1985): 330-43.

13. Rosalind Pollak Petchevsky, *Abortion and Woman's Choice: The State, Sexuality and the Condition of Reproductive Freedom* (New York: Longman, 1984), pp. 262-76.

14. Patricia Hennessey and Jay L. Garfield, eds., *Abortion: Moral and Legal Perspectives* (Amherst: University of Massachusetts Press, 1984). Contains a good current bibliography.

15. Sylvia Law, "Rethinking Sex and the Constitution," *University of Pennsylvania Law Review* 132 (June 1984):955-1040.

16. Eva R. Rubin, *The Supreme Court and the American Family: Ideology and Issues.* (Westport, Conn.: Greenwood Press, 1986).

17. Gilbert Y. Steiner, *The Abortion Dispute and the American System,* pp. 3-6. See also Richard McCormick, "Abortion: Rules for Debate," *America,* July 22, 1978.

Selected Bibliography

Newsletters and newspaper and newsmagazine accounts of developing events are not listed separately. For such references, see the footnotes to each chapter. The *Congressional Quarterly Weekly Report* was used extensively in following legislative activity in Congress. Planned Parenthood Federation of America's *Family Planning/Population Reporter* was the source for much of the material on state abortion legislation, and *Planned Parenthood—World Population Washington Memo* was also used extensively. Footnotes to these publications indicate the precise material used.

Government Documents

U.S., Congress, Senate, Committee on the Judiciary. *Hearings before the Subcommittee on Constitutional Amendments.* 93rd Cong., 2d sess.; 94th Cong., 1st sess., 1974-76, 4 parts.

U.S., Commission on Civil Rights. *Report. Constitutional Aspects of the Right to Limit Childbearing,* April 1975.

U.S., Department of Health, Education and Welfare. *Report and Recommendations: Research on the Fetus.* "Report on the Viability and Non-Viability of the Fetus," by R. E. Behrman and T. S. Rosen, 1975.

U.S., Congress, House. Committee on the Judiciary, Subcommittee on Civil and Constitutional Rights. *Hearings on Proposed Constitutional Amendments.* 94th Cong., 2d sess., February-March 1976.

U.S., Congress, Senate, Committee on the Judiciary. *Hearings on the Nomination of Sandra Day O'Connor to be Associate Justice of the Supreme Court.* 97th Cong., 1st sess., 1981.

U.S., Congress, Senate, Committee on the Judiciary, Subcommittee on the Constitution. *Hearings on Constitutional Amendments Relating to Abortion.* 97th Cong., 1st sess., October-December 1981. 2 vols.

U.S., Library of Congress Research Service. Issue Brief #1B 74019. "Abortion: Judicial and Legislative Control," 1981.

U.S., Congress, Senate, Committee on the Judiciary, Subcommittee on Separation of Powers. *Hearings on S. 158, H.R. 900, The Human Life Bill.* 97th Cong. 1st sess., 1982.

U.S., Congress, Senate, Committee on the Judiciary, Subcommittee on the Constitution. *Hearings on the Constitutional Convention Implementation Act of 1981.* 98th Cong., 2d sess., April 1984.

U.S., Congress, Senate, Committee on the Judiciary. Senate Report 98-594, on S. 119, S. 2812, H.R. 3373. (Constitutional Convention Implementation Act), 98th Cong., 2d sess., August 1984.

U.S., Congress, Senate, Committee on the Judiciary, Subcommittee on the Constitution. *Report.* "Amendments to the Constitution: A Brief Legislative History." 99th Cong., 1st sess., October 1985.

Books and Articles

"Abortion: Next Round." *Commonweal*, March 23, 1973, pp. 51-52.

Ambrose, Linda. "The McRae Case: A Record of the Hyde Amendment's Impact on Religious Freedom and Health Care." *Family Planning/ Population Reporter* 7 (April 1978): 26-28.

"American Adults Approval of Legal Abortion Has Remained Virtually Unchanged since 1972," *Family Planning Perspectives* 17 (July/August 1985): 181.

American Bar Association. Special Constitutional Study Committee. *Amendment of the Constitution by Convention Method under Article V.* Chicago, Ill.: 1974.

American Enterprise Institute for Public Policy Research. Legislative Analysis No. 46, 98th Congress, September 1984. *Proposed Procedures for a Limited Constitutional Convention, 1984.*

Armstrong, James. "The Politics of Abortion." *Christian Century*, March 10, 1976, pp. 215-16.

Auerbach, Carl A. "The Unconstitutionality of Congressional Proposals to Limit the Jurisdiction of the Federal Courts." *Missouri Law Review* 47 (Winter 1982): 47-58.

Barton, Judy, "Abortion Clinics under Siege," *The Progressive* 43 (March 1979): 27-29.

Beal, Ron. "Can I Sue Mommy? An Analysis of a Woman's Tort Liability for Prenatal Injuries to Her Child Born Alive." *San Diego Law Review* 21 (March 1984): 325-70.

Berman, Daniel M. *A Bill Becomes a Law: Congress Enacts Civil Rights Legislation.* 2nd ed. New York: Macmillan, 1966.

Black, Jonathan, ed. *Radical Lawyers.* New York: Avon Books, 1971.

Blake, Judith. "Abortion and Public Opinion: The 1960-1970 Decade." *Science* 171 (February 12, 1971): 540-49.

———. "The Supreme Court's Abortion Decisions and Public Opinion in the United States." *Population and Development Review* 3 (March-June 1977): 45-71.

Brown, Wendy. "Reproductive Freedom and the Right to Privacy: A Paradox for Feminists." In *Family, Politics and Public Policy*, edited by Irene Diamond, pp. 322-38. New York: Longman, 1985.

Bush, Diane. "Fertililty Related State Laws Enacted in 1982." *Family Planning Perspectives* 15 (May/June 1983): pp. 111-16.

Burgess, Anthony. *The Wanting Seed.* New York: Ballantine Books, 1970.

Cahodas, Nadine. "Array of Anti-Abortion Amendments Planned (Appropriations)." *Congressional Quarterly Weekly Report* (hereafter cited as *CQ Weekly Report*), November 2, 1985, pp. 2201-2.

——— CQ Special Report: Alternatives to Abortion. "Federal Abortion

Alternatives Cut." *CQ Weekly Report*, November 17, 1984, pp. 2949-55.

Callahan, Daniel. *Abortion: Law, Choice and Morality*. New York: Macmillan, 1970.

Callahan, Sidney, and Daniel Callahan, eds. *Abortion: Understanding Differences*. New York: Plenum Press, 1984.

Carmen, Arlene, and Moody, Howard. *Abortion Counseling and Social Change*. Valley Forge, Pa.: Judson Press, 1973.

Castelli, Jim, "Anti-Abortion, the Bishops and the Crusaders." *America*, May 22, 1976, pp. 442-43.

Chayes, Abram, "The Role of the Judge in Public Law Litigation," *Harvard Law Review* 89 (May 1976): 1281-1316.

Cigler, Allan J., and Burdett A. Loomis, eds. *Interest Group Politics*. Washington, D.C.: Congressional Quarterly Press, 1983.

Cisler, Lucinda. "Unfinished Business: Birth Control and Women's Liberation." In *Sisterhood Is Powerful*, edited by Robin Morgan, pp. 245-89. New York: Vintage Books, 1970.

Clark, Tom C. "Religion, Morality and Abortion: A Constitutional Appraisal." *Loyola (Los Angeles) Law Review* 2 (April 1969): 1-11.

Conover, Pamela Johnston and Gray, Virginia. *Feminism and the New Right: Conflict over the American Family*. New York: Praeger, 1983.

Cowan, Ruth B. "Women's Rights through Litigation: An Examination of the American Civil Liberties Union Women's Rights Project, 1971-1976." *Columbia Human Rights Law Review* 8 (Spring-Summer 1976): 373-412.

Cox, Archibald. *The Role of the Supreme Court in American Government*. New York: Oxford University Press, 1976.

Crawford, Alan. *Thunder on the Right*. New York: Pantheon Books, 1980.

Davis, Nanette J. *From Crime to Choice: The Transformation of Abortion in America*. Westport, Conn.: Greenwood Press, 1985.

Deckard, Barbara. *The Women's Movement*. New York: Harper and Row, 1975.

Dellinger, Walter. "Con Con Con." *New Republic*, April 7, 1986, pp. 10-11.

Destro, Robert A. "Abortion and the Constitution: The Need for a Life Protective Amendment." *University of California Law Review* 63 (September 1975): 1250-71.

Diamond, Irene, ed. *Families, Politics and Public Policy*. New York: Longman, 1983.

Dienes, C. Thomas. *Law, Politics and Birth Control*. Urbana: University of Illinois Press, 1972.

Djerassi, Carl. "Abortion in the United States: Politics or Policy?" *Bulletin of the Atomic Scientists* 42 (April 1986): 38-41.

Donovan, Patricia. "Fertility-Related State Laws Enacted in 1981." *Family Planning Perspectives* 14 (March/April 1982): 63-67.

_____. "The Holy War." *Family Planning Perspectives* 17 (January/ February 1985): 5-9.

_____. "The People Vote on Abortion Funding: Colorado and Washington." *Family Planning Perspectives* 17 (July/August 1985): 155-57.

_____. State Funding of Abortion: Restrictions Prevail, Liberal Policies Face Challenges." *Family Planning/Population Reporter* 7 (April 1978): 20-21.

Drinan, Robert F. "The Inviolability of the Right to be Born." In *Abortion and the Law*, edited by David T. Smith, pp. 107-23. Cleveland: Case Western Reserve University, 1967.

Ehrlich, Paul R. *The Population Bomb*. New York: Ballantine Books, 1968.

Ely, John Hart. "The Wages of Crying Wolf: A Comment on Roe v. Wade." *Yale Law Journal* 82 (April 1973): 920-49.

Emerson, Thomas I. "Nine Justices in Search of a Doctrine." *Michigan Law Review* 64 (December 1965): 219-34.

_____. "The Power of Congress to Change Constitutional Decisions of the Supreme Court: The Human Life Bill." *Northwestern University Law Review* 77 (April 1982): 129-42.

Epstein, Lee. *Conservatives in Court*. Knoxville: University of Tennessee Press, 1985.

Epstein, Richard A. "Substantive Due Process by Any Other Name: The Abortion Cases." *Supreme Court Review* (1974): 159-65.

Falik, Marilyn, *Ideology and Abortion Policy Politics*. New York: Praeger, 1983.

Fleming, Thomas "Divided Shepherds of a Restive Flock." *New York Times Magazine*, January 16, 1977, pp. 9, 34-44.

Francome, Colin. *Abortion Freedom: A Worldwide Movement*. London and Boston: Allen & Unwin, 1984.

Freedman, Anne. "Sex Equality, Sex Differences and the Supreme Court." *Yale Law Journal* 92 (May 1984): 913-68.

Freeman, Jo. *The Politics of Women's Liberation*. New York; McKay, 1975.

Friedman, Lawrence M. "The Conflict over Constitutional Legitimacy," In *The Abortion Dispute and the American System*, edited by Gilbert Y. Steiner, pp. 13-29. Washington, D.C.: Congressional Quarterly Press, 1983.

Frohock, Fred M. *Abortion: A Case Study in Law and Morals*. Westport, Conn.: Greenwood Press, 1983.

Garfield, Jay L., and Hennessey, Patricia, eds. *Abortion: Moral and Legal Perspectives*. Amherst: The University of Massachusetts Press, 1984.

George, James, Jr. "The Evolving Law of Abortion." In *Abortion, Society and the Law*, edited by David F. Walbert and J. Douglas Butler, pp. 3-32. Cleveland: Case Western Reserve University, 1973.

Gilligan, Carol. *In a Different Voice.* Cambridge: Harvard University Press, 1982.

Ginsburg, Ruth Bader. "Some Thoughts on Autonomy and Equality in Relation to Roe v. Wade." *North Carolina Law Review* 63 (January 1985): 375-86.

Goodman, Janice; Schoenbrod, Rhonda Copelon; and Stearns, Nancy. "Doe and Roe: Where Do We Go From Here?" *Women's Rights Law Reporter* 1 (Spring 1973): 2-38.

Gordon, Linda. *Woman's Body, Woman's Right.* New York: Penguin Books, 1977.

Gratz, Roberta Brandes. "Never Again." *Ms.*, April 1973, pp. 44-45.

Gray, Jan Charles. "Compulsory Sterilization in a Free Society: Choices and Dilemmas." *University of Cincinnati Law Review* 41, no. 3 (1972): 529-87.

Greeley, Andrew M. *The American Catholic: A Social Portrait.* New York: Basic Books, 1977.

Greenberg, Jack. *Judicial Process and Social Change: Constitutional Litigation.* St. Paul: West Publishing Co., 1977.

Greenhouse, Linda. "Abortion Issue Weaves an Intricate Web." *New York Times*, April 22, 1986, p. 10.

Gunther, Gerald. "The Subtle Vices of the 'Passive Virtues'—A Comment on Principle and Expediency in Judicial Review." *Columbia Law Review* 64 (January 1964): 1-25.

Harrison, Beverly Wildung. *Our Right to Choose: Toward a New Ethic of Abortion.* Boston: Beacon Press, 1983.

Hawkins, William A. *A Treatise on the Pleas of the Crown.* 4th ed. London: Richardson and Lintot, 1762.

Henshaw, Stanley K. and Wallesch, Lynn S. "The Medical Cutoff and Abortion Services for the Poor." *Family Planning Perspectives* 16 (July/August 1984): 170-80.

Hershey, Marjorie Randon, and West, Darrell M. "Single-Issue Politics: Pro-Life Groups and the 1980 Senate Campaign." In *Interest Group Politics*, edited by Allan J. Cigler and Burdett A. Loomis, pp. 31-59. Washington, D.C.: Congressional Quarterly Press, 1983.

Hilgers, Thomas W.; Horan, Dennis J.; and Mall, David. *New Perspectives on Abortion.* Frederick, Md.: University Press of America, 1981.

Hill, Samuel S. and Owen, Dennis. *The New Religious Political Right in America.* Nashville: Abington Press, 1982.

Hines, Norman E. "A Decade of Progress in Birth Control." *Annals of the American Academy* 212 (1940): 88-95.

Hodge, Hugh L. "Foeticide, or Criminal Abortion, A Lecture Introductory to the Course of Obstetrics." In *Abortion in Nineteenth Century America*. Sex, Marriage and Society series. New York: Arno Press, 1974.

Horowitz, Donald L. *The Courts and Social Policy*. Washington, D.C.: Brookings, 1977.

"How Women Live, Vote, Think." (Louis Harris National Survey) *Ms.*, July, 1984, pp. 51-66.

Huddlesworth, H. Martin. "Comment. The Law of Therapeutic Abortion: A Social Commentary on Proposed Reform." *Journal of Public Law* 15, no. 2 (1966): 386-400.

Jackson, John E., and Vinovskis, Maris A. "Public Opinion, Elections and 'Single Issue.'"In *The Abortion Dispute and the American System*, edited by Gilbert Y. Steiner, pp. 64-81. Washington, D.C.: Brookings, 1983.

Jaffe, Frederick S.; Lindheim, Barbara L.; and Lee, Philip R. *Abortion Politics*. New York: McGraw-Hill, 1981.

Jaffe, Louis L. "The Citizen as Litigant in Public Actions: The Non-Hohfeldian or Ideological Plaintiff." *University of Pennsylvania Law Review* 116 (1968): 1033-47.

Jain, Sagar C., and Sinding, Steven W. *North Carolina Abortion Law: 1967*. Carolina Population Center Monograph No. 2. Chapel Hill: University of North Carolina, 1968.

_____. and Gooch, Laurel F. *Georgia Abortion Act, 1968: A Study in Legislative Process*. School of Public Health Monograph. Chapel Hill: University of North Carolina, 1972.

Johnsen, Dawn E. "The Creation of Fetal Rights: Conflicts with Women's Constitutional Rights to Liberty, Privacy and Equal Protection." *Yale Law Journal* 95 (January 1986): 599-625.

Johnson, Charles A., and Canon, Bradley C. *Judicial Policies: Implementation and Impact*. Washington, D.C.: Congressional Quarterly Press, 1984.

Kaye, Tony. "Are You for RU-486?" *New Republic*, January 27, 1986, pp. 13-15.

Koop, C. Everett, and Shaeffer, Frances A. *Whatever Happened to the Human Race?* Westchester, Ill.: Good News Publications, 1983.

Krason, Stephen M. *Abortion: Politics, Morality and the Constitution: A Critical Study of Roe v. Wade and Doe v. Bolton and a Basis for Change*. Lanham, Md.: University Press of America, 1984.

Kuzma, Abigail Lawles. "The Legislative Response to Infant Doe." *Indiana Law Journal* 59 (April 1983-4): 377-416.

Ladd, Everett Carll, Jr. *Where Have All the Voters Gone?* New York: Norton, 1978.

Lader, Lawrence. *Abortion*. Boston: Beacon Press, 1967.

————. *Abortion II: Making the Revolution*. Boston: Beacon Press, 1973.

Langer, William L. "Europe's Initial Population Explosion." *American Historical Review* 69 (October 1963): 8-10.

"Late Abortion and Technical Advances in Fetal Viability." *Family Planning Perspectives* 17 (July/August 1983): 160-4.

"Law and the Status of Women: An International Symposium." *Columbia Human Rights Law Review* 8 (Spring-Summer 1976).

Law, Sylvia. "Rethinking Sex and the Constitution." *University of Pennsylvania Law Review*, 132 (June 1984): 955-1040.

Leavy, Zad, and Kummer, Jerome M. "Criminal Abortion: Human Hard-Ship and Unyielding Laws." *Southern California Law Review* 35 (Winter 1962): 123-48.

Legge, Jerome S. *Abortion Policy: An Evaluation of the Consequences for Maternal and Infant Health*. Albany: University of New York Press, 1985.

Lowi, Theodore J. *The Politics of Disorder*. New York: Norton, 1971.

Lucas, Roy. "Federal Constitutional Limitations on the Enforcement and Administration of State Abortion Statutes." *North Carolina Law Review* 46 (June 1968): 730-78.

Luker, Kristin. *Abortion and the Politics of Motherhood*. Berkeley and Los Angeles: University of California Press, 1984.

Lynch, Robert N. "'Abortion' and 1976 Politics." *America*, March 6, 1976, pp. 177-78.

MacKenzie, G. Calvin. "A Test of Fitness for Presidential Appointment?" In *The Abortion Dispute and the American System*, edited by Gilbert Y. Steiner, pp. 47-62. Washington, D.C.: Brookings, 1983.

Means, Cyril C., Jr. "The Law of New York Concerning Abortion and the State of the Foetus, 1664-1968: A Case of Cessation of Constitutionality." *New York Law Forum* 14 (Fall 1968): 411-515.

————. "The Phoenix of Abortional Freedom: Is a Penumbral or Ninth Amendment Right about to Arise from Nineteenth-Century Legislative Ashes of a Fourteenth-Century Common Law Liberty?" *New York Law Forum* 17, no. 2 (1971): 335-410.

Menendez, Albert J. *Religion at the Polls*. Philadelphia: Westminster Press, 1977.

Miller, Arthur S. *Social Change and Fundamental Law*. Westport, Conn.: Greenwood Press, 1979.

————. *The Supreme Court and American Capitalism*. New York: The Free Press, 1968.

————. *The Supreme Court: Myth and Reality*. Westport, Conn.: Greenwood Press, 1978.

Mnookin, Robert H. *In the Interest of Children: Advocacy, Law Reform and Public Policy*. New York: W. H. Freeman, 1985.

Mohr, James C. *Abortion in America: The Origins and Evolution of National Policy*. New York: Oxford University Press, 1978.

Monroe, Keith. "How California's Abortion Law Isn't Working." *New York Times Magazine*, December 29, 1968, pp. 10-11.

Moorman, Keith. "Kentucky's New Abortion Law: Searching for the Outer Limits of Permissible Regulation." *Kentucky Law Journal* 71, no. 3 (1982-3): 617-46.

Morgan, Robin, ed. *Sisterhood Is Powerful*. New York: Vintage Books, 1970.

Murphy, Walter F. *Elements of Judicial Strategy*. Chicago: University of Chicago Press, 1964.

Nathanson, Bernard N. *Aborting America*. Garden City, N.Y.: Doubleday, 1979.

Nicholson, Jeanne Bell and Stewart, Debra W. "Abortion Policy in 1978." *Publius* 9 (Winter 1979): 161-67.

———. "The Court, Abortion Policy and State Response: A Preliminary Analysis." *Publius* 8 (Winter 1978): 159-78.

Nie, Norman H.; Verba, Sidney; and Petrocik, John R. *The Changing American Voter*. Cambridge, Mass.: Harvard University Press, 1976.

Nolen, William A. *The Baby in the Bottle*. New York: Coward, McCann, & Geoghegan, 1978.

Noonan, John T., Jr. "The Hatch Amendment and the New Federalism." *Harvard Journal of Law and Public Policy*. 6 (1982): 93-102.

"Note: Declaratory Relief in Criminal Law." *Harvard Law Review* 80 (May 1967): 1490-1507.

O'Connor, Karen. *Women's Organizations' Use of the Courts*. Lexington, Mass.: Lexington Books, 1980.

Ooms, Theodora, ed. *Teenage Pregnancy in a Family Context: Implications for Policy*. Philadelphia: Temple University Press, 1981.

Packer, Herbert L. *The Limits of the Criminal Sanction*. Stanford: Stanford University Press, 1968.

Paige, Connie. *The Right to Lifers: Who They Are, Where They Operate, Where They Get Their Money*. N.Y.: Summit Books, 1983.

Petchevsky, Rosalind Pollak *Abortion and Woman's Choice: The State, Sexuality and the Conditions of Reproductive Freedom*. New York: Longman, 1984.

"Politics and Abortion," *Commonweal*, February 27, 1976, p. 131.

Pritchett, C. Herman. *Congress versus the Supreme Court, 1957-1960*. Minneapolis: University of Minnesota Press, 1961.

Rebell, Michael A. and Block, Arthur R. *Educational Policy-Making and the Courts.* Chicago: University of Chicago Press, 1982.

"Religious Right: Trying to Link Poll Power and Lobby Muscle." *CQ Weekly Report,* September 22, 1984, pp. 2315-19.

Rhoden, Nancy K. "Should Medical Technology Dictate a Woman's Right to Choose?" *Technology Review* 89 (April 1, 1986): 21-22.

Rosen, Harold, ed. *Abortion in America.* Boston: Beacon Press, 1967.

Rossiter, Clinton. *Parties and Politics in America.* Ithaca, N.Y.: Cornell University Press, 1960.

Rubin, Eva R. *The Supreme Court and the American Family: Ideology and Issues.* Westport, Conn.: Greenwood Press, 1986.

Sabo, William S. "The New Right and the Fragmentation of American Conservatism." *Journal of the North Carolina Political Science Association* 3 (1983): 24-37.

Sanders, Marion K. "Enemies of Abortion." *Harpers,* March 1974, pp. 26-30.

Sarat, Austin. "Abortion and the Courts: Uncertain Boundaries of Law and Politics." In *American Politics and Public Policy,* edited by Allan Sindler. Washington, D.C.: Congressional Quarterly Press, 1982.

Sarvis, Betty, and Rodman, Hyman. *The Abortion Controversy.* New York: Columbia University Press, 1973.

Schneider, Carl, and Vinovskis, Maris A., eds. *The Law and Politics of Abortion.* Lexington, Mass.: Lexington Books, 1980.

Schram, Martin. *Running for President: A Journal of the Carter Campaign.* New York: Pocket Books, 1976.

Schulder, Diane, and Kennedy, Florynce. *Abortion Rap.* New York: McGraw-Hill, 1971.

Sendor, Benjamin B. "Medical Responsibility for Fetal Survival under Roe and Doe." *Harvard Civil Rights-Civil Liberties Law Review* 10 (Spring 1975): 444-71.

Shapiro, Laura. "Abortion: Back to Square One," *Mother Jones,* September-October 1977, pp. 13-14.

Sigworth, Heather. "Abortion Laws in the Federal Courts: The Supreme Court as Platonic Guardian." *Indiana Legal Forum* 5 (Fall 1971): 130-42.

Smith, David T., ed. *Abortion and the Law.* Cleveland: Case Western University, 1967.

Sollom, Terry, and Donovan, Patricia. "State Laws and the Provision of Family Planning and Abortion Services in 1985." *Family Planning Perspectives* 17 (December 1985): 262-66.

Sorenson, Theodore C. *Kennedy.* New York: Harper and Row, 1965.

Sperry, Peter. "The Class Conflict over Abortion." *The Public Interest* 52 (Summer 1978):69-84.

Stedman, Murray S., Jr. *Religion and Politics in America*. New York: Harcourt, Brace and World, 1964.

Steiner, Gilbert Y., ed. *The Abortion Dispute and the American System*. Washington, D.C.: Brookings Institute, 1983.

Stern, Marc D. "Abortion Conscience Clauses." *Columbia Journal of Law and Social Problems* 11 (Summer 1975):571-627.

"A Stunning Approval for Abortion." *Time*, February 5, 1973, pp. 50-51.

"Summary of State Legislation, 1984." *Planned Parenthood-World Population Washington Memo*, January 14, 1985, pp. 5-6.

Swisher, Carl B. *American Constitutional Development*. Boston: Houghton Mifflin, 1943.

"Symposium on McRae v. Califano." *Christianity and Crisis*, March 5, 1979, pp. 34-43.

Tannenbaum, Jeffrey A. "A New Cause: Many Americans Join Move to Ban Abortion." *Wall Street Journal*, 2 August 1973.

Thayer, George. *The Farther Shores of Politics*. 2nd ed. New York: Simon and Schuster, 1968.

Tribe, Laurence H. *American Constitutional Law*. Mineola, N.Y.: Foundation Press, 1978.

_____. "The Abortion Funding Conundrum: Inalienable Rights, Affirmative Duties and the Dilemma of Dependence." *Harvard Law Review* 99 (November 1985): 330-43.

Trippett, Frank. "The Menace of Fanatic Factions." *Time*, October 23, 1978, pp. 73-74.

Vergata, Pat, et al. "Abortion Cases in the United States." *Women's Rights Law Reporter* 1 (Spring 1972): 50-55.

Vitiello, Michael. "The Baby Jane Doe Litigation and Section 504: An Exercise in Raw Executive Power." *Connecticut Law Review* 17 (Fall 1984): 95-164.

Vose, Clement E. *Constitutional Change: Amendment Politics and Supreme Court Litigation since 1900*. Lexington, Mass: D. C. Heath, 1972.

Walker, Robert H. *Reform in America: The Continuing Frontier*. Lexington: University Press of Kentucky, 1985.

Wardle, Lynn D. *The Abortion Privacy Doctrine: A Compendium and Critique of Federal Court Abortion Cases*. Buffalo, N.Y.: W. S. Hein and Co., 1980.

Wardle, Lynn D., and Wood, Mary A. *A Lawyer Looks at Abortion*. Provo, Utah: Brigham Young University Press, 1982.

Ware, Cellestine. *Woman Power: The Movement for Women's Liberation*. New York: Tower Publications, 1970.

Wasby, Stephen. *The Impact of the U.S. Supreme Court: Some Per-*

spectives. Homewood, Ill.: The Dorsey Press, 1970.

"Was the Court Bamboozled?" *National Law Journal,* June 10, 1985.

Weber, Paul J. "Bishops in Politics: The Big Plunge." *America,* May 22, 1976, pp. 220-23.

Westfall, David. "Beyond Abortion: The Potential Reach of a Human Life Amendment." *American Journal of Law and Medicine.* 8 (1982): 97-135.

Westin, Alan F. *Privacy and Freedom.* New York: Atheneum, 1967.

Westoff, Charles F., and Ryder, Norman B. *The Contraceptive Revolution.* Princeton: Princeton University Press, 1977.

Williams, Glanville. *The Sanctity of Life and the Criminal Law.* New York: Knopf, 1957.

Williams, Roger M. "The Power of Fetal Politics," *Saturday Review,* June 9, 1979, pp. 12-15.

Woodward, Bob, and Armstrong, Scott. *The Brethren.* New York: Simon and Schuster, 1979.

Yarbrough, Tinsley E. "Abortion Funding Issue: A Study in Mixed Constitutional Cues." *North Carolina Law Review* (1981): 611-27.

Index to Cases

Subject Index

Intervenors, 3
Involuntary servitude, 33
Iowa caucus (1976), 95-96

Jackson, Henry M., 95, 98
James Madison Constitutional Law
  Institute, 51
Japan, 19
Jefferson, Mildred, 123-24
Johnson, Charles A., 186
Jones, Arthur, 27
Judicial activism, 179, 189
Judicial appointments, 179-83, 187
Judicial policymakng, 59-62
Judicial self-restraint, 83, 84, 175
Justice, Department of, 147, 149
Justiciability, 33-34, 68

Kansas, abortion laws, 139
Kemp, Jack, 176
Kemp Amendment, 177
Kennedy, Edward M., 102, 104
Kennedy, John F., 102
Kennedy Foundation, 25
Kentucky: abortion funding, 166;
  abortion laws, 15
King, Edward J., 109-10
King, Jim, 104
Kinsey, Alfred, 18
Krol, John, 90, 105, 124

Lader, Lawrence, 88
Law, Sylvia, 6
Law Center for Constitutional
  Rights, 49-50
Lawsuits, traditional, 2
Leahy, Frank, 110
Lefkowitz, Louis J., 50
Legal Services Corporation Act,
  163
Legislatures, versus courts, 31-38

Liberty, 141, 148, 190, 191
Life Amendment Political Action
  Committee (LAPAC), 110, 112
Literacy tests, 160
Litigation, 61-62, 63, 89-90, 118,
  137-38; abortion, 43-57; cam-
  paigns, 1-8, 54; for social
  change, 31, 32, 33
Locke, Jon, 80-81
Louisiana: abortion funding, 166;
  abortion laws, 85-86, 130, 139
Lucas, Roy, 5, 43, 44, 47, 51, 54
Lyons, Jesse, 50

McCarthy, Eugene, 98
McCormack, Ellen, 99-101
McGovern, George, 106, 110, 112
McGuire, James C., 122
McIntire, Thomas, 109
McRae, Cora, 171
Maginnis, Patricia, 24
Maine, abortion laws, 23
Manslaughter prosecutions, 122-24,
  126, 132
Margold, Nathan, 32
Marriage, 42, 187
Marshall, Thurgood, 32, 56, 66,
  141, 148, 168
Maryland, abortion laws, 23
Massachusetts, abortion laws,
  121-26, 134-37
Massachusetts Civil Liberties
  Union, 135
Massachusetts primary (1976), 99
Maternal health, 145, 147, 148,
  178
Mayo Clinic, 65, 69
Means, C. C., 47
Medicaid, 54, 90, 107, 118, 129,
  162, 165-75, 176; and abortion
  funding, 163-75

About the Author

EVA R. RUBIN is Associate Professor in the Department of Political Science and Public Administration at North Carolina State University. In addition to the first edition of *Abortion, Politics, and the Courts,* she is the author of *The Supreme Court and the American Family* (Greenwood Press, 1986).